W9-CSY-355

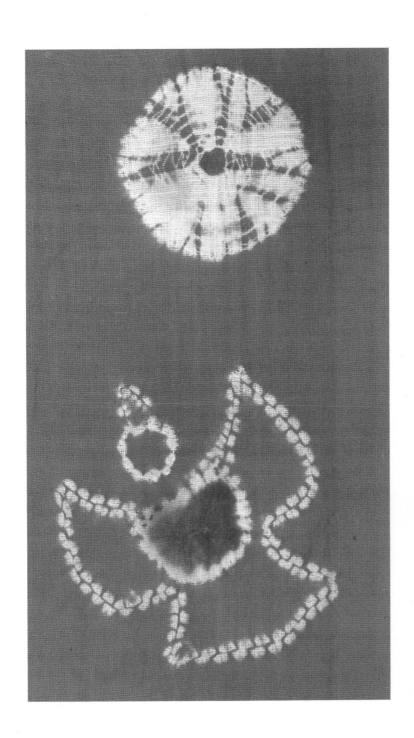

# The Inventive Art c

Yoshiko Wada

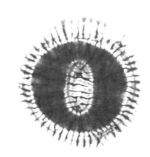

# B O R I

## apanese Shaped Resist Dyeing

### Tradition  Techniques  Innovation

Jane Barton

Mary Kellogg Rice

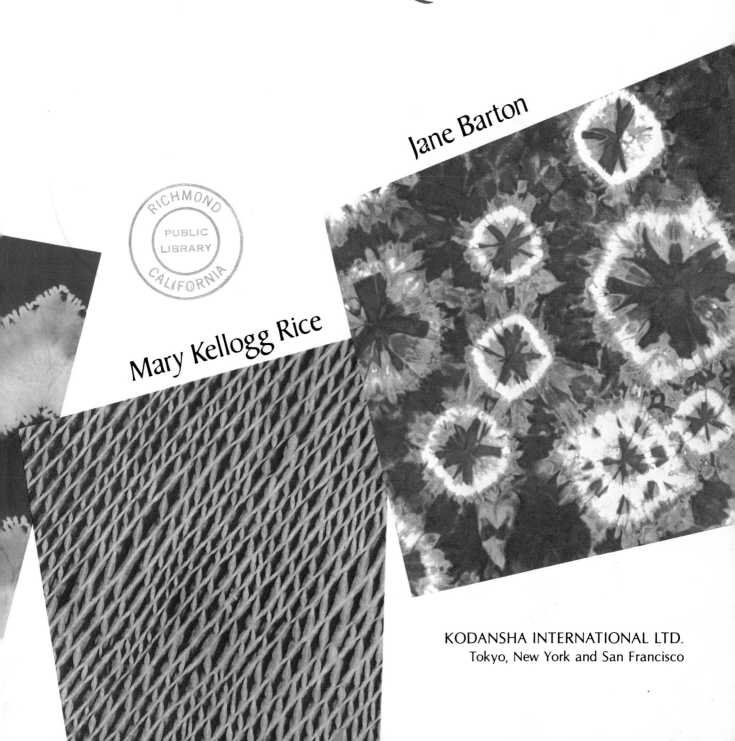

KODANSHA INTERNATIONAL LTD.
Tokyo, New York and San Francisco

distributed in the United States by Kodansha International/USA, Ltd.,
through Harper & Row, Publishers, Inc., 10 East 53rd Street,
New York, New York 10022

published by Kodansha International Ltd., 2-2 Otowa 1-chome,
Bunkyo-ku, Tokyo 112 and Kodansha International/USA, Ltd., 10 East
53rd Street, New York, New York 10022 and 44 Montgomery Street,
San Francisco, California 94104

LCC 82-48789
ISBN 0-87011-559-6
ISBN 4-7700-1063-X (in Japan)

# CONTENTS

# Shibori—A Definition

*Shibori* is the Japanese word for a variety of ways of embellishing textiles by shaping cloth and securing it before dyeing. The word comes from the verb root *shiboru*, "to wring, squeeze, press." Although shibori is used to designate a particular group of resist-dyed textiles, the verb root of the word emphasizes the action performed on cloth, the process of manipulating fabric. Rather than treating cloth as a two-dimensional surface, with shibori it is given a three-dimensional form by folding, crumpling, stitching, plaiting, or plucking and twisting. Cloth shaped by these methods is secured in a number of ways, such as binding and knotting. It is the pliancy of a textile and its potential for creating a multitude of shape-resisted designs that the Japanese concept of shibori recognizes and explores. The shibori family of techniques includes numerous resist processes practiced throughout the world.

Shibori is used as an English word throughout this book because there is no English equivalent. In fact, most languages have no term that encompasses all the various shibori techniques, nor is there English terminology for individual methods, which often have been incorrectly lumped together as "tie-and-dye." Three terms for separate shibori methods have come into international usage: *plangi*, a Malay-Indonesian word for the process of gathering and binding cloth; *banda*, an Indian term for the same process; and *tritik*, a Malay-Indonesian word for stitch-resist. However, these three terms represent only two of the major shibori techniques. In this context, the word shibori seems the most useful term for the entire group of shaped resist textiles. It is the hope of the authors that "shibori" will win acceptance in the international textile vocabulary.

The special characteristic of shibori resist is a soft- or blurry-edged pattern. This effect is quite different from the sharp-edged resist obtained with stencil, paste, and wax. With shibori the dyer works in concert with the materials, not in an effort to overcome their limitations but to allow them full expression. And, an element of the unexpected is always present.

All the variables attendant on shaping the cloth and all the influences that control the events in the dye vat or pot conspire to remove some of the shibori process from human control. An analogy is that of a potter firing a wood-burning kiln. All the technical conditions have been met, but what happens in the kiln may be a miracle or a disaster. Chance and accident also give life to the shibori process, and this is its special magic and strongest appeal.

7

# Tradition

# Tradition

ASUKA (552–645) AND NARA (645–794) PERIODS

In A.D. 749 Emperor Shōmu proceeded in state to Tōdai-ji, the great Buddhist temple in Nara, to celebrate the completion of its enormous bronze image of Buddha and the fortuitous discovery in a remote part of Japan of gold, needed to coat the figure itself and the large bronze lotus upon which it is seated. There, with all the court nobles, the ministers of state, and religious, civil, and military figures, the emperor assumed a position facing north in front of the image, the position of a subject in audience before his sovereign. A minister of the imperial household then addressed the image on the emperor's behalf, describing him as a servant of the Buddha and giving thanks for the timely discovery of the gold, regarded as an auspicious sign. That same year, after a reign of twenty-four years, the emperor abdicated and took religious vows, and in 756, after his death, the empress donated all his household and personal possessions to the Tōdai-ji. There they were placed in a wooden storehouse known as the Shōsō-in, where they remain today. Included among them, protected from Japan's humid climate, are the earliest existing examples in Japan of resist-dyed cloth.

The textiles preserved in the Shōsō-in include three types of resist-dyed fabric: *kōkechi*, tied or bound resist; *rōkechi*, wax resist; and *kyōkechi*, a resist process in which cloth is folded and then clamped between carved wooden blocks. One might speculate that the word *kechi*—which is not a native Japanese term, but the Chinese *xie* (纈)—had come to mean "resist," as evidenced by its use as suffix for the three processes, only one of which is a type of shibori. The three types of resist-dyed fabrics were fairly well known in Japan at the time—all three terms were used, at any rate, in an inventory of gifts made in 756 to the Hōryū-ji temple.

Although the Shōsō-in pieces are the earliest existing examples in Japan of resist-dyed cloth, at least some of them are of non-Japanese origin. It seems likely, because some examples are of textiles probably not yet made in Japan—specifically, brocade and gauze—that these came from China, with which Japan had been enjoying a lively interchange dating back to the sixth century. One early Japanese contact with China is recorded in the Chinese *Chronicles of Wei (Wei chih)*, where it is recorded that in the year corresponding to A.D. 238 the Japanese Queen Himiko gave the emperor of the Chinese Wei dynasty more than two hundred yards of "spotted cloth." It seems possible that the textile referred to was a kind of resist-dyed cloth.

Many of the other possessions of Emperor Shōmu stored in the Shōsō-in are of foreign origin, and it may be that all the textile pieces in its collection are, as has been asserted, of Chinese provenance. Cloth being perishable and the circumstances of preservation in the Shōsō-in unique, there are no eighth century examples of indubitably Japanese origin with which comparison might be made, so the controversy cannot be resolved one way or the other.

Etymological evidence, however, indicates that the Japanese used resist dyeing prior to the sixth century, which is when Buddhism and writing were introduced from the continent and assimilated in the islands. That is, resist dyeing was practiced before the advent of strong continental influence. The native Japanese word *yūhata*, referring to "knotting" cloth, was assigned Chinese characters when writing was introduced. This indicates that this process—a type of shibori, it can be assumed—was a native technique or at least antedates the introduction of both Chinese writing and Chinese resist-dyeing techniques into Japan. If this technique had been Chinese, it is likely that it would have received and retained a non-Japanese name. This argument is based on indirect evidence and on conjecture. With its many flaws, still, it points to a fruitful direction for research.

Indeed, Toshiko Itō, in *Tsujigahana, The Flower of Japanese Textiles,* expresses the opinion that the use of resist dyeing in Japan goes back to prehistory, and that the Japanese then already knew how to bind off sections of cloth so that they remained undyed. Her opinion is reinforced by the eminent Swiss anthropologist Alfred Bühler, who has made a special study of resist dyeing. He thinks it is of spontaneous origin, occurring at an early stage of man's technological development, and that in areas favorable to its use more elaborate techniques were developed. These more advanced methods then spread through trade and other contact between peoples.

During the Nara period the interchange between Japan and China increased greatly, borne upon the rising tide of Japan's acceptance of Buddhism, then flourishing on the continent, facilitated by political reunification of China under the short-lived Sui dynasty, and enriched by the cultural brilliance of the Tang dynasty, which succeeded it. The Japanese missions sent to the Chinese court during the early and middle years of that dynasty sometimes numbered hundreds of people and included a variety of specialists, among them artists and craftsmen, intent upon acquiring new skills and knowledge. And at the Chinese capital of Changan they found a cosmopolitan city with many foreign residents—Persians, Indians, Turks, and various peoples from central Asia—as well as a court hospitable to foreigners and interested in what the outside world had to offer.

Of the three resist processes represented in the Shōsō-in, the more advanced are those using wax *(rōkechi)* and clamped wooden blocks *(kyōkechi),* and they undoubtedly were continental in origin. They were frequently cited in accounts of the Nara period, but they were seldom referred to after that, and their use appears to have died out. The *Chronicles of Japan (Nihon shoki),* published in 720, lists nineteen bolts of resist-dyed cloth *(kechi)* among items presented by the Japanese emperor to foreign ambassadors. This is clear indication that Japanese resist-dyed textiles reached a high technical and aesthetic level at an early date. The nature, extent, and role of Chinese resist (including shibori) in this development is not even known in the vaguest terms and remains a matter of speculation only. One rewarding avenue of preliminary research would be a comparison of the patterns on clothing worn in China and Japan during this period.

The earliest shibori fabrics found to date in China are several centuries older than those in the Shōsō-in. They were excavated from a tomb in the ruins of Astana, one of a number of former oasis towns along the Silk Road, the great trade route that connected East Asia with the centers of western civilizations. Fabrics found there are illustrated in a Chinese book whose English summary is entitled *The Silk Road: Fabrics from the Han to the T'ang Dynasty,* with this description: "Two kinds of *jiao-xie* (絞 纈) were taken from a tomb at Astana in 1967. Both the pongee's basic material and method of decoration are like pieces found here in 1963 in a tomb of Western Liang built in A.D.

418. They are the oldest pieces of *jiao-xie* in existence." The character 絞 *(jiao)* is the one used in Japan as "shibori," and these examples are of a type of shibori using binding that is known in Japan as *meyui*. The patterns of two of the fragments are of uniform, half-centimeter resisted squares, repeated in rows over the entire surface of the cloth. In the center of each undyed square is a small dot. The pattern of a third fragment is the same, but the resisted squares are larger and not as uniform in size.

In a tomb at the same site dated 683, a fragment was found in which stitching was used to achieve the resist. It is interesting to note that its diamond pattern was made by pleating and then stitching through the resulting layers of cloth: large needle holes are clearly evident in each resisted area.

At Astana a number of wooden burial figurines were discovered. They are colorfully painted, and, on some, part of the clothing is of cloth. Among them are two delightful Tang dynasty ladies with high-piled black hair. Their clothes consist of a long skirt, tight bodice, and a shawl caught into a fitted belt on one side of the waist and draped around the shoulders. The shawls of both figurines are resist dyed in a pattern of tiny squared rings *(meyui)* arranged in groups of threes. The dress of the two ladies is of particular interest because the style is the one adopted with but little change by the Japanese court ladies of the eighth century.

It is possible by examining such fabrics to ascertain the way in which many of them were made. Tetsurō Kitamura, a scholar who has examined the Shōsō-in pieces, has set forth his findings in his book *Shibori*. The majority of the pieces were patterned by drawing up and binding portions of the cloth. He found only two pieces of stitch resist. Plate 2 The pieces made by binding include those in which the drawn-up cloth is bound in only one place, which results in a single resisted ring, and those bound in two places to create two concentric rings. One of the examples (Plate 1) illustrates both types of binding; Plate 1 each design motif, composed of a central unit of concentric rings that is surrounded by

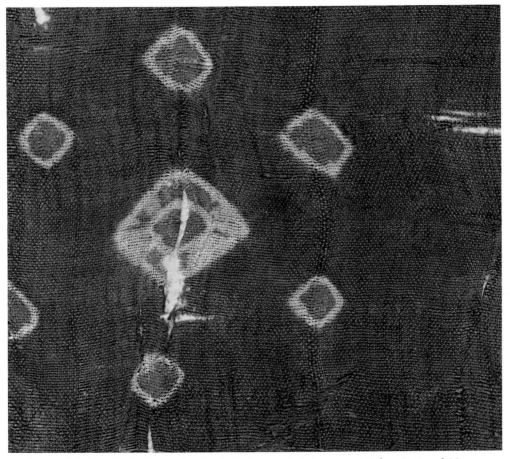

1.   Bound shibori, red silk, "seven luminaries" pattern. Eighth century. Tokyo National Museum.

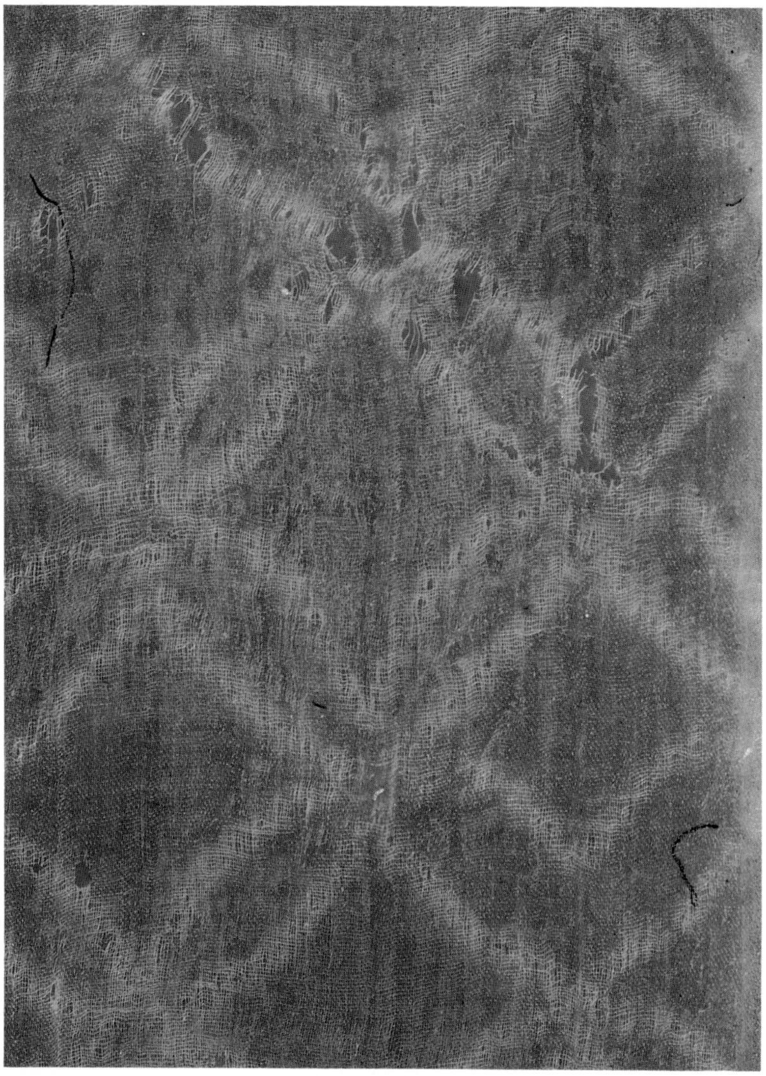

2. Stitched shibori, brown silk gauze. Eighth century. Tokyo National Museum.

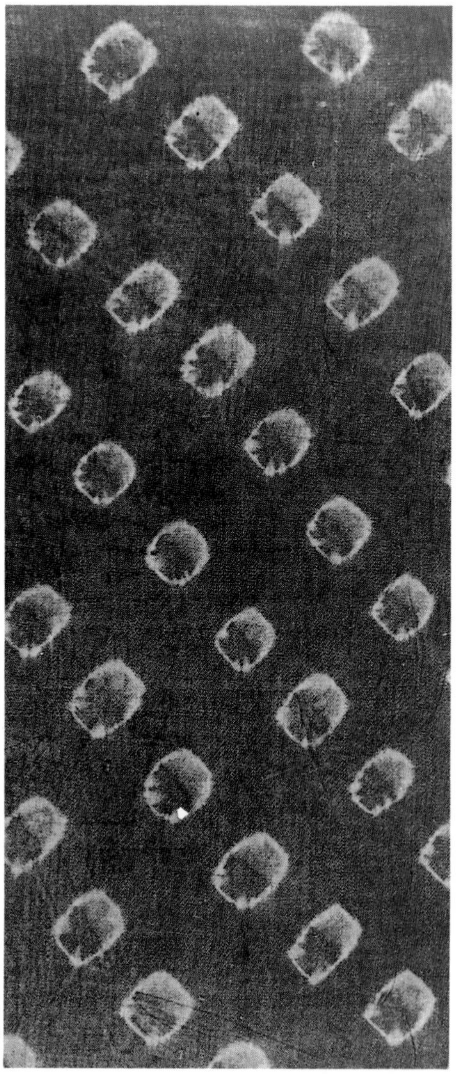

3. Bound shibori, green silk, *te-hitome kanoko* variation. Eighth century. Tokyo National Museum.

six smaller single rings, forms the pattern known as "seven luminaries." The large unit represents the sun, and the six rings encircling it represent the moon and planets. The clarity of the resisted rings in this example suggests that the cloth was bound over a core of some sort. Kitamura thinks bamboo was used.

Among the other types he studied is one resembling present-day *bai* shibori (see page 68), in which the thread is bound several times around the drawn-up cloth with

Plate 3

intervals left between each turn of thread. Still another of the Shōsō-in pieces (Plate 3) bears a close resemblance to the resist effect of half-dots achieved by *te-hitome*, a type of *kanoko* still being made in which the drawn-up cloth is folded two or three times before it is bound (see page 65). In addition to the pieces made by stitching and binding,

Plate 11

there are several that may have been made by folding and clamping.

The pieces of shibori in Emperor Shōmu's effects undoubtedly were particularly fine ones, but possession of this kind of patterned cloth was not confined to one of his lofty position. A poem appearing in the *Man'yōshū*, an eighth century anthology of Japanese poetry written between 557 and 764, cited by Mitsukuni Yoshida in the book *Kyō kanoko*, shows that children were wearing garments patterned with shibori *(yūhata)* by the latter half of the eighth century. Two lines in one poem appearing in that anthology have been translated as follows:

*When I was a child with hair down to my shoulders*
*I wore a sleeved robe of shibori cloth.*

The site chosen for a new capital to supplant Nara was to the north, the site of present-day Kyoto. The city was planned in the grand Chinese style with wide avenues running north-south and east-west and numerous narrower intersecting streets and lanes. The emperor moved into his new palace in the year 794. It was here in this city that a truly native Japanese style developed and flourished in all the arts.

layered robes—*jūni-hitoe*

In 894 the Japanese court, feeling confident and secure in their beautiful capital and having learned that the Tang empire was disintegrating, stopped sending official missions to Changan. They had learned from China; now they would make the knowledge their own. In the three hundred years that followed, the Japanese assimilated and transformed the continental culture that had swept onto their shores during the sixth, seventh, and eighth centuries. This process of opening the country to outside influences and then closing them off—made possible by the islands' location—of first borrowing and then assimilating, is a recurrent one in Japanese history. The result is a culture and art uniquely Japanese.

The cultural life of the new capital was centered in the court and affected a relatively small segment of society. The court, where tastes ran more to luxury than to Buddhist practices, was secluded, isolated from the rough life of the country at large and the pressing problems of the times. The life of the court was hidden behind garden walls in palace apartments divided with silken hangings and screened from view with delicate blinds of bamboo. Politics and administration were left to the Fujiwara regents while the emperor was preoccupied with ceremonies, rituals, and etiquette, the courtiers and their ladies with art, beauty, love, and intrigue. The arts flourished; fashions changed.

The high style of the Tang ladies, consisting of a long shirt, short tight bodice, and shawl draped gracefully over the shoulders, adopted with but little change by the Japanese court ladies during the Nara period, gave way to a uniquely Japanese dress style of many-layered robes—*jūni-hitoe*—literally, "twelve unlined robes," each one dyed in a different shade or color and all worn in a way calculated to show in subtle combination at neck and sleeves and hem. These layered robes were worn over full, skirtlike trousers. The Heian beauties appear in the paintings of the times almost completely enveloped in the voluminous folds of their garments.

However, the fashions of the court depended on patterned textiles also. There are many references to shibori-dyed cloth in the copious literature of the times—chronicles, diaries, romances, and codes of dress—and it is seen in paintings as well. Moreover, it is possible from such sources to sketch with some certainty the development of shibori and its use in the three hundred years that followed the break with China.

For example, in the *Ryō no gige*, the great ninth century exposition of the administrative codes (*Yōrō ritsuryō*) of a century earlier, Book Six deals with codes of dress for the twelve ranks of officers and the common classes. *Kechi* (纐) is mentioned in descriptions of clothing worn by women of the imperial family and their attendants and ladies-in-waiting. It was also used for uniforms of court officers of ranks one through six (*chōfuku*) and for garments of civil employees without rank (*seifuku*) and by commoners.

Toshiko Itō in her splendid book *Tsujigahana zome* (not the English adaptation) cites this as evidence that resist techniques, which had continued from the Nara period, began to take different directions. The methods of wax resist (*rōkechi*) and clamped wooden block resist (*kyōkechi*), imported from China and often noted in Nara records but seldom mentioned after the ninth century, evidently disappeared, while during Heian times shibori resist dyeing became increasingly important and widespread.

Itō cites a passage in the *Engi shiki*—a fifty-volume history that is a valuable source of information about tenth century Japan—dealing with dress codes and describing the types of garments and fabrics to be worn by the empress, her mother, and her grandmother. Shibori-patterned cloth (*yūhata* and *narabi-sakume*) was considered suitable for the robes of these high-ranking ladies. *Yūhata* is the same, ancient, general term for shibori noted in the previous section. *Narabi-sakume* is an obsolete term. Itō thinks that it refers to a specific kind of shibori, a very fine type that may have been similar to the *hitta kanoko* of a much later period.

In the book *Kyō kanoko*, Mitsukuni Yoshida cites a description, also from the *Engi shiki*, of a ceremony in which mounted imperial soldiers wore garments decorated with large shibori (*dai-kechi* or *ō-yūhata*), while palanquin carriers wore garments with a shiborilike pattern stenciled on the cloth (*dai-kechi suri*). Yoshida concludes that the larger, coarser shibori designs and stenciled imitation shibori were used for the dress of soldiers and servants, while the type referred to in the *Engi shiki* as *sakume* or *narabi-sakume* was reserved for garments worn by the empress and other women of high rank. These references indicate that by the end of the tenth century different types of shibori were being made and that they were worn by soldiers, servants, and—if the quality was very fine—by the highest ranking women of the court.

Tax records also found in the *Engi shiki*, and cited by Yoshida, show that shibori-dyed silk was accepted as tax by the imperial court, an indication that it was valued and much used by the court. In this connection, it is interesting to note that shibori-dyed fabrics were paid as tax from two widely separated areas of Japan: thirty double bolts of red silk shibori (*yūhata*) were collected from Dazaifu (in today's Fukuoka Prefecture) in northern Kyushu and from Hitachi (now Ibaraki Prefecture) on the eastern coast of Honshu. It is clear from this record that shibori dyeing was not limited to the capital, where dyeing was done for the court, but was being done in other places as well; nor was it restricted only to silk—the same tax record lists thirty pieces of shibori-dyed leather (*yūhata kawa*) from Dazaifu.

The literature of the eleventh and twelfth centuries contains many references to shibori. A number of these, cited in Itō's *Tsujigahana zome*, provide evidence that garments made of shibori-patterned cloth were increasingly worn by all classes and that such cloth was being put to a variety of other uses.

Murasaki Shikibu, the court lady whose keen and sensitive observations of Heian society are recorded in the world's first novel, *The Tale of Genji*, describes a group of courtiers as they set off on an outing, a casual visit to the Ishiyama temple, decked out for travel in damask and shibori robes. And in another passage she writes: "The covers for the votive stands were in splendid shibori, the colors beautifully matched, the dyeing done with skill rarely seen."

A document bearing the date 1088 tells of a ship belonging to a Fujiwara nobleman that flew a large banner of shibori (*kōkechi*). Shibori-dyed fabrics were also used in religious ceremonies and were part of the appointments of the emperor's palace, as a Taira clan nobleman records in his diary. In the entry for October 18, 1154, he tells of a Buddhist ceremony in an area partly enclosed by a canopy above and curtains on the three sides of shibori (*kōkechi*). And in a description of the imperial palace he notes that the large interior spaces were partitioned with shibori (*kōkechi*) hangings. At a festival held at the imperial court, according to an entry in the same diary, courtiers above the fifth rank and their wives all wore garments of shibori (*kōkechi*). The women who cooked and served the meals (*uneme*) also wore skirts of shibori (*kōkechi*) and sashes of a fine patterned shibori (*mezome*) tied in formal style.

The first visual representations of Japanese shibori fabrics are found in paintings of the late twelfth century. By that time Japanese artists had developed a style of painting entirely their own, dealing with essentially Japanese topics. The scrolls on which these pictures are painted, unrolled section by section as one sequence follows another, represent a dynamic form of storytelling and a way of adding the time element to pictorial art. The draftsmanship, quality of observation, and sense of humor shown in these scrolls are often of the highest order, and in one of the finest, "Legends of Shigi-san Temple" (Shigi-san engi emaki), lower-class people are shown wearing what may well be shibori-patterned garments. On one man's clothing, the large circular motifs seem to be the type of shibori made by drawing up a portion of cloth with the fingers and binding it round and round with thread before immersing it in the dye. The resulting pattern resembles a web, and in later times it came to be called kumo ("spider-web") shibori.

Another important source of visual references to shibori is provided by the paintings on fan-shaped pieces of paper on which Buddhist sutras are written. A number of these, containing sections of the Lotus Sutra, Myōhō renge kyō, were made into a set of seven scrolls at the end of the twelfth century. Five of them are preserved in the Shitennō-ji temple in Osaka; one is in the National Museum in Tokyo; and scattered fragments from the remaining scrolls are in private collections, small museums, and libraries. These genre paintings are a remarkable source of information about the life of the twelfth century. Several of them are reproduced in full color, together with scroll paintings, including the "Legends of Shigi-san Temple," in Volume 8, Emakimono ("Picture Scrolls"), in the series Nihon no Genshoku Bijutsu published (in Japanese) by Shogakukan.

In one of the fan sutra paintings (below) a servant girl is seen dressed in a short sleeveless garment worn over a simple skirt. The short wrapped garment she wears is

textile pattern motif from "Legends of Shigi-san Temple"

Plate 4

4. Detail of fan sutra (Myōhō renge kyō), late twelfth century (courtesy of Shitennō-ji temple, Osaka)

patterned with the same large circular shiborilike motifs seen in the "Legends of Shigi-san Temple" scroll. The sheer robe, however, that she has hung on a bamboo pole, is decorated in a design made up of small squarish resisted rings. The robe most likely belongs to her mistress, because the pattern of its sheer fabric is similar to the fabrics of the robes worn by an upper-class woman in yet another of these paintings. The scene in the second painting is of several women cooling off on a hot summer day. One dangles her bare feet in a garden pond, another is seen reclining on a raised platform above the pond. The one who reclines wears a red robe, patterned in small resisted squares arranged in groups of three *(mitsu meyui)*, and over it is a second robe of sheer fabric dyed pale indigo in the same shibori pattern. The red of the underrobe showing through the sheer outer one, with patterns overlaid, creates a lovely effect.

The numerous visual and written references of the Heian period to shibori clearly indicate that by the end of the era different types of shibori-patterned cloth were being made and that its distinctive designs were being imitated with stenciled patterns of silver and gold. The decorative cloth so produced was used for temple banners and canopies, the flags of ships, palace curtains, and for garments worn by different classes of society.

Plate 5

5.  Sutra scroll lining, red silk, *ori-nui* and *karamatsu* shibori. Kamakura period. Tō-ji temple, Kyoto.

### KAMAKURA PERIOD (1185–1333)

The late twelfth century marked the rise to power of the leaders of two warrior clans, the Taira and the Minamoto, at the expense of the Fujiwara regents, who had dominated Heian politics for centuries. The Taira clan was at first in the ascendant, but in the Gempei War of 1180–85 it was defeated by the Minamoto clan under the leadership of Minamoto no Yoritomo.

In the year 1185 Yoritomo established a military government with its headquarters at Kamakura, far to the east of the imperial capital and away from what he considered—and not without reason—the debilitating influence of the imperial court. Yoritomo demanded and obtained the powers of taxation and of appointment from the emperor, who remained with his court at Kyoto and carried on the ceremonial duties of his office. Life at court continued for a time in its old ways, but the power to influence society had shifted to a different breed of men in another part of the land.

The advent of military government naturally saw changes in styles of dress, reflecting the needs of the new leading class. The new leaders were men much influenced by Zen Buddhism. Its frugality, simplicity, and discipline appealed to fighting men. The elaborate and restrictive style of dress worn by the Fujiwara nobles was unsuited to the active life of warriors, and its opulence was alien to their tastes. As fighting men, the new leaders adapted the garment *(suikan)* worn by lower-class men to their particular needs. This three-quarter length upper garment was tied at the neck, had large sleeves, and was always tucked into the trousers.

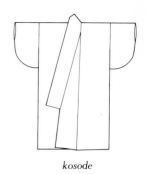

*kosode*

The many-layered robes worn by the ladies of the imperial court were deemed unsuitable for the wives of such sober men. They, in turn, adopted the simple wrapped garment with narrow sleeves that was worn as an undergarment by the court ladies of the preceding era. Called *kosode*, literally, "small sleeves," it was the garment that for centuries had been worn by commoners. On formal occasions they wore a robe *(uchiki)* over the *kosode*, and in time these two garments became the informal dress of the imperial court ladies.

*suikan*

The dress of courtiers, like that of the court ladies, was affected, and, following the example of the warriors, they adopted the *suikan* for informal wear. However, their style was neither drab nor simple: as though in compensation for abandoning the opulent garments of earlier times and adopting what had been the garments of commoners, they went in for the elaborately decorative. A detailed description of clothing worn on one occasion during this time is noted in the diary of Sanjō Saneatsu and is cited by Itō in *Tsujigahana zome*. He was one of a large band of courtiers who accompanied the abdicated emperor Kameyama, in the autumn of 1285, on a trip to the Bay of Sakai, perhaps to enjoy the nearby hot springs, and in one diary entry he describes the garments worn by some of his companions. A nobleman named Sanetoki wore a *suikan* made of a fabric woven of *kuzu (Pueraria lobata)* fiber. Its natural glossiness must have given a shimmering quality to the green of the shibori *(kanoko yui)* decorated cloth, and over the dyed pattern motifs of exotic birds had been painted (not stenciled) with gold and silver. Under this garment he wore an unlined summer *kosode*, called *katabira*, that was patterned in the same type of shibori *(kanoko yui)*, dyed red. His black, somewhat stiff and full-cut trousers also were decorated with shibori. The entry continues with a description of the dress of the high-ranking noble Kanetsugu, who was wearing a deep blue *suikan* patterned with a different kind of shibori *(maki zome)*. On this fabric was the motif of a meandering stream in applied gold and silver leaf; the same motif, embroidered in graduated shades of blue, decorated his trousers.

The adoption of the *kosode* by the ladies of the court and the wives of military men was a revolutionary change in dress style. The *kosode* long continued to be worn by women of all classes, and although its decoration and the manner in which it was worn reflected changing ideas and taste, its basic shape has remained unchanged. It is the simple wrapped garment known today as the kimono.

For a time the *kosode* may have been worn undecorated, a style of utmost simplicity reflecting the rigorous ideals of the military rulers. However, these ideals were not adhered to for long—women's love of color and pattern and the gradual relaxation of the austerity that characterized the early years of the shogunate ensured the emergence of changing styles. Instead of utilizing the subtle color combinations of many robes, decorative effect was achieved by the embellishment of one garment. A good example of this style change is seen in a scroll painting of the late Kamakura period. In this painting, the *kosode* worn by the sleeping woman is decorated only at the shoulders and hem. Itō is of the opinion that its design of tidepools was created by divided dyeing *(somewake)*. This is a process in which the outline of the design is delineated with stitches and the stitching thread is drawn up, making it possible to protect ground areas

*kosode* showing earliest known example of "divided dyeing" *(somewake)*; dated 1309

from the dye; the drawn-up stitching thread precisely reproduces the outline of the design. Refined stitch resists were being used during Kamakura times. The further development of stitched shibori that takes place in the Muromachi period reaches a peak of perfection in the superb *tsujigahana* textiles of the sixteenth century.

## MUROMACHI PERIOD (1333–1513)

The Kamakura shogunate, its hand no longer firm, came under serious challenge early in the fourteenth century with the accession in Kyoto of Godaigo, an emperor who wanted not only to reign but to rule as well. After the armed adherents attracted to his cause had become a threat to its Kyoto garrison, the shogunate sent off an army that was intended to reassert its authority in the imperial capital. The army was commanded by a trusted daimyo, Ashikaga Takauji, but he went over to the imperial cause. This led to the overthrow of the Kamakura shogunate and the establishment of a new shogunate by Ashikaga Takauji. His headquarters were located in the Muromachi quarter of Kyoto, which gave its name to the period he had ushered in.

The Ashikaga shoguns never established the degree of authority over the feudal lords that their Kamakura predecessors had exercised. Civil war continued for over half a century after the establishment of the Ashikaga shogunate in 1333; the sanguinary Ōnin War, during which Kyoto was reduced to ashes, raged from 1467 through 1477; and at the close of the fifteenth century there began a period of civil warfare that lasted a hundred years. However, although the Muromachi period was one of great turbulence, it also was one of economic growth, cultural ferment, and artistic development.

Indeed, the civil wars, although sometimes destructive, served in some respects to stimulate economic activity rather than to inhibit it. The armies that took to the field had to be supported, and this gave rise to a class of contractors who procured, stored, and transported foodstuffs and other supplies for the military. The port of Sakai, near Osaka, benefited from this business, and even more from a lucrative trade carried on with Ming dynasty China, with which official relations were resumed. That trade, sponsored by leading lords and great monasteries, gave rise to a class of rich and influential merchants. Sakai also benefited during the Ōnin War by an influx of refugees from Kyoto, where a great part of the fighting took place. The refugees included many skilled artisans, and they contributed greatly to the prosperity of Sakai.

In the ferment of the Muromachi period, cultural activities, previously confined largely to the capital and to Buddhist centers of learning, spread throughout the land. Feudal lords and successful warriors, established in strongholds and not completely satisfied by the arts of war, found satisfaction also in the peaceful arts. When not engaged in military pursuits, some of them wrote poetry, collected paintings, and invited theatrical companies to put on performances.

It was during this time that the dyers developed an ingenious way of using stitching as a shibori technique to create designs of stylized natural motifs. By the end of the sixteenth century this dye-patterned cloth was worn by people of all classes and by men and women alike. This new style of textile decoration is unlike any other in Japan or elsewhere; obscure in origin and short-lived in its fullest flowering, it was later to become an outstanding expression of a remarkable time in Japanese history—the few decades known as the Momoyama period.

Precisely where or exactly when this development of shibori began is unknown. The techniques were all known in Japan by the early fourteenth century, but it was the way in which they were used, and later combined, that was new. Since there is no direct evidence of its origin, one can only conjecture that commoners living in and around the cities and in the towns that grew up around the larger castles created a demand for garments that were different from those of lower-class country people, who had worn indigo-dyed, shibori-patterned cloth for centuries. The shibori dyers responded by creating designs using motifs derived from nature.

Until the emergence of the new style of shibori patterns, binding was the primary shibori method used. The motifs created by bound shibori are determined by the placement and pressure of the binding thread on the folds of a drawn-up portion of cloth. Freely drawn forms cannot be resisted in this way—the very nature of the binding process limits the type of motif that can be resisted to rings and other forms that are circular or squarish. However, by outlining a motif with stitches and drawing the thread up tight, the form of the motif is reserved when the cloth is dyed. When the process was developed further by covering the portions of drawn-up cloth within each of the stitch-outlined motifs and immersing the entire cloth in dye, a design composed of motifs reserved on a dyed ground became possible. Carried one step further, by protecting the area surrounding the stitch-enclosed portions of drawn-up cloth, and by dipping only the uncovered portions of cloth in dyes of different colors, it became possible to create multicolored designs composed of motifs on a reserved ground. This Plate 12 was a breakthrough in the dyer's art that occurred in Japan during the fourteenth century. It is this development in the resist process that later made possible the superb dyed textiles of the sixteenth and early seventeenth centuries.

It is not known where these new patterns were first made or what they looked like. At any rate, the first written reference to them appears in a poem entered in a competition held around the end of the fourteenth century. The subject of the competition was artisans and tradespeople, and one of the poems selected by the judge for special comment was about a woman fish vendor from Katsura outside Kyoto. The word *tsujigahana*, a compound containing the words for a crossroads *(tsuji)* and for flowers *(hana)*, was used to describe a sleeve of her garment; the judge said that it evoked a vision of spring flowers. Some existing examples of *tsujigahana* patterns contain crossed lines, which create the effect of a lattice, and almost all of them contain flowers, making the name an appropriate as well as a poetic one.

That the women of Katsura dressed attractively may be inferred from an entry made during 1416 in the diary of Prince Fushimi Sadafusa concerning a party given by another person of high rank. The prince wrote that his host's servants were dressed like women of Katsura *(Katsurame)*, and remarked on the beauty of the *kosode* that they wore. Ten years later another diarist wrote that at the New Year, when people from the different districts of Kyoto danced in celebration, the women from the Sanjō district affected the dress of *Katsurame*—an indication that the women of the capital found the style attractive.

The wearing of *tsujigahana* apparently had become fashionable well before the end of the fifteenth century, and it is clear that some men wore it, at least on informal occasions. An entry in the diary of a retainer of the Ashikaga shogunate, describing a chase conducted by the Hosogawa family in 1465, mentions one of the participants as wearing a *katabira* (a lightweight *kosode*) of *tsujigahana* without red—a comment that suggests that red was often used in *tsujigahana*. In 1528 an official named Ise Sadayori, who had served four successive Ashikaga shoguns, wrote a book of etiquette and guidance entitled *Sōgo daisōshi*, in which he declared: "*Tsujigahana*, gold imprint, and the like are suitable for children, ladies, and youths, but not for adult males."

If the wearing of *tsujigahana* by males then signified a lack of maturity, if not effeminacy, it did not long continue to do so. Itō's book *Tsujigahana: The Flower of Japanese Textile Art* contains a reproduction of a sixteenth century portrait of Takeda Shingen, who died in 1573. Takeda Shingen was noted for his bellicosity, and the portrait is that of a formidable man, sword at hand, with a bull neck and massively square body—the kind of build likely to belong to a successful warrior in any army of whatever country in any age. Shingen is clad in a wraparound garment that opens sufficiently in front to reveal an undergarment decorated with a *tsujigahana* pattern. Moreover, military leaders more redoubtable than he would shortly be wearing outer garments decorated with shibori—if, indeed, they had not already begun to do so.

The earliest existing examples of *tsujigahana* are not garments but a group of banners made to be placed around Buddhist temples during special religious ceremonies. Their silk could have been patterned expressly for these banners, or the banners may have been made from *kosode*. When a woman died it was customary to take her *kosode* apart and donate the cloth strips to her family temple. If the cloth was brocade, it was likely to be used in making the shawllike priest's vestment called a *kesa*. This was often made of patchwork to suggest the patched clothing of the poor—a symbol of poverty worn long after poverty itself had been abandoned. Lightweight silks were made into the covers for votive stands or into temple banners. Accordingly one cannot tell whether these earliest existing examples of *tsujigahana* were made of newly patterned cloth or from an old *kosode*, but the time that the banners were made is precisely documented, as recounted by Itō in *Tsujigahana: The Flower of Japanese Textile Art*. She states that when one of the banners became worn, it was cut apart, and found stitched in the selvage was a piece of paper on which was written: "Chōzembō, an inhabitant of the village of Ōno, Kaisō County, Kii Province, and priest of Negoro-dera, has planned the presentation of these banners to the temple. Their making began in 1528 and was completed in the hour of the monkey [between 3:00 and 5:00 p.m.] on the twenty-first day of the twelfth month of 1530. It is hoped that people in later ages who see these banners will pray for the pious Chōzembō."

The motifs in the silk of these banners, wisteria flowers, waves, and maple leaves, are all executed with stitch resists; accents of sumi ink can be detected, and the forms of the flowers are overlaid with silver leaf. In style and technique the banners reflect an advanced state of the art, suggesting a considerable period of development.

At least part of that development undoubtedly took place in the thriving port city of Sakai. With the influx of upper-class society from Kyoto, fleeing the destruction of the Ōnin War, and the stimuli from abroad resulting from foreign trade, Sakai had grown to be a cultured, fashionable, and wealthy city. Artisans, too, had fled from Kyoto, and it seems likely that among them were dyers who brought the new shibori techniques to Sakai. Itō states that much of the *tsujigahana* was made there, and it is clear that the producers did not all move back to Kyoto after the end of the Ōnin War. A record in a local shrine shows that there was a *tsujigahana* workshop in Sakai in 1535, long after Kyoto had been rebuilt.

Shibori dyeing continued to develop during the last years of the Muromachi period, but it was during the brief, joyful, extravagant period of Momoyama that followed that it attained its peak of perfection.

## MOMOYAMA PERIOD (1573–1615)

During the last three decades of the sixteenth century three great generals—Oda Nobunaga, Toyotomi Hideyoshi, and Tokugawa Ieyasu—through force of arms and character, unified Japan and brought the powerful, independent feudal lords under a strong central authority. Unification of the divided land was begun by Nobunaga and completed after his untimely death in 1582 by Hideyoshi. Following the death of Hideyoshi in 1598, Ieyasu established the capital in the east at Edo—present-day Tokyo—and set the country on the road to an unprecedented period of peace that lasted for 250 years.

All of Hideyoshi's undertakings were conceived on a grand scale. After unifying the country, he embarked on a vast building program, one that involved, if contemporary records are to be believed, tens or even hundreds of thousands of workers. Nobunaga had built his castle at Azuchi on the shore of Lake Biwa, Hideyoshi built his on a grander scale at Osaka. In Kyoto he built a palace, the Jurakudai, and saw to the reconstruction of the emperor's palace. A few years later Hideyoshi ordered a palace built for himself in Kyoto on rising ground, which came to be called Momoyama, "peach hill," for the abundance of peach trees on the slope. Nothing remains of the palace, but the name Momoyama is given to the period. It was a time in which the arts took directions outside the old traditions, a time lasting little more than half a century that fell between two eras, one of war and violence and the other of a strictly controlled society. This period of great prosperity, expansiveness, and freedom, dominated by men risen to power from undistinguished origins—Hideyoshi was the son of a common soldier and had himself risen from the ranks in Nobunaga's army—generated and released a powerful creative energy that produced an art imbued with a native Japanese love of decoration and feel for bold eccentric design.

Hideyoshi's building projects stimulated the economy and provided work for artists and artisans alike. The great halls of castles and palaces demanded an entirely new style of decoration. Hideyoshi found in the artist Kanō Eitoku, who had worked on Nobunaga's castle at Azuchi, a man who met the challenge. Eitoku developed a bold style of painting admirably suited to the large scale of the numerous rooms—several hundred in Osaka castle—a style that with its strength, bright colors, and expanses of gold appealed to Hideyoshi and greatly impressed his vassals. It was Hideyoshi's pleasure to conduct his guests through the castle audience chambers to view the magnificent paintings on gold-covered panels and screens and then on to the treasure vaults to see the piles of gold and other precious objects kept there.

The role of Kanō Eitoku and other lesser artists in the employ of powerful and wealthy men in the latter part of the sixteenth century was perhaps not only one of a painter of great screens, but of a designer as well. Eitoku designed a lacquered saddle, for example, and Seiroku Noma in *Japanese Costume and Textile Arts* expresses the opinion that well-known painters designed clothes for the ruling class as well as the superb Nō costumes of the period. This dramatic brilliance, as effective as the screen paintings, is characteristic of Momoyama clothing. A *dōfuku* (cloak) that may have belonged to Hideyoshi, known from its design as the Arrow Dōfuku, still exists and is a good example of this type of boldly conceived decoration, which demanded great skill from the shibori artisans and dyers who executed it.

Arrow Dōfuku

The fabric used for that garment, as well as for all of the fine shibori of the period, is a silk that is no longer woven, whose particular sheen depends on the degree of its degumming (i.e., the degree to which the natural gum called sericin is removed from silk thread). The late Shōzo Takeuchi, who in 1965 successfully reproduced the Hideyoshi Arrow Dōfuku for display at Osaka Castle, spent two years in his search for comparable silk and finally had to have it specially woven. He commented that after three hundred years the silk of the original garment "retains the sheen of a pearl."

By the end of the sixteenth century, Itō tells us, even the noble ladies of the imperial court were wearing the simplified garment style and *tsujigahana*-patterned silk. Sakai evidently was still a center for this work, for a diarist known as the "lord of Nishi-tō-in" noted in 1596 that his ladies got their *tsujigahana katabira*—unlined summer *kosode*—from a man named Kamo. In that same year, when the ambassador from the Ming court returned to China, Hideyoshi made him a gift of two unglossed *katabira* with leaf imprint of incomparable workmanship and ten *katabira* of *tsujigahana*. That Hideyoshi chose to give *tsujigahana* as a gift to a foreign envoy is a good indication of its high quality.

The most creative of the shibori producers served the most influential, wealthy, and powerful patrons. Working with the finest silks and the most skillful artisans, they produced garments of the highest quality. To meet the growing demand of the commoners, standardized patterns requiring less skill and pongee, a coarser silk, were used. A kind of mass production in small workshops was developed so that the work could be turned out rapidly. In reflection of these differences the extant *tsujigahana* fabrics display a wide range in quality. In short, during this brief and brilliant age, these colorfully patterned garments were worn by old and young, men and women, upper-class people and commoners. Seiroku Noma comments that "at no other time in Japan's long history were the streets so full of color."

Ieyasu, after the death in 1598 of Hideyoshi, set about consolidating his own power. After his decisive victory at Sekigahara two years later over rivals for the leadership, he moved the capital to Edo, the stronghold of his own eastern domain, where he had resided for over a decade. In establishing his authority, he confiscated the fief lands of ninety daimyo who had opposed him, retaining a large proportion of those lands for his own Tokugawa family and distributing the rest as rewards among the daimyo who had fought for him. And in 1603 the emperor granted Ieyasu, now firmly in power, the title of shogun.

Although a rigidly ordered feudal society was created under the domination of the Tokugawa family, such a society was not achieved all at once. It took some time for the vigor of the past half century to be subdued and society to be reshaped. But the energy of the Momoyama could not be indefinitely maintained, and the need for some reshaping of society was inherent in the age's very extravagance.

The Keichō era (1596–1615; eras reflect emperors' reigns) almost coincides with the dates of the death of Hideyoshi in 1598 and that of Ieyasu in 1616. Most of the shibori-dyed garments in the *tsujigahana* style that exist today are from that time. That they have survived for so long is due to one or the other of two related circumstances. Many of the garments were made expressly for Ieyasu and members of his family, and the Tokugawa rule of the country for almost three hundred years ensured the protection of the possessions of the founder and his family. In addition, some pieces of clothing were

6. Robe owned by Tokugawa Ieyasu, given to a gunsmith named Kunitomo. Early seventeenth century. This marvelous shibori garment came to light as this book was being completed (courtesy of Kunitomo family).

carefully preserved for reasons related to a custom going back to Heian times of rewarding faithful retainers with gifts of cloth or costume. On occasion the great man might so reward a retainer by taking off an item of clothing and presenting it to him. Plate 6 The recipient, draping the garment about his shoulders would then take his leave. An aura of greatness flowing from the donor was inevitably associated with garments acquired in this way and was likely to ensure that they would be cared for as family heirlooms. Two noteworthy garments that had belonged to Ieyasu have been preserved in consequence of his having followed that custom. One is a short garment worn under armor presented by Ieyasu to Inagaki Nagashige in 1590 in return for a pledge of fealty. The other is a robe, splendidly designed with wide horizontal bands of red on a yellow ground with motifs of clove flowers, their sharply tapered points shibori dyed with incomparable skill. It was presented to Yasuhara Dembei, who was in charge of silver mining at Iwami, as a reward for the discovery of a vein that resulted in dramatically increased production. It is possible to tell from these and many other existing garments, as well as from surviving fragments, the techniques that were used to create these striking textiles.

Many of Ieyasu's garments, like Hideyoshi's *dōfuku* with arrow design, are executed solely with stitched shibori in the manner already described, and they show the greatest possible skill. However, more typically, the *tsujigahana* style is characterized by a combination of shibori-dyed designs and decorative detail added in sumi ink. Stitch-resisted lines and motif outlines have a distinct soft-edged quality. Motifs that are Plate 13 outlined with stitches and covered to prevent dye from reaching the cloth within the stitch-enclosed portion may give a feeling of emptiness. It was to overcome this sense of incompleteness that decorative details were added to the forms with sumi ink painting. The exceptionally fine detailing, especially of flower forms, provides an elegant touch. The contrast of sharply drawn details with the soft edges of the resisted motifs and the tonal contrast of the dark ink with the delicate blues, greens, and yellows the dyers often used give the designs a unique quality. The beauty of *tsujigahana* lies in the balance of these contrasts. Besides the sumi ink detail, hand-painted dyes, embroidery, and gold and Plates 16, 17 silver leaf were often added to create a textile of extreme elegance and luxury.

Stitching provides not only the means to delineate motifs that are dyed or reserved, but a way of creating a textural design effect as well. This application of stitching in resist dyeing had developed during the Muromachi period—or possibly earlier, though there are no earlier existing examples. Later known as *mokume* (wood grain) shibori, Plate 7

7.   Detail of Bugaku costume, indigo silk, wood-grain (*mokume*) shibori. Sixteenth century. Amano-Yashiro, Kōya-san.

the subtlety of the effect that results from the repetition of parallel rows of stitches drawn up before the cloth is dyed belies the simplicity of the technique.

Bound resists, which were paramount before the development of stitch resists, continued to be used but played a minor role. Tiny resisted dots (*kanoko* shibori) were used in the *tsujigahana* style to create textured effects or to add details to stitch-resisted motifs. Dyed in pale shades, they were usually only delicate elements in the overall design. Rarely, to judge from existing examples, was *kanoko* the sole technique used in a garment. Among these exceptions are two of Ieyasu's *kosode* in which the tiny resisted square dots create floral arabesques on very dark grounds of blue and green. Another of his garments, a wadded *kosode*, uses *kanoko* to create the outlines of fan motifs on a ground of palest indigo.

The shibori artisans of the period who worked for patrons at the pinnacle of the social order, such as Ieyasu, had developed their skill to the highest level. By using extremely small stitches—taking up only two or three of the fine threads of the cloth with each stitch—they were able to achieve sharp instead of fuzzy-edged resists; that they could do this with motifs placed very close together is particularly remarkable. Indeed, the process was sometimes stretched to the limits of human skill, achieving a perfection such as we associate with the output of the error-free machine. One marvels at the skill that made this possible, yet, as with all art carried to that stage, something was lost. Perhaps it is the human evidence of imperfection that is missed.

Change was in the offing, and towards the end of the Keichō era, a new style of textile decoration developed. The design of the *kosode* becomes divided into large asymmetrical interlocking areas of color that are filled in with disparate patterns. *Kanoko* shibori in combination with embroidery and gold leaf create a style that is strong and rhythmical in an almost jazzy way, with large areas of color and of black cutting across the garment. These bold, contrasting diagonals seem to be drawn from the "pine bark lozenge" motif (*matsukawabishi*) of *tsujigahana* textiles, but the two styles are totally different. At this time a change also occurred in the relative importance of bound and stitched resists; *kanoko*, which had played a minor role during the Momoyama period, emerged as the dominant shibori technique. Stitched shibori, which was so important in *tsujigahana* textiles, became less important—limited to dividing the large design areas so that they could be dyed in different colors in the process called "divided dyeing" (*somewake*).

The shift to *kanoko* and the decline of *tsujigahana* shibori, in the opinion of Itō, came about when the process of weaving figured silk was introduced from China in the first decade of the seventeenth century. At first these silks were used undyed, appreciated for their woven patterns—Ieyasu owned a large number of garments made from them. However, by the end of the Keichō era they began to be used as a base for pattern dyeing. The popularity of the novel silks discouraged the weaving of plain weave glossed silk, and they eventually replaced it. However, the uneven textures of these figured weaves proved unsuitable for the type of stitch resists used in *tsujigahana*, as well as for the finely drawn lines of sumi ink painting. Both were replaced by *kanoko* dots, for which the new silks were not unsuited. By the Keichō era, in the opinion of Yoshida, *kanoko* shibori had become an established craft specialty in Kyoto. It was destined to develop to its peak of artistic perfection in the first half of the seventeenth century.

During Muromachi and Momoyama, two textile traditions emerged. Each had elements rooted in the past, but with the growth of urban centers and a class of townspeople, their distinguishing characteristics became clear. One was elegant, refined, colorful for an upper-class elite, rich merchants, and city-dwelling commoners and used silks and fine hemp textiles; the other, natural, robust and typically indigo-dyed for country people, using hemp, other rough fibers, and later cotton. In the last

Plate 15

Plate 18

Plate 19

Plate 8

Plate 15

8. *Kosode* displaying interlocking and overlapping color areas (*somewake*) and *kanoko* shibori. Early seventeenth century. Kanebo Collection.

years of the seventeenth century and the first decade of the eighteenth, the bold steps taken by Ieyasu to consolidate his power and construct the framework for the new Tokugawa shogunate would set in motion events affecting both textile traditions as well as every aspect of Japanese life.

EDO PERIOD (1615–1868)

Shogun Tokugawa Ieyasu, in redistributing feudal lands for the purposes of consolidating his power and insuring the dominance of his family, awarded to one of his younger sons the fief of Owari, a strategically located province lying between Nara and Kyoto to the west and the more distant lands to the east, where Edo was situated. A castle was to be built for his son, and to help with the planning and construction Ieyasu commanded the assistance of twenty of the lords. One of them, according to Hiroko Andō and Hiroko Harada in an article in *Textile Arts*, was Shigetoshi Takenaka, whose fief in the southern island of Kyushu included the shibori producing village of Kodata, and the workers he brought to help with construction of the castle wore garments of distinctively patterned shibori cloth. The castle was completed in 1612, and a castle town began to grow up around it, now the city of Nagoya.

In 1601, shortly after his victory in the battle of Sekigahara, Ieyasu had required the feudal lords to sign an oath of loyalty, pledging to obey all orders sent from his headquarters at Edo. Upon his installation as shogun in 1603, the feudal lords journeyed to Edo to declare their fealty, and to facilitate their travel then and on subsequent occasions, the government established rest stations, fifty-three in number, on the eastern coastal route, known as the Tōkaidō, connecting the two capitals of Edo and Kyoto. At these stations travelers could obtain palanquin bearers and porters for the onward journey, and inns and shops that catered to their wants sprang up.

The expectation that the feudal lords would journey to Edo from time to time to declare anew their fealty became a formalized requirement. In order to ensure their obedience, and as a precaution against their attempting rebellion, the lords were required to maintain residences in Edo, to live there for stated periods, and to leave their wives and children there upon returning to their fiefs. With the establishing of that requirement, and the setting up of a courier service linking the old and new capitals, there was a permanent increase in official travel on the Tōkaidō. In addition, it was used by merchants going to Edo on business, by pilgrims, and by other travelers.

The Tōkaidō passed through some uninhabited areas of Owari that held danger for travelers, prompting the lord of Owari to encourage new settlements with promises of free land and exemption from taxation on it. In response, a man named Takeda and eight fellow villagers from a cotton-growing region on the nearby Chita Peninsula, together with their families, established a settlement on the Tōkaidō at a place that was first called Aramachi, meaning "new town," and later changed to Arimatsu, meaning "place of the pines." It was, of course, not an official station providing overnight accommodations, but the settlers quickly began to cater to the needs of passing travelers. Tea shops were opened, and the villagers began to make straw sandals for wayfarers traveling on foot and simple bound shibori *tenugui*, small all-purpose towels.

The making of the patterned *tenugui* represented the modest beginning at Arimatsu of a thriving village shibori industry, one that is unique in having an unbroken development to the present day. The location of the village on the Tōkaidō tended to ensure that it would enjoy prosperity in normal times, and the interest that the Owari fief took in Arimatsu helped enable it to survive hardship. The first settlers came with some knowledge of basic shibori processes, and those who followed, if they lacked the skill, could learn it after their arrival. Cotton, which had been introduced into Japan early in the fifteenth century, was grown in Owari and presumably was being woven there by the early years of the seventeenth century, when Arimatsu was established. There were many dyers already established in the province of Owari, and dyes were readily available. Indigo for blue in its many shades was locally grown, additional supplies of it came in from Shikoku, and in later years there would come into use the red derived from the safflower and the purple of gromwell.

The first patterns produced in Arimatsu were simply variations of the bound shibori called *kumo*, which resembles a spider's web, that had been used for centuries to pattern cloth for the garments of common people. However, because the feudal lords with their retainers made repeated trips to and from Edo, as did other travelers, there was a constant demand for new patterns, and particularly for cloth and garments with patterns that made them suitable for the gifts that Japanese travelers seem constrained to buy. As early as 1624 Takeda Shōkurō Takenori, one of the original settlers, was producing a pattern of stripes and bands, on hemp and also silk cloth. This was made by pleating and binding the cloth, creating an effect similar to that of medieval armor. Another pattern, according to local lore, was introduced by the wife of a doctor named Miura Genchū, who had accompanied Lord Takenaka from Kyushu at the time Owari Castle was being built and had later returned to Owari and settled in Arimatsu. She was familiar with the shibori made in Kyushu and taught people in Arimatsu a kind of looped binding, a method of binding employing a hook to hold the cloth. This method, as well as the distinctive patterning it creates, were later named after Mrs. Miura, and shibori-dyed cloth of the *miura* pattern is still being produced in Arimatsu (see pages 70ff). The hook used in binding *miura* shibori was adapted for use in the binding of *kumo* shibori, perhaps shortly after its introduction. Use of the hook, besides speeding the process, makes it possible to shape the cloth into even pleats and to hold them taut while the cloth is bound, producing a much more refined effect. Arimatsu was now producing attractive cloth of distinctive designs, it was being bought by increasing numbers of travelers, and the Owari clan benefited from taxes levied on its sale.

In 1641 the second lord of Owari, Tokugawa Mitsutomo, accompanied by his retinue, passed through Arimatsu on his way to Owari Castle. The villagers had all turned out to line the way in order to watch him pass and make their obeisances, and when he arrived they presented him with a pair of horse reins made of shibori-decorated cloth. It must be that he appreciated the gift, and that the horse reins continued to be produced; when the fifth Tokugawa shogun was installed in Edo in 1680, the lords who gathered from around the country brought gifts—products made in their respective fiefs—and among the gifts from the lord of Owari were ceremonial horse reins decorated in the "armor" pattern of stripes and bands.

By the middle of the seventeenth century, with peace in the land and growing prosperity, the lords and their retainers, officials on missions for the shogunate and people on errands for the merchant houses traveling over the Tōkaidō were joined by more and more commoners making pilgrimages to the great Atsuta Shrine, located in the Owari fief a few miles from Arimatsu, and the more distant Ise shrines. In Arimatsu they found the shibori temptingly displayed by the enterprising local merchants, who called attention to it by hanging great lengths of the decorated cloth near the open fronts of their shops, where it fluttered like colorful banners in the wind. With a bit more money to spend than in former years, many could afford the purchase of some decorated cloth or perhaps a shibori garment. Kahei Takeda, a fourteenth-generation producer of shibori, has expressed in his book *Arimatsu shibori* the opinion that those garments represented the origin of the *yukata*, an unlined light cotton kimono that later gained general acceptance for casual summer wear.

Increased sales and a greater variety of patterns led to the introduction of a division of labor in the production of shibori: there were those who bound or stitched or pleated the cloth; those who dyed it; and merchants who sold it. In the opinion of Takeda, it had begun by the middle of the seventeenth century. The Owari fief had given the villagers of Arimatsu exclusive rights for the sale of shibori to members of the clan as well as the right to put a stamp representing the clan seal upon their products—much as chosen producers in Great Britain may place on their goods a replica of the royal arms and a notation that they are supplied by appointment to the reigning sovereign. To assure the high quality of shibori bearing that stamp of approval, the merchant producers of the village organized an association, set up quality controls, and agreed to cooperate for mutual benefit.

The members of the association were men whose families had been engaged in shibori production in Arimatsu since shortly after the founding of the village. However, in time people of nearby areas, who were beyond the control of the village association, began to make and sell shibori cloth of inferior quality, and this became a source of worry to the merchant producers of Arimatsu, who feared that a lowering of standards would damage the reputation for high quality of their own shibori cloth and might ultimately destroy the regional craft. In addition, the shibori fabrics and garments made in Arimatsu began to encounter competition from the nearby town of Narumi, which enjoyed the advantage of being an overnight station on the Tōkaidō, and where the local women had begun to make and sell their own shibori products. In fact, shibori

Plates 9, 10, 23, 24

fabrics made in Arimatsu were sold quite early in Narumi shops, and were often erroneously called Narumi shibori. The Arimatsu merchants took their grievances to the Owari fief officials, and in 1781 a compromise was reached. Fourteen producers outside the village were also to be included in the production and sales monopoly, and they joined the Arimatsu merchants in forming a new association of merchant producers.

In 1784 a fire swept through Arimatsu, completely destroying it. Again the Owari fief stepped in and gave financial assistance to rebuild the village. The new shops and houses along its main street, two storied and tile roofed, were a great improvement over the original buildings, and some of them remain to this day. In twenty years the village had not only completely recovered; it was producing shibori cloth of finer quality than ever before.

The agreement reached in 1781 did not mark the end of friction between Arimatsu and Narumi over the production and sale of shibori. It would appear that under the agreement some restriction had been placed on shibori production in Narumi, perhaps under a system of producers' quotas. At any rate, in 1804 Arimatsu merchants filed complaints over illegal sales of Narumi shibori, alleging that quantities of it were being distributed through pawnbrokers in the guise of second-hand goods. This ingenious scheme was not easily stamped out, as evidenced by renewed complaints lodged against the practice in subsequent years.

The early *ukiyo-e* paintings, the subsequent hand-tinted woodblock prints, and the color block prints that supplanted them attest to the popularity of shibori-decorated garments and provide a means of tracing the development of shibori patterns. They also suggest that the early Edo fashions were the loveliest. The unusual and striking
Plate 8  style of the Keichō years, which featured disparate interlocking design areas and strongly contrasting colors, gave way to quieter and more refined designs, which came
Plate 22  to be known as the Kanbun style. The style persisted long after the short reign era from which it takes its name. Motifs were dramatically increased in size and placed at one shoulder of the *kosode* or grouped across both shoulders and arranged to sweep down to the hem. *Kanoko* was skillfully used by the designers to enhance a form or to create a lively contrast between tiny individual resists and greatly enlarged motifs. In one version of the style, large motifs intricately detailed with *kanoko* are contrasted with
Plate 20  areas of undecorated ground (Plate 20). In a much more luxurious treatment of the same design style, the ground of the *kosode* is filled with the tiny resisted squares,
Plate 21  leaving only the lines of the design free of them (Plate 21).

A Kyoto specialty with a history of development since the Nara period, expensive because making it took much labor and time and required great skill, *kanoko* was the type of shibori in greatest demand among the affluent city dwellers, and because it was expensive the Tokugawa regime frowned on it. Trying to maintain the conservative class distinctions, which placed the warrior class at the top of the social scale, meant that repeated attempts had to be made to restrain conspicuous consumption by everyone else. The shogunate issued decrees in which the clothing appropriate for each class was specified, but the merchants, who theoretically occupied the lowest position— below the farmers of the countryside and the artisans of the urban centers—had the most money and were intent on enjoying the benefits it might bring. In 1683 the government, as part of its sumptuary edicts and a new effort to limit sums spent for new garments, specifically prohibited the use of *sō kanoko*, the allover *kanoko* used to fill large areas. It did succeed, then or later, in suppressing its use, if not in eliminating it entirely. However, official efforts to discourage the creation of all garments with *kanoko* patterns were to no avail. A popular writer of the day tells of a gathering of people in the spring of 1687 at Ueno in Edo to view the cherry blossoms. On outings such as this, samurai families cordoned off areas with curtains bearing the family crest, while others happily hung up their brightly colored *kosode* on ropes stretched between the trees. On this particular day not a single *kosode* was seen that was not decorated with *kanoko*.

During the latter part of the eighteenth century and the first years of the nineteenth, townspeople and city dwellers continued to enjoy great affluence. The merchants, in particular, had gained a position of real importance, which the military class no longer enjoyed. The military still had a consciousness of high social standing, but it was commoners who had most of the money and most of the fun. They became inveterate consumers. It was to them that the works of novelists, painters, and playwrights were addressed; they crowded the theaters, and the favored actors and courtesans received popularity and fame. Indeed, it was these people, and especially the courtesans, who set the fashions. They provided subjects for color prints, which sold for only a few small coins and pictured women wearing attractive clothes in the newest style, serving as fashion plates for the style conscious.

The *ukiyo-e* prints of the last decades of the eighteenth century and the first years of the nineteenth by Utamaro and other artists, depicting the people of the entertainment quarter of Edo, show that this period was one in which *kanoko* still retained its popularity. However, the tiny resisted squares now were being used sparingly to create linear designs rather than in the allover patterning of *sō kanoko*. Conspicuous among the shibori types appearing in the *ukiyo-e* prints is spiderweb *(kumo)* shibori (see page 69), for the making of which a special hook was developed in Arimatsu. This type of

9. Woodblock print by Kunichika, titled ''Narumi,'' from a series depicting the fifty-three stages on the Tōkaidō highway. Shibori cloth hangs on display, and a woman binds cloth. Note the *mame* shibori towel on the shoulder of the standing woman (Plate 225).

10. Woodblock print by Hiroshige, titled "Fujieda," from a series depicting the fifty-three stages on the Tōkaidō highway. Both women being carried across a river by porters wear shibori kimono.

motif was being used in many ways—large and small, squarish and circular, scattered or closely repeated—to decorate cotton kimono, *jiban* (underkimono), the obi, scarves, and even fans. A block print by the artist Toyokuni I shows the actor Matsumoto Kōshirō wearing a garment patterned with squarish *kumo* motifs grouped together in fours to suggest a design popular in the dress of warriors of the Kamakura period.

A member of a Dutch mission traveling over the Tōkaidō in 1691 and 1692 is quoted by Sansom as declaring that it was "on some days more crowded than the public streets in any of the more populous towns of Europe." This gives an indication of the amount of foot traffic on the road at even this early date. A century later, in order to make the quantities of shibori required to meet the needs of urban dwellers and the demands of travelers on the Tōkaidō, production at Arimatsu was stepped up and the work spread to adjacent areas, employing many thousands of people on either a full- or a part-time basis. It also became more specialized. Go-betweens were hired to carry orders and materials from the merchants to the appropriate specialists—those who worked out the designs, those who stitched or bound or pleated or capped the cloth, and those who dyed it, and many of these people developed very high skills in their specialties.

Then, in the first half of the nineteenth century the shogunate, which had been vainly trying to preserve stability by preventing change, became increasingly unable to cope with domestic problems. The autonomy of the daimyo grew, at the expense of the central government. Some fiefs were plagued by troubles, while others remained strong. Social and economic problems increased.

The Owari fief was among those that were able to withstand much of the turmoil of the times, but its shibori industry depended on outside markets, which were in trouble. The fief did what it could to help sustain the shibori business for a while, but the great demand of previous times declined, and the region fell onto hard times. *Kanoko* shibori continued to be made in Kyoto—as, indeed, it is at the present day. In part, this was simply because it was expensive, for the merchants of nearby Osaka had prospered and now were paying even less attention than before to official efforts to restrain their habits of conspicuous consumption. Some exceptionally fine *kanoko* kimono were made during the last days of Edo, but in general the quality declined. Designs became more realistic and elaborate. With the advent of wide obi made of sumptuous, thick brocades, the design of the kimono was often restrained or simply neglected and the focus of attention given to the highly decorated obi. More basic, with *kanoko*, stencils began to be used to mark the location on the cloth for each tiny resist. In consequence, the work became more mechanical and dull; the subtle effect, the lively quality created when the repeated resisted squares were made and arranged solely by eye and touch was lost.

Elsewhere in Japan, shibori, produced by local people for local or regional use still was being made. Research into the extent to which shibori was made in such places has only recently begun and remains inconclusive. For example, there is evidence that shibori was produced in Kyushu since Heian times. The tax record in the *Engi shiki* (see page 16) refers to shibori paid as tax from Daizaifu. In accounts of the construction of Owari Castle in 1610, mention exists of the shibori garments worn by the workers from Kyushu who came to help in the building. Between 1837 and 1853 an essayist named Morisada Mankō, who was a keen and careful observer, included numerous descriptions of different kinds of shibori from different areas of the country in his writings about Owari. Shibori from Hakata in Kyushu is mentioned, which he describes as being of large white flowers on a blue lapislike ground. In 1877, the first trade fair in Japan published a map of locations of shibori production throughout the country. In Kyushu, the cities of Amagi and Hakata and the regions of Bungo, Higo, and Chikuzen are cited. Other areas of the country, also, certainly had traditions of shibori production of equal antiquity. Likely as not, such shibori was mainly for local consumption, made, presumably, by farmers for their own use, or possibly by specialist dyers in small country towns. The nineteenth century also saw the widespread growing and use of cotton and the industrialization of the textile industry. *Kasuri* (ikat) patterns assumed great popularity in the countryside. What happened to locally produced shibori? Future research will shed some light on this.

THE MEIJI PERIOD (1868–1912)
AND THE EARLY TWENTIETH CENTURY

In the early seventeenth century the Tokugawa shogunate, in keeping with its efforts to maintain stability, adopted an isolationist policy under which foreigners were excluded from the country. It was not only that foreigners, westerners in particular, were suspect as possible agents of aggressive foreign powers, they were associated with Christianity, regarded by the shogunate as a threat to its determination to control all aspects of Japanese life, social and moral as well as economic and political. So nearly complete was the application of this exclusionist policy that no westerners were permitted to remain except for a few Dutch traders, who were allowed to reside on the tiny island of Deshima at the head of Nagasaki Bay. However, by the middle of the nineteenth century, in consequence of the economic and technological advances that western nations had been making, the exclusionist policy had become impossible.

Those advances were symbolized by Commodore Perry's naval squadron, which included two powerful steam frigates and which arrived in Japan in 1853. Perry presented a letter from President Fillmore addressed to the emperor asking protection for shipwrecked American seamen, the right for ships to buy coal, and the opening of one or more ports to trade. This led to the signing of treaties, between 1854 and 1858, which reopened Japan to the outside world. That reopening was attended by new problems, which the shogunate—no longer in capable hands or able to enforce the obedience of the more powerful daimyo—was incapable of solving. With the shogunate's decline, the country turned more and more to the imperial court for the solution of its problems. Indeed, in 1863 the shogun journeyed to Kyoto in obedience to a command of the court—the first one to do so in over two hundred years—to consult with the nobles about the future government of Japan. In 1867, after some further troubles, the shogun resigned, and in 1868 the emperor moved from Kyoto to Edo, renamed Tokyo ("eastern capital") and was installed in the great castle that had been the stronghold of the shoguns. This change of rule—the Meiji Restoration—ushered in a period of momentous change.

With the transfer of power, Arimatsu largely lost the market for its shibori. The annual travel to Edo of lords and their retainers over the Tōkaidō became a thing of the past, and the construction of a railway, which passed through Arimatsu without stopping there, eliminated what little traffic had remained on the Tōkaidō. The advantages of its location destroyed, the villagers of Arimatsu now were competing with shibori produced elsewhere and at a time when inflation had reduced people's buying power and hence the volume of goods that could be sold. Moreover, with the change of regime, the Owari fief could no longer support Arimatsu's shibori industry. This time the people of Arimatsu were saved by a man of inventive bent from their own village, who helped them adapt to the requirements of the changed age, which had so far been their undoing.

Suzuki Kanezō had been born in 1837 into a prosperous shibori-producing family in Arimatsu. It is said that when he was only fourteen he originated the shibori process called *shirokage* (literally, "white shadow"). Later he invented a machine for polishing rice, after which he set up and operated a rice mill for the Owari fief. He left that job a few years after the change of government and returned to Arimatsu to help his aging parents. Seeing the plight of the village, he turned his mind to the problem of finding a new and faster method of dye-patterning cloth. This led to his devising an ingenious way of creating patterns by wrapping the cloth around long poles, pushing it along the pole into tightly compressed folds, and immersing it, pole and all, in a long vat of indigo. With this method, production increased at least tenfold over that of other shibori methods. Formerly a worker needed one day to make a bolt of patterned cloth using the simplest of shibori patterns and up to six days for others; now two workers were able to produce twenty bolts in a day. This proved to be a boon to the village—not only was production increased, making the cloth very competitive with types of printed cloth, but the patterns had an entirely new look. They became very popular.

During the eight years it took Suzuki to perfect the new process, he and several of the leading merchant-producers of shibori organized a group to find other ways of rehabilitating the village craft. They realized that in order to find customers they would have to create new patterns, and that processes for patterning the cloth more quickly would have to be devised if shibori-decorated cloth was to compete successfully in an age of machine production. Suzuki's pole-wrapping process, which produced a kind of shibori poetically named *arashi* (see pages 123ff), which means "storm," had been a good beginning, and he is also credited with developing the folding and clamping process of *itajime* (board-clamped) dyeing.

In 1897 a small manually operated machine for shaping and binding cloth for the spiderweb pattern was patented and a faster way of making patterns of reserved rings (*chikuwa* shibori; page 58) was devised. This process involved substituting small rings of bamboo for binding thread and use of a long hook fastened to a stand or workbench; the rings of hollow bamboo were strung on the hook and slipped over the cloth held by the point of the hook. This easy, quick method led a local man, Matsujirō Okada, to try using the hook to create a patterned cloth with an effect similar to that of *kanoko* shibori. Having the hook in a fixed position, rather than hanging by a cord as in looped binding and *kumo* shibori, made it possible to quickly bind a thread around a very small bit of cloth. The pressure of the thread left an undyed ring in the cloth. At first the process was called *kikai* ("machine") *kanoko*; it is now known as *yokobiki kanoko* (page 62).

Okada found that the new method was more satisfactory for silk than for cotton, since the binding thread was easier to remove from silk after the cloth had been dyed and, of greater importance, the silk retained a crimped texture. This led him to contact wholesale dealers in Kyoto, and from them he received a contract to produce *kanoko*-patterned silk for hair ornaments and for kimono collar bands. This marked the beginning of the production in Arimatsu of shibori-dyed silk for merchants in Kyoto. This production for the Kyoto market proved profitable for a decade or so, but in 1927 Kyoto merchants took the process to Korea, where, employing young girls, they established a production center that turned out *yokobiki* shibori that was less expensive, though of inferior quality.

With the need to speed up production and reduce the labor costs of shibori, around the turn of the century workshops were set up in and around Arimatsu and Narumi in which small groups of workers were taught to use a recently invented pleating machine as well as other new devices and where they worked full time under supervisors intent on maintaining the quality of the work. However, the traditional techniques of looped binding and also stitching continued to be done in the workers' homes. Chemical dyes came into use at this time also.

It was not long before a small group of merchants financed the connecting of Arimatsu with the outside world by telephone and telegraph, and in 1917 rail service was extended to it, making it easier to receive needed materials and to ship out finished goods. The members of the association of shibori merchants were enterprising—they showed at the Paris World Fair of 1900, winning a bronze medal—and were successful in gaining wide recognition for the shibori products of the Arimatsu area within the domestic market. In the years following World War I, a period of great prosperity and extravagance, they adapted shibori for western style clothes, which had been growing in popularity. The changeover to foreign fashions brought added profits to the merchants; viewed retrospectively, however, this use of shibori was aesthetically unfortunate. But, such mistakes were a symptom of vigor rather than of decadence. Marvelously spirited shibori light cotton kimono *(yukata)* and underkimono *(jiban)* were made until the Pacific War, and this vigor is still evident today on a smaller scale.

The shibori of Kyushu evidently had remained in regional use through the Edo years and the succeeding Meiji era. But, beginning in 1912, according to Kahei Takeda, Kyushu shibori cloth made at Amagi was exported to Korea, Taiwan, Singapore, and even to Africa. In 1937, Arimatsu merchants were approached by an American trading company based in Kobe and asked to make samples of shibori cloth suited to African tastes, using wide cloth suited to the African garments. The Arimatsu producers used binding, stitching, and pleating to create designs on cloth dyed in red, yellow, or green and overdyed the cloth with natural indigo, which was preferred in Africa over the chemical dyes in use. A profitable trade resulted, but it was cut short after the outbreak in 1937 of the Sino-Japanese War, bringing with it controls on cotton and unfavorable rates of exchange.

Trade with Africa was reestablished after World War II through the same group of

Americans, who were aware that there was a good market for shibori-dyed cloth in the uranium-rich Belgian Congo. The trade was so profitable that the shibori merchants were able to regain their prewar prosperity, but it lasted only a short time. In the meantime, changes in social life in Japan following the war deeply affected the demand for shibori. The adoption of western dress by the great majority of women, except for very formal occasions, the reluctance of many young people to carry on traditional crafts, and competition from machine-printed cloth combined to cause a decline in the production and use of shibori to the point where the Japanese public's knowledge of shibori was limited mainly to *kanoko* by, say, 1978.

Like all books dealing with declining and dying craft traditions, this book was initiated by a sense of need. Yet, in Japan in 1981 and 1982 the interest of hobbyists—mainly housewives with spare time—in shibori blossomed. As of this writing, it is still too early to tell what the effects of this interest will be, but this is a welcome and healthy development. The more people interested in shibori, the better. All handwork and craft traditions seem fated to produce objects mainly for a luxury or gift market. Shibori is no exception. Yet hobbyist interest has created a demand and brought a number of shibori objects reflecting different techniques onto the market—purses, kimono, dresses, and neckties, etc. It is hoped that henceforth this increased attention will both save the craft from total oblivion on a popular level as well as stimulate serious artists with the challenge of creating beautiful objects with the unique techniques of this tradition.

11. *Kōkechi* fragment, silk. Folding and binding; exact process unknown. Eighth century. Tokyo National Museum. Two grid patterns give an illusion of depth to this superb example. The small, relatively sharply dyed squares are seen as if from a distance through the larger, soft lines that frame them.

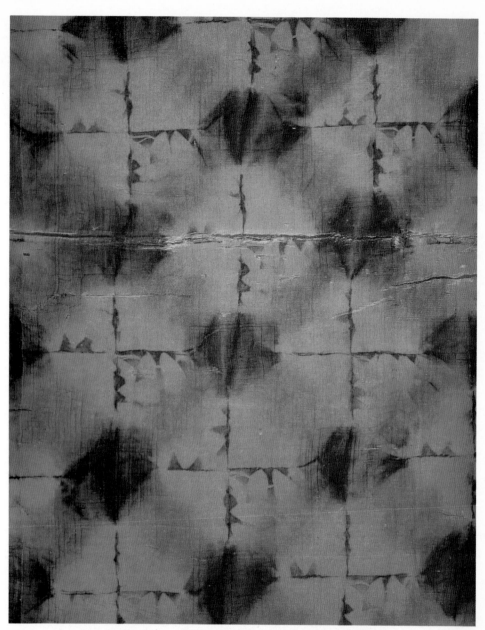

12. *Tsujigahana* fragment, pongee. Stitching and capping; resisted motifs dip dyed. Late Muromachi period. Lively and direct, these simple forms reveal the typical soft edges of stitched and capped shibori.

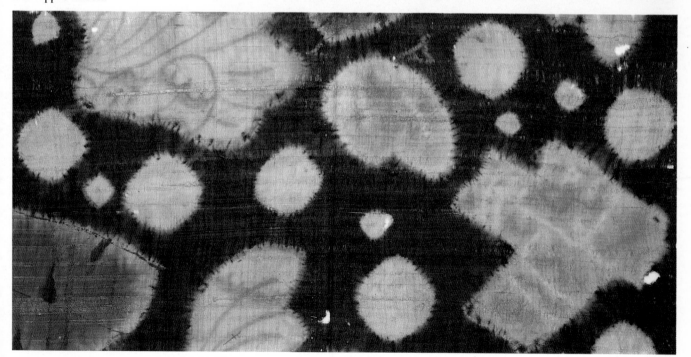

37

14. Detail of *tsujigahana* garment (*kosode*), glossed silk. Stitching and capping; bound dots (*hitta kanoko*); divided dyeing (*somewake*) and sumi ink painting. Early seventeenth century. Tokyo National Museum. Shibori techniques are utilized both to outline massive color areas and to create a textural pattern with small dots. In both Plates 14 and 15, the designs are large yet show a mixture of boldness and subdued, almost fragile delicacy.

15. Detail of *tsujigahana* fragment, light figured silk twill. Stitching and capping; bound dots (*hitta kanoko*); dip-dyeing and sumi ink painting. Early seventeenth century. The use of *kanoko* dots is developed in relationship to color areas and negative space to create both linear effects and full, textured designs.

13. *Tsujigahana* fragment, silk. Stitching and capping, bound dots (*hitta kanoko*); divided dyeing (*somewake*), dip-dyeing, and sumi ink painting. Momoyama period. Massive "pine bark lozenge" (*matsukawabishi*) motifs divide the textile into bold areas. In one, the same motif is used to form a complex lattice vigorously defined in black; another is filled with a soft, textured ground of *kanoko* dots. These bold forms contrast with the delicate, shaded flowers and leaves.

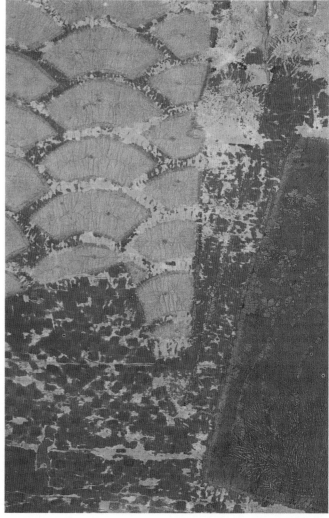

16, 17.  Details of fragments, silk. Stitching and capping; bound dots (large *kanoko*) in Plate 16, stenciled gold leaf. Momoyama period. These two examples are a type of *tsujigahana*, featuring patchwork-like interlocking of complex and disparate designs. The shibori techniques are basic and simple, yet the result is highly sophisticated.

18, 19.    Details of garment (*kosode*) fragments, figured satin-weave silk (*rinzu*). Divided dyeing (*somewake*), bound dots (*hitta kanoko*), and embroidery. Keichō era (1596–1615). Plate 19, Tokyo National Museum. Typical examples of Keichō period textiles, these two fragments display dark colors and massive dyed areas embellished by large quantities of delicate detail, including embroidery. Note how the stitched and capped areas have taken on complex, irregular outlines echoing the "pine bark lozenge" (*matsukawabishi*) motif.

20. *Kosode*, silk. Stylized leaf design in bound dots (*hitta kanoko*) and embroidery. Seventeenth century. Tokyo National Museum. *Kanoko* dots create the design of one of these *kosode* and almost entirely cover the other. These two examples represent the highest development of the use of *kanoko*.

21. *Kosode*, silk. Negative linear design (*ji-ochi*) of cherry blossoms and snow-covered bamboo leaves against a ground of bound dots (*kanoko*). Seventeenth century. Tokyo National Museum.

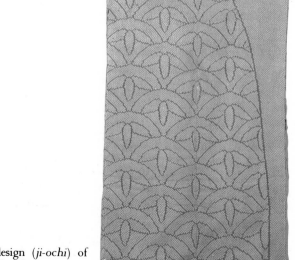

22.   Painting: "Kanbun Beauty," woman wearing *kosode* embellished by shibori. Kanbun era (1661–73). Mounting: *tsujigahana* textile.

23. Woodblock print by Hokusai, titled "Narumi," from a series depicting the fifty-three stages on the Tōkaidō highway. Nineteenth century. Kahei Takeda. One of the two women, thread held taut in her mouth, is binding cloth while the other examines folded lengths of shibori. A bundle of finished cloth lies between them.

24. Woodblock print by Hiroshige. The cartouche reads "Fifty-three Stages of the Tōkaidō. Number forty-two. Narumi. A shop selling Arimatsu shibori." Nineteenth century. Kahei Takeda. This animated scene in front of a shop selling Arimatsu shibori appears to involve a sale to a passing traveler, who holds a bolt of cloth in his hands.

25.   Detail of fragment, silk and purple-root dye. "Pine bark lozenge" (*matsukawabishi*) pattern; stitching and binding (*maki-age*). Eighteenth century. Evidencing careful control of the folds in each stitched motif, the spiderweb pattern formed by the binding threads appears only on vertical and horizontal axes of the motifs. The ground forms a lattice reminiscent of the one in the *tsujigahana* textile of Plate 13.

26.   Garment worn under armor, cotton and indigo dye. Stitched (*ori-nui*) and bound (*kumo*) motifs. Eighteenth century. Hiroshi Fujimoto. This well-worn warrior's garment shows a strength and simplicity of decoration that undoubtedly characterized many early shibori garments. Few remain. One can be sure that the resisted lines and forms were created directly in the cloth—no artist drew them first.

27. Detail of fragment, silk and indigo dye. Design of plovers and stream; stitched (*ori-nui*) motifs and capping. Nineteenth century. Yoshiko I. Wada. This masterpiece of folk shibori is created by the simplest and most direct techniques. The plovers seem to be carried along on the stream's current, and its depths and shallows are suggested by shading of the indigo.

28. Man's short underkimono (*han-jiban*), cotton and purple-root dye. "Small" squares (*komasu*); folding, stitching, and binding. Nineteenth century. Hitoshi Fujimoto. The bold artlessness of both the pattern and the construction of this garment give this example of Hanawa shibori great appeal.

29. Underkimono (*jiban*), hemp and safflower dye. Willow (*yanagi*) shibori with cherry blossoms, butterflies; and plovers; pleating, stitching (*hira-nui*), and stitched and bound motifs (*maki-age*). Nineteenth century. Keisuke Serizawa. The willow shibori dyed red on a lighter red ground creates an unusual effect in which the small motifs catch the eye and the graceful lines remain part of the ground, giving an effect of flowing water or wind.

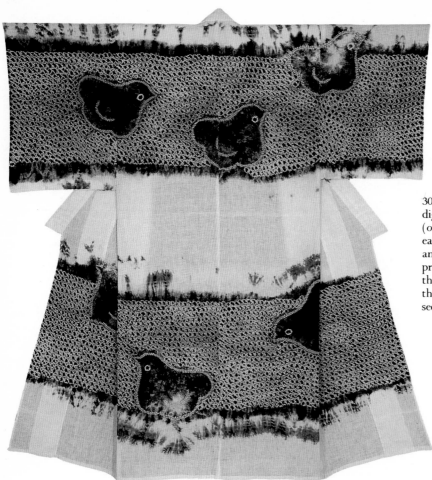

30. Man's underkimono (*jiban*), cotton and indigo. Plover and stream design; dip-dyeing; stitching (*ori-nui*) and loop binding (*hira miura*). Arimatsu, early twentieth century. Kahei Takeda. The binding and design of this traditional motif seems done by a practiced hand, but the indigo dyeing is nothing less than sloppy, which adds to the vigor and delight of the garment. The stream, done in *miura* shibori, seems to flow over pebbles.

31. Man's underkimono (*jiban*), cotton and indigo. "Mountain path" (*yamamichi*) shibori; dip-dyeing; pleating and bound units (*kumo* variations). Arimatsu, early twentieth century. Kahei Takeda. A study of this garment reveals a highly subtle and sophisticated design sense in the ways bound diamond-shaped motifs are incorporated into the dyed and reserved bands to break monotony and in the way the garment is constructed.

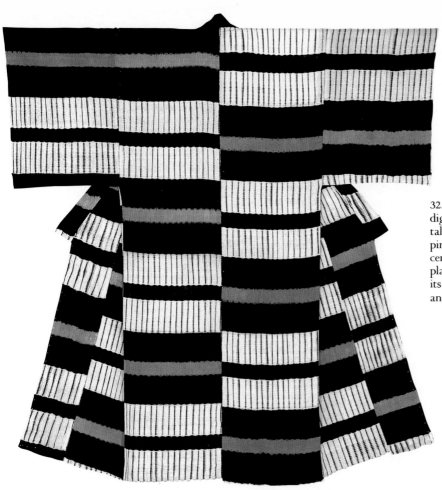

32. Man's light kimono, cotton and indigo. Pattern of vertical stripes and horizontal bands; pleating (*tesuji*) and paper wrapping (*kami maki*). Arimatsu, early twentieth century. Kahei Takeda. This kimono displays a strength equal to that in Plate 31, but its rhythm is more direct and less nervous and complex.

33. Man's light kimono, cotton and indigo. Design of train (and signal lights?—telegraph poles?) celebrating the establishment of railway service through Arimatsu in 1917; stitching (*ori-nui* and *awase-nui*) and capping. Kahei Takeda. This piece of folk art is unsurpassed. There is no aspect of it that does not elicit pleasure, from the lighted windows and remarkable wheels to the swooping birds and brightly highlighted insulators or signal lights.

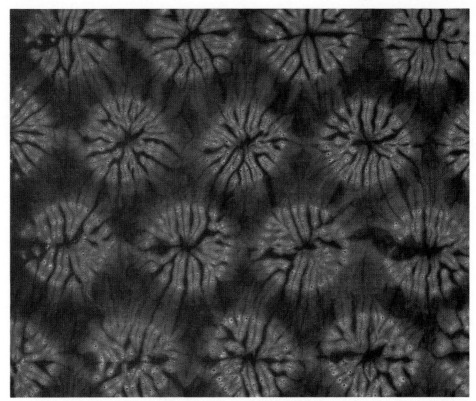

34. Japanese larch (*karamatsu*)

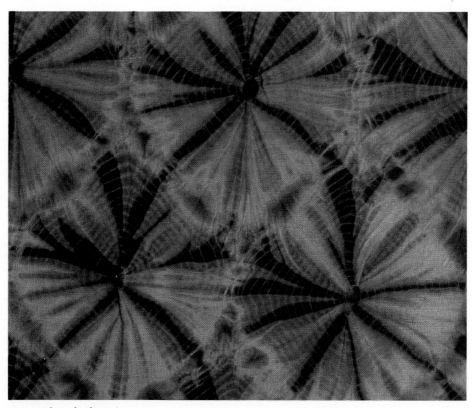

35. spiderweb (*kumo*)

36.   small capped motifs (*kobōshi* or *kawamaki*)

37.   pole-wrapping (*arashi*)

34–37.   Arimatsu design samples, cotton and indigo. Indigo, yielding the blues of ice crystals, spring sky, and winter's night, works in perfect harmony with shibori, recording the pressure of every knot, stitch, and binding, the depth of every fold, imprinting them in the cloth.

38. *Haori* coat, figured silk (*saya*) and purple-root dye. Hanawa shibori. Early twentieth century. This woman's garment showing an arrow-feather pattern of stitched and bound diamonds shows the same vigor and directness of the underkimono in Plate 28, though it is of a much later date.

39.  Detail of quilt in kimono shape (*yōgi*), pongee and purple-root dye. Stitching (*hira-nui*) and bound motifs (*kumo*). Late nineteenth century. Takumi Sugawara. This unusual pattern of interlocking six-lobed figures—six small ones surrounding a large central one—is created by large stitches, while the central motifs are bound *kumo* units.

40.  Detail of middle kimono of set of three worn together (*kasane*), silk. Glimpses of the pattern appear as the wearer walks. Hemp leaf (*asa-no-ha*) pattern; bound dots (*kanoko*). Late nineteenth century. Takumi Sugawara. The radiating lines of small *kanoko* dots highlighted by larger dots seem somehow to add vibrancy to the already brilliant red.

# Techniques

## SHAPED CLOTH RESIST

Shibori has been defined in the beginning of the book as cloth that is given three-dimensional shape and then dyed. After the cloth is returned to its two-dimensional form, the design that emerges is the result of the three-dimensional shape of the cloth, the type of resist, and the amount of pressure exerted by the thread or clamp that secured the shape during the cloth's exposure to the dye. The cloth sensitively records both the shape and the pressure; it is the "memory" of the shape that remains imprinted in the cloth. This is the essence of shibori.

In Japan shibori designs and patterns are created by shaping the cloth in many ways. Some of the ways have been widely used in other places by other peoples, some are unique to Japan. Cloth may be drawn up and bound; stitched and gathered up; pleated and bound; folded and clamped between boards; or wrapped around a pole then pushed along it to compress the fabric into folds. Further, a cloth may be dyed repeatedly, using a different shaping method each time.

Designs created in this way clearly reflect the touch of each worker. No two persons fold or bind or stitch in exactly the same way—the work of one may be very precise and even, that of another, looser and more free. Likewise, the amount of force exerted on the binding thread, or in drawing up the stitching thread, or in compressing the cloth into folds on the pole, varies from person to person. The effect of each person's hand, and indeed temperament, on the shaping of the cloth becomes imprinted by the dye in the finished piece. This characteristic makes for highly individual results, even within a traditional framework.

In this book, different shibori designs are classified by the way the cloth is shaped and secured, not by historical period or place of origin. Traditional resist-dyeing techniques are described in detail to record old ways that have died or are dying and to open a world of creative possibilities.

# Binding

Designs are created by drawing up portions of cloth and binding each such shape with thread. The shape of the cloth, the tension on the thread, and the resisting action of the thread determine the configuration of each unit, while the placement, spacing, and amount of thread affect the way the dye penetrates. The nature of the binding process itself limits the type of motif to circles and modified squares. The Japanese, working within the limitation imposed by the process, have exploited its design possibilities by increasing or decreasing the size of the bound unit. Great circular motifs are depicted in kimono worn by beautiful women in the woodblock prints of Utamaro, while one style of the Edo period is composed of units reduced to the absolute minimum of cloth that it is possible to grasp and bind.

A small hook was invented in Japan to hold the drawn-up portion of cloth taut while it is bound. This tool allows both speed and control of the shape of the cloth. Besides dramatic differences in the size of the bound units and the use of devices such as hooks, the variety of designs and patterns and unique textured surface of Japanese bound shibori are the result as well of the skill of those who shape, bind, and knot the cloth.

## CLOSE-WOUND BINDING

A portion of cloth is drawn up with the fingers and held while a thread is wound around it. Each turn of thread must be in tight contact with the previous one. Space between binding threads allows dye to penetrate and mar the clarity of the resisted ring. The amount of cloth that is drawn up determines the diameter of the ring, and the number of turns of thread determines the width of the resisted area.

Resisted ring motifs created by close-wound binding are called *ne-maki* shibori. Dots within tiny resisted areas (*kanoko*; pages 58ff) are also bound by the close-wound method.

## RING SHIBORI

Undyed rings on a dyed ground is the simplest design possible to achieve with shibori —and may be the oldest. The fan sutra painting from twelfth century Japan shows a short garment decorated in this way. Plate 4

**Thread-Resisted Rings** (*ne-maki* shibori): White rings on a dark ground may be used as single design elements or grouped and arranged in various ways. The name *ne-maki* shibori, literally, "base-wound shibori," is used by the Japanese to describe the design as well as the way the cloth is bound. Plates 41, 99

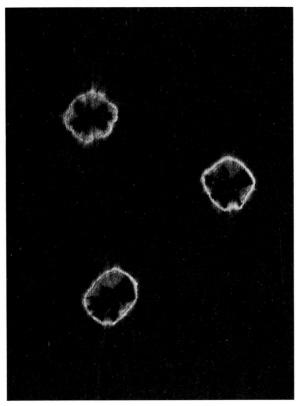

41.  Thread-resisted rings (*ne-maki* shibori)

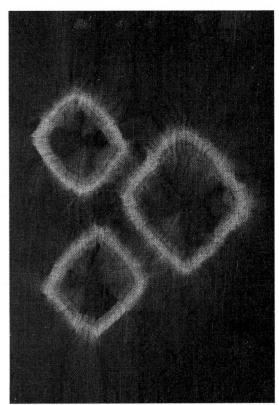

42.  Bamboo-resisted rings (*chikuwa* shibori)

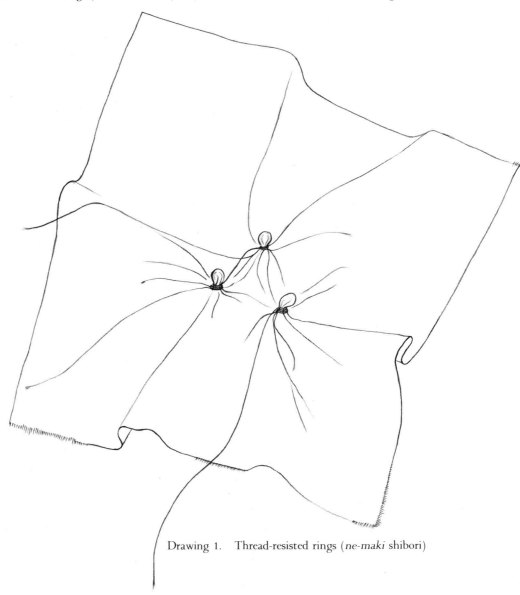

Drawing 1.   Thread-resisted rings (*ne-maki* shibori)

■*Shaping and Binding:*    A portion of cloth is drawn up with the right thumb and index finger and held firmly between the left thumbnail and left index finger. The binding thread is brought three or four times around the shaped cloth at the point where the cloth is held, but care must be taken to avoid any space between the turns of thread as it is wound around the cloth. The thread is secured with a special single knot (*kamosage*; see below). The number of turns of binding thread controls the width of the resisted ring. The greater the tension of the thread and the more care taken to achieve a uniform, closely bound layer of thread, the clearer the resisted ring will be. Drawing 1

■*Kamosage Knot*:    This simple knot is secured by friction, which makes it indispensable in binding *kanoko* and many other types of shibori as well. This also allows the worker to remove the binding thread by just pulling the cloth taut—the knots pop right off. The thread is looped clockwise once around the shaped cloth, with the short end held against the cloth under the left thumb. The right hand, holding the long thread between thumb and index finger, is then rotated so the palm is up, and the thumb at the same time moves so that it is holding the thread tight against the lower joint of the ring finger. The thread passes behind the index finger and middle finger, which are spread apart as the hand rotates, and passes around the index finger to the front of the hand. Drawing 2

Now the right hand is brought toward the cloth, and the top of the cloth shape is slipped under the thread passing in front of the fingers, then brought up between the index and middle fingers so that a loop is formed around the cloth. Holding this loop in place with the index finger of the left hand, the thread is drawn down and tight with the right hand. This description is general. This knot is executed quickly, with fluid movement of both hands. As with most such simple processes, the worker will find his own method and rhythm after a few trials.

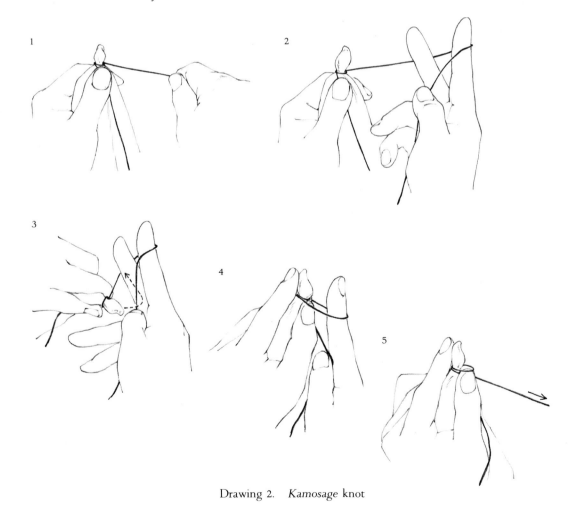

Drawing 2.    *Kamosage* knot

Plate 42 **Bamboo-Resisted Rings** *(chikuwa* shibori*)*:    Rings that are resisted with bamboo are softer and more square than those bound with thread.

■*Shaping*:    Rings of bamboo (5 to 7 mm in diameter and 7 to 10 mm in length) are strung on a long hook, which is fixed to a support. A latchet hook with a long shank (available at sewing shops) clamped to a tabletop works well. The cloth is caught in the hook and held taut while each bamboo ring is slipped over the fabric until the ring can no longer move. Rings made of any material may be used.

DOTS (*KANOKO* SHIBORI)

The tiny bound resists so often seen in Japanese textiles may at first seem similar in appearance but they differ in form, in use, and in the way they are bound. Confusion exists among westerners about these minute resists, and in Japan itself there are differences of opinion about types and names. Regional differences in the names and processes add to the confusion.

One simple and convenient classification of these dots is to call them all *kanoko shibori* and divide them into five types: Dots Within Squares *(hitta kanoko)*; Square Ring Dots *(yokobiki kanoko)*; Linked Dots *(tatebiki kanoko)*; Half Dots *(tehitome kanoko)*; and Spaced Dots *(tsukidashi kanoko)*. This is the system used in this book. It is hoped that an analysis of the methods together with typical examples will clarify differences and dispel misconceptions that have grown up in the West about this type of shibori.

Tiny resisted units are used to create a variety of pattern effects as well as a unique texture and useful elasticity in silk. The individual units vary from minute dots in the center of small undyed squares to small round dots outlined by the thinnest of undyed lines. Dots may be repeated to fill ground or motif areas; they may be widely scattered, used to outline designs, and if they are densely packed throughout a length of silk and the silk is left unpressed, a deeply textured textile that is also elastic is the result.

For all types of *kanoko*, silk is favored for its suppleness, sheen, and luxurious quality and for another important and enhancing characteristic—silk's natural tendency to retain, after it is dry, sharp creases made in it when it is wet. This characteristic is important because it preserves the crinkling or crimping effect of the binding thread on the silk when it is dyed, resulting in the kind of textured, elastic textile mentioned above, a unique characteristic of many Japanese *kanoko* shibori fabrics.

Plate 43 **Dots Within Squares** *(hon hitta kanoko)*:    The clear square form of the tiny resisted area and the extremely small size of the center dot are the distinguishing characteristics of *hon hitta kanoko*. The resisted squares are usually repeated very close together, and the lines separating them create a grid. One of the characters used in writing *hitta* is 田, meaning "field," which suggests this arrangement. When silk decorated with these tiny square resists is pressed flat after it is dyed, it can be seen that most of the area of the fabric is resisted—only the tiny dots and narrow spaces between resists receive dye. The unpressed silk presents an entirely different effect. Each of the tiny shapes raised in the silk by the binding process catch the light, and as the fabric moves and shifts, it shimmers, jewellike, in changing patterns.

In older fabrics, individual tiny squares are sometimes scattered *(bara hitta)* or arranged in lines. Today these scattered or linear resisted units have been largely replaced by similar effects created by faster, less labor-intensive techniques.

*Hon hitta kanoko* decorated the silks of the Muromachi, Momoyama, and Edo periods. In the earlier periods, its use was characterized by a delicate restraint, and the quality of the resisted squares was free of the relentless, mechanical perfection that developed later.

The use of *hon hitta kanoko* hit its peak in the Edo period, when silks for sumptuous kimono were decorated by filling the entire ground with these tiny resisted squares *(sō-hitta)*, leaving only lines and small areas of design free of resist (the effect known as *ji-ochi*, "omitted ground"). The design was drawn on the silk, but no guiding marks were made to indicate where each tiny unit was to be bound. The worker had to shift the rows of them ever so slightly to compensate for the design without destroying the grid arrangement of the squares. The dots were bound on the bias of the cloth by touch, the fingers sensing the diagonal direction in the cloth's weave. The slight changes and shifts in the uniformity of the grid create patterning of great subtlety in the ground.

Plates 21, 105

Maintaining the smoothly flowing lines of the intricate designs without destroying the grid arrangement of the minute bound units demanded a high level of artistry and skill. Hundreds of thousands of dots, each bound with as many as eight turns of thread, were needed for a single kimono. This most difficult way of binding, which maintains the grid arrangement by touch, has entirely disappeared, replaced by dots stenciled on the cloth to indicate the location of each bound unit, a development that has made both the manner of working and the result more mechanical.

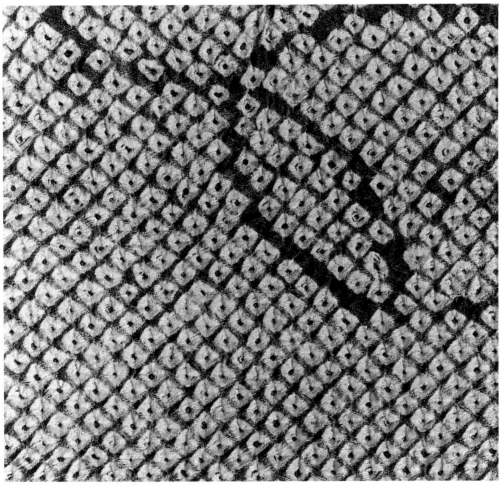

43.   Dots within squares (*hon hitta kanoko*)

■*Cloth and Thread*:    The thread used for binding is a reeled silk made up of eighteen to twenty-three filaments. Reeled silk contains the natural gum, sericin, which gives it a slight stiffness and a sticky quality when moistened. The natural stiffness and slight adhesive quality of this silk thread make it possible to bind each minute bit of cloth almost completely without the thread unraveling from the tip of the cloth.

The fabric most frequently used for this type of *kanoko* is a monochrome figured silk *(rinzu)* of great suppleness. The weave is a satin damask and must be woven in a wider than standard kimono width to allow for the 10 percent shrinkage that results from the texture produced by the multiplicity of minute bindings.

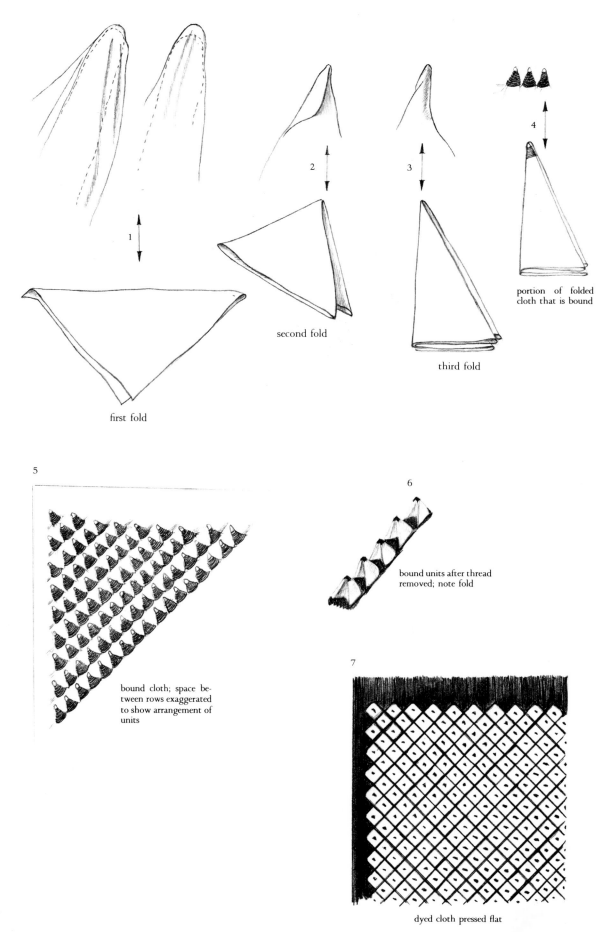

1

first fold

2

second fold

3

third fold

4

portion of folded
cloth that is bound

5

bound cloth; space be-
tween rows exaggerated
to show arrangement of
units

6

bound units after thread
removed; note fold

7

dyed cloth pressed flat

Drawing 3.   Dots within squares (*hon hitta kanoko*)

■*Preparing the Cloth and Stenciling the Design*: The preparation of the silk, the method of stenciling a design, the dyeing of the cloth, and steaming the cloth to stretch it are the same for all types of silk shibori. The following discussion is for *kanoko*, but in general applies to other silk shibori as well.

Bamboo stretchers *(shinshi)* are placed at intervals across the width of the silk fabric, parallel to the weft threads. Wooden bars *(harite)* are fastened at both ends of the length of silk to allow the entire bolt to be worked on at one time and to be stretched in

Drawing 4

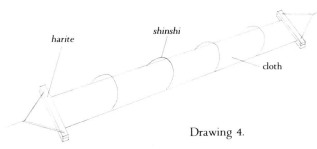

harite    shinshi    cloth

Drawing 4.

the direction of the warp. Sizing is brushed onto the stretched silk. The stretching and sizing process is called *shita bari*. Although this is the old and best way, at the present time a roller mechanism is used to apply sizing. The sizing gives body to the silk and makes it easier to stencil the design onto it and to remove the stencil marks; and perhaps most important of all, the sized silk is easier to bind, since it holds any creases and helps prevent the binding thread from slipping.

As mentioned above, originally the binding was done freely, without any marks on the silk to indicate the individual bound units; only the design areas were drawn on the fabric. In present-day Kyoto, dots are stenciled on the silk to indicate each unit to be bound. The location and density are determined by the designer, and directions are sent, with the design and the sized silk, to a stencil-maker, who cuts the required stencils and stencils the silk, using a fugitive blue color *(aobana)*. The stencil-maker keeps a file of the stencils ordered by each kimono dealer.

■*Shaping and Binding*: The cloth is bound on the bias in diagonal rows. The work progresses from lower left to upper right. The cloth is shaped by placing the left index finger underneath it, with one of the stenciled marks directly over the corner of the fingernail. It is held taut in this position by the pressure of the left thumb. The cloth is drawn up from above, pinching a fold on the bias between the right thumbnail and right index finger. The left index finger is removed from underneath the cloth, and the bias fold is held in place between the left thumb and index finger. The cloth is folded again, doubling the bias fold. The doubled fold is held in place between the left thumb and index finger. The tiny folded point of cloth is given a 180-degree counterclockwise twist with the right thumb and index finger, compressing it into a conical shape. This nub of cloth is held pinched between the left thumbnail and left index finger while it is bound.

Drawing 3
Drawing 3.1
Drawing 3.2
Drawing 3.3

The length and tension of the binding thread is controlled by looping it a few times around the little finger of the right hand.

The thread is wrapped in a clockwise direction five or six (or sometimes as many as eight) times around the tiny nub of cloth and fastened with two *kamosage* knots (page 57). The thread is moistened on the lips or tongue before the securing knots are tied; it is not cut, but continues to the next unit.

Drawing 3.4

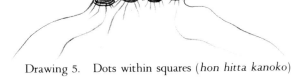

Drawing 5.   Dots within squares (*hon hitta kanoko*)

■*Dyeing and Finishing*:   After the cloth is bound, it is returned to the dye shop, where it is thoroughly soaked to remove the stenciled marks and any dirt and at the same time is lightly bleached. The cloth is dyed and dried and returned to the dealer, who has it finished. First the bindings are removed by stretching the cloth, which causes the threads to pop off. To keep the weave of the fabric straight and to avoid tearing the silk during this operation, the cloth must be stretched evenly, and this stretching must be on the bias. Finally, the cloth is passed over a special steamer and stretched to the standard kimono width. If no textural quality is desired, the silk is pressed flat. The steam finishing of the silk softens and imparts a sheen to it. The cloth is rolled and sent to be hand-sewn into a kimono.

Plate 44    **Medium Dots Within Squares** *(chū hitta kanoko)*:    This coarser type of resisted dot pattern differs from the preceding *hon hitta kanoko* in several respects: the dots within each of the square units are larger and somewhat irregular; the square form of the resisted units is not as clear, which reduces the sharpness and precision of the grid.

Fabric and thread are the same as those used for *hon hitta*, as is the preparation, stenciling, dyeing, and finishing of the silk. The manner of shaping the cloth is different in only two important aspects.

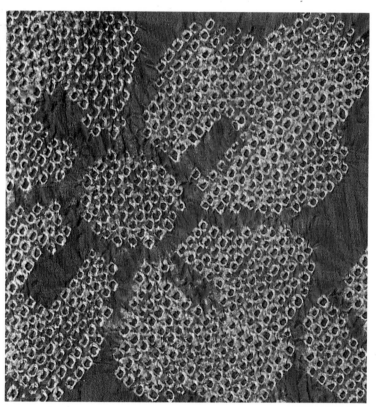

44.   Medium dots within squares (*chū hitta kanoko*)

■*Shaping and Binding*:    The point of cloth to be bound is drawn up instead of being raised from underneath it. Up until the binding, the steps are the same as *hon hitta kanoko*. The thread is wound around the bit of raised cloth three to five times (as compared to five to eight times for *hon hitta*). The thread is moistened on the lips or tongue and secured with one or two *kamosage* knots (page 57). The thread is left uncut and continues to the next unit.

Plate 45    **Square Ring Dots** *(yokobiki kanoko)*:    Square or rectangular resisted rings against a dark ground characterize this type of *kanoko*. The rings are usually somewhat irregular in size and form, creating a casual effect that reflects the fast method of binding. Left unpressed, the silk is textured but it is neither as light-reflecting nor as elastic as textured *hitta kanoko*.

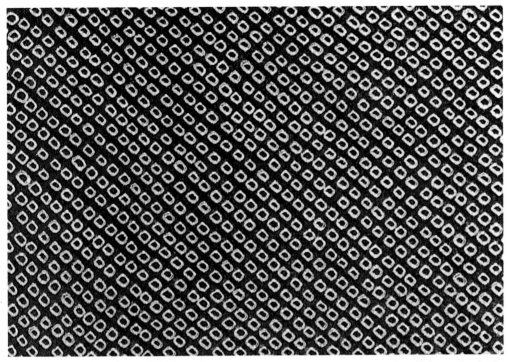

45.  Square ring dots (*yokobiki kanoko*)

■*Equipment, Cloth, and Thread*:    A tying stand *(yokobiki dai)* is used. It has a metal    Drawing 6
arm fitted with a very fine hook, like a bent needle. The worker sits on the base of the    Drawings 43, 44
stand facing the hook. A short bobbin with knob ends holds the thread.

The cloth is silk or cotton; the thread is cotton (20/4), which, being heavier than silk
thread, creates the resisted ring with fewer bindings. The pattern of dots is stenciled on
the silk.

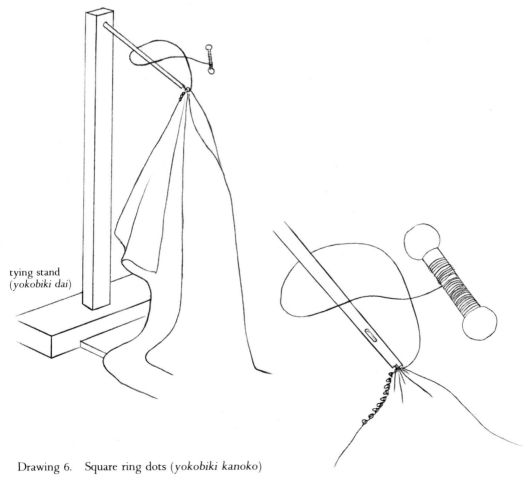

tying stand
(*yokobiki dai*)

Drawing 6.    Square ring dots (*yokobiki kanoko*)

•*Shaping and Binding*:    Binding with the hook is fast and relatively easy to master. It was developed in the Arimatsu–Narumi area for the binding of cotton cloth. The lower prices made possible by this fast method led Kyoto kimono dealers to send silk to Arimatsu–Narumi to be bound. This is a practice that continues to some extent at the present time. However, now much of the work is sent to be bound in Korea, where labor costs are lower than in Japan.

The cloth is shaped by folding the cloth on the bias across a stenciled mark. It is then caught onto the hook at the stenciled mark and held taut with the left hand. The right edge of the cloth is brought over to align it with the left edge, forming a second fold. The bobbin is passed under and over the metal arm and dropped through the loop of thread that is formed. The loop is slipped down over the tautly held cloth, and the thread is pulled sharply to the right to tighten the loop. Each loop of the thread forms a single knot (not a *kamosage*). The more loops that are made, the wider the resisted ring will be. The coarsest type is bound with only two loops.

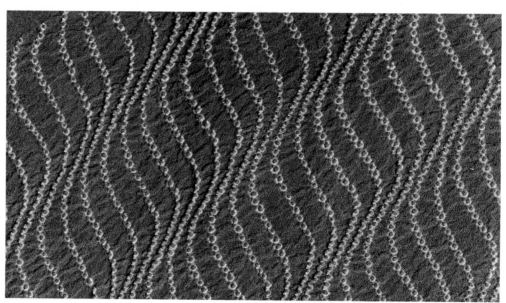

46.   Linked dots (*tatebiki kanoko*)

Plate 46  **Linked Dots** (*tatebiki kanoko*):    The small round dots of *tatebiki kanoko* are always repeated close together and have the appearance of tiny beads on a string. Although they are most frequently employed in the creation of linear designs, for which they are ideally suited, rows of linked dots repeated close together are sometimes used to create a fine jewellike textured surface.

•*Equipment, Cloth and Thread*:    The stand, hook, bobbin, cloth, and thread are the same as those used for the preceding *yokobiki kanoko*, except that there is no projection beneath the hook. This means that the cloth will not fold as neatly and the resists will be rounder.

•*Shaping and Binding*:    The cloth is shaped and bound in the same way as *yokobiki kanoko* with these exceptions: the cloth is not folded on the bias but is folded only once on the stenciled lines indicating the linear dot design, and the binding thread is pulled down and towards the worker instead of to the right to tighten each loop of thread. The direction of pulling the thread acts to fold or gather the cloth, but the effect is, again, rounder and smaller than *yokobiki*.

Plates 47, 48  **Half Dots** (*te-hitome kanoko*):    In this distinctive form, the dot fills one-half of the resisted area, which is usually oval or almond shaped. However, examples in the Shōsō-
Plate 3  in (possibly eighth century) show half dots within resisted circles. This may well have been the original type of *hitome kanoko*, for circles and ovals are shaped and tied in

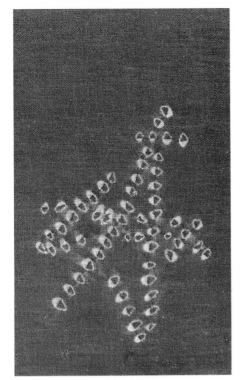 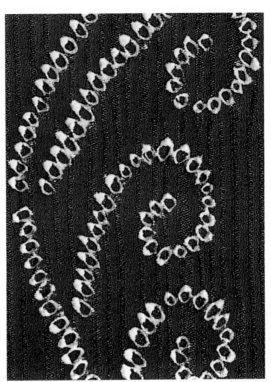

47.  Half dots (*te-hitome kanoko*), cotton    48.  Half dots (*te-hitome kanoko*), silk (Kyoto)

much the same way. The oval-shaped resist is faster to tie; it is presently used in Kyoto silks to create linear design elements. In the indigo-dyed cotton fragment illustrated, a more casual use is made of the dots, and they are large enough to reveal their distinctive shape. The grouping of the dots into motifs is spontaneous and more interesting than the dots repeated mechanically to form lines.

■*Cloth and Thread:*    Silk fabric and reeled silk thread containing eighteen to twenty filaments are now used exclusively. The linear dot design is stenciled on the silk with broken lines.

■*Shaping and Binding:*    The cloth is folded on a stenciled line of the design and then is folded a second time at right angles to the first fold. The folded triangular bit of cloth is held between the left thumb and index finger, while two *kamosage* knots (page 57) are tied.

The circular resist shapes with half dots are made by folding either of the two edges of the triangle-shaped fold of cloth either under or over. The minimum amount of cloth is turned at either edge, and two *kamosage* knots are tied.

**Spaced Dots** (*tsukidashi kanoko*):    Silks bound with spaced dots are prized for the subtle and subdued effect created by the small size of the dots and their spacing. *Hon hitta kanoko* is dazzling, jewellike; *tsukidashi kanoko* is finer and more restrained. This quiet, restrained effect is considered appropriate to kimono worn by older women as well as for the soft sashes *(heko* obi*)* worn by men.    Plates 49, 50

When the bound cloth is not pressed flat, the distinctive crinkled texture composed of the many minute shaped units makes the minute dots appear to be raised on the surface of the cloth like tiny seeds. This textured surface is more delicate than that of the textured *hon hitta kanoko,* and silk bound in this way is used for accessories such as *obiage,* the sashes that are worn to hold the knot of the obi in place.

■*Equipment, Cloth, and Thread:*    The tying stand that is used consists of a flat wooden base with an upright that holds a blunt needle. The worker sits on the wooden base. A satisfactory substitute is made by inserting a blunt-pointed tapestry needle (4 to 6 cm long) in a piece of soft wood and clamping it to a tabletop.

49, 50.   Spaced dots (*tsukidashi kanoko*)          50.

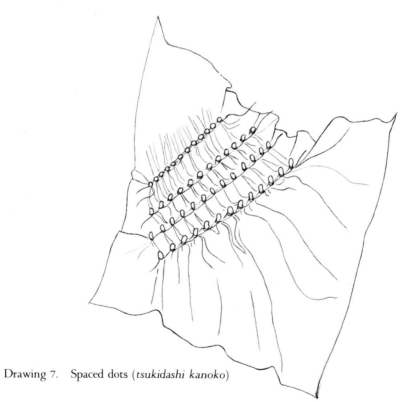

Drawing 7.   Spaced dots (*tsukidashi kanoko*)

Silk cloth and mercerized cotton thread (numbers 40/3–50/3) are used in Japan. Cotton cloth may be bound in this way, but it will not retain a crinkled texture.

Drawing 7 ■*Shaping and Binding*:    The cloth is held down over the needle with the left hand, and two turns of the thread are made. One or two *kamosage* knots (page 57) are used, depending on your skill. The cloth is raised free of the needle, the fingers are withdrawn from the loop, and the thread is tightened. This is tricky. As this is being done, the tip of the raised bit of cloth is gently held in place by the left index finger, which prevents the thread from slipping as the knot is tightened.

## OPEN-WOUND BINDING

The special hook and blunt point (Drawings 43, 44) used for open-wound binding in Japan allow tension to be maintained on the cloth—the hook makes possible tiny resist units, fine pleating, and evenly spaced binding threads, and the blunt point enables one to obtain specific effects not possible with the hook. In both cases the thread is wound counterclockwise around the shaped cloth, leaving uniform intervals between the turns of thread.

Drawings 43, 44

If the thread is wound from base to top of the shaped cloth, the lines resisted directly by the thread form a spiral (which is broken by the pleats in the shaped motif). However, if the thread is bound from base to top and back to the base, the thread-resisted lines cross, the result of crisscrossing the thread. This same effect is obtained by using the fast crisscross binding method described on pages 57 and 58.

Plate 53

Plate 62

### SPIRAL AND SHELL SHIBORI

Binding cloth with three or four turns of thread creates small circular or modified square motifs. The cloth may be drawn up with the fingers and held pinched between them while it is bound or it may be held down over a blunt needle as in *tsukidashi kanoko*. The motifs are called *rasen* (spiral) shibori in Arimatsu, where the needle is used, and *bai* (shell) shibori in Kyoto, where the cloth is usually shaped with the fingers. Each bit of cloth bound in this way resembles a tiny conical shell, which is why Kyoto has adopted this name.

Drawing 8

**Spiral** (*rasen* shibori): The small, soft square motifs in this design are uniform in size and shape. A resisted spiral line is clearly seen within each square. These lines set up a dynamic movement, enlivening the simple design. This type of allover pattern reflects the simpler style of Arimatsu and Narumi shibori, where the worker simply repeats a design element over and over to create a pattern in a length of cloth. In Kyoto, on the other hand, shibori is consciously designed into a large composition that may include various shibori types or other decorative textile techniques.

Plate 51

51.  Spiral (*rasen* shibori)

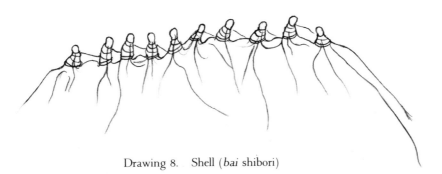

Drawing 8.  Shell (*bai* shibori)

■*Equipment, Cloth, and Thread*: The blunt needle described under *tsukidashi kano-ko* is used. Cotton cloth and thread are used exclusively in Arimatsu for *rasen* shibori. Traditionally this is used for cotton and thin silk for children's obi.

■*Shaping and Binding*: The cloth is shaped by drawing it down over the blunt needle; the thread is given three turns and secured with one *kamosage* knot (page 57).

Plate 52    **Shell** (*bai* shibori): The small motifs of shell shibori, in Kyoto silk shaped with the fingers instead of over the blunt needle, are not as refined in size and form as those from Arimatsu. The piece reflects the Kyoto style of shibori, where shibori units form arrangements and motifs in a large design.

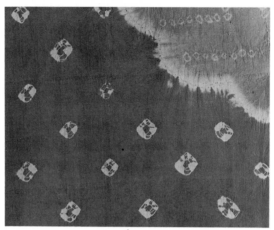

52. Shell (*bai* shibori)

### SPIDERWEB *(KUMO)* SHIBORI

Spiderweb shibori has long been known in Japan. The fan sutra painting from the twelfth century shows a simple hemp garment with a pattern that resembles this type of shibori. It

Plate 4    seems likely that it continued to be used, because it is frequently depicted in the *ukiyo-e* prints of the Edo period.

In the late Edo period, an unusually fine type of spiderweb shibori *(hidatori kumo)* was done in Arimatsu and Narumi for indigo-dyed cloth of the light cotton kimono that had become fashionable. The individual resisted elements were set very close together, finely pleated—*hidatori* means pleated—and precisely bound to create an unusually delicate spiderweb pattern; often with an almost undyed ground, resulting from the fact that the resist units are so close together. Cloth patterned with this exceptionally fine tracery became popular, and because it required unusual skill and much time to produce, it was not possible to meet the demand. This led to the invention in 1911 of various mechanical means to shape the cloth more quickly. With the advent of these devices, this special type of spiderweb was less frequently made by hand, and today no one is left in Arimatsu or Narumi who can create this pattern.

Plate 53    Illustrated is a twentieth century example from Arimatsu of hand-bound spiderweb *(te-kumo)* shibori. Although the units are set farther apart, resulting in a dyed ground, and the shaping of the cloth is not as regular and fine as the finest type *(hidatori kumo)*, it effectively conveys the idea of small spiderwebs. The variations that occur in the squarish resisted shapes—no two are ever precisely the same—the fineness of the resisted lines, and the variations in depth and tone of indigo dye, create a design simple in structure but complex in its varied detail.

Drawings 9, 43    ■*Equipment, Cloth, and Thread*: A metal hook attached by a cord to the upright of a tying stand is used to hold the cloth taut while it is shaped and bound. The cloth must be closely woven and strong to prevent it from being torn by the hook. Cotton cloth and cotton thread (number 20/4) are generally used.

53. Hand-bound spiderweb (*te-kumo* shibori)

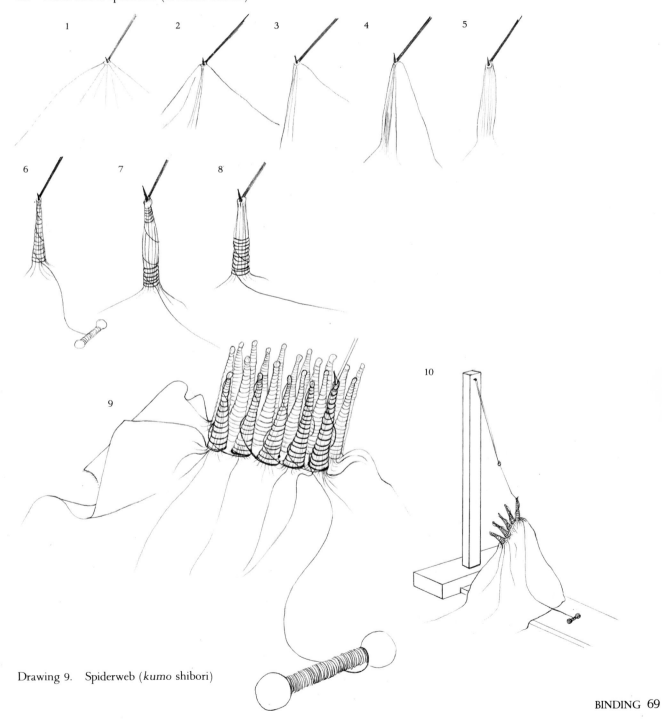

Drawing 9.   Spiderweb (*kumo* shibori)

∎*Shaping and Binding*:    One width of kimono cloth (36 cm/14 in) generally contains about fourteen design units. This size of unit seems to be the most attractive. The units are arranged in staggered rows.

The cloth, dampened slightly, is pushed up from underneath by the left index finger, caught on the hook, pulled taut on it, and drawn into folds. With the shaped cloth held firmly in the left hand, the thread is bound from the base of the unit, where the folds are held gathered together, to the top near the hook. The spacing of the thread is even. The thread is brought back to the starting point at the base by making several turns around the bound cloth. The thread is neither knotted nor cut, but is carried to the next unit.

## LOOPED BINDING (*MIURA* SHIBORI)

Another type of special hook is used in looped binding in order to control the size and shape of the bound units. The cloth is shaped by pushing up a portion of it with the index finger from the underside. The binding thread is looped around the tip of the cloth-covered finger, the cloth within the loop of thread is caught and held by the hook, and the finger is withdrawn from the cloth as the loop is drawn tight. The hook is left in place in the drawn-up cloth until it is needed to catch and hold the cloth of the next unit. The thread is not knotted on each loop-bound unit. Rather, the various tensions on the binding thread hold the loops in place.

The small motifs created by looped binding and the process itself are called *miura* shibori.

In the Nagoya area, where looped binding has been known since its introduction from Kyushu in the seventeenth century, the technique is used to create a variety of effects. The small resisted motifs have a characteristic irregular form and are always repeated in rows. The size of the motifs may be uniform within the rows (*hira* and *hitta miura*) or varied to create more random patterns (*ishigaki* and *yatara miura*). The binding may be done along the warp grain of the cloth to create vertical stripes *(suji miura)*, or tiny units of cloth may be bound on the bias *(hitta miura)*, creating an effect reminiscent of the dot patterns of *kanoko* shibori.

**Small Shapes Bound on the Weft Grain** (*hira miura* shibori):    The example
Plate 54 illustrated shows the small resisted shapes with soft outlines that appear to join them together in rows.

∎*Equipment, Cloth, and Thread*:    A metal hook is used that is longer and somewhat different in shape from the one used for spiderweb *(kumo)* shibori. It hangs by a cord from the upright of the tying stand. The cloth is cotton or silk; thread is number 20/4 twist cotton; 30/4 is used for *hitta miura*.

∎*Shaping and Binding*:    It is important to note that, unlike other types of binding, the thread is not knotted on each resist unit. This type of binding depends upon constant and even tension on the cloth and the thread.

Traditionally, with the exception of *hitta miura*, no stenciled guide marks are used.

In order to anchor the cloth, it is caught in the hook at a point just to the right of the first unit to be bound. It is important that the hook remains caught in one bound unit until it is moved to the next unit in order to maintain the proper tension.

The left index finger is placed underneath the cloth at the point where the cloth is to be raised, and the left thumb on the cloth helps control the tension. A loop of thread is made around the portion of cloth to be bound. The right hand moves the hook to catch the center of the cloth within this loop of thread. Once the cloth is caught in the hook, the left index finger is withdrawn and the cloth is pulled taut (still on the hook) with the left hand. At the same time, the right hand tightens the loop of thread. The shaped bit of cloth, which is held at its base by the thread, is left in place in the hook

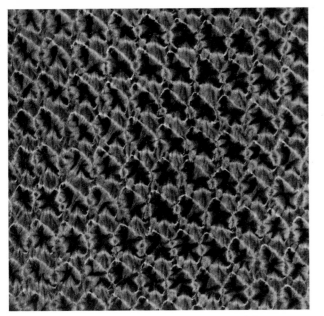

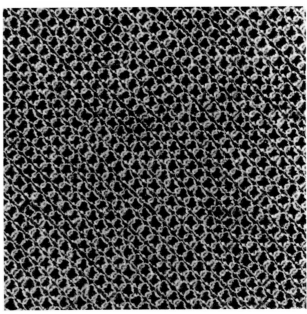

54. Small shapes bound on weft (*hira miura* shibori)

55. Small shapes bound on bias (*hitta miura* shibori)

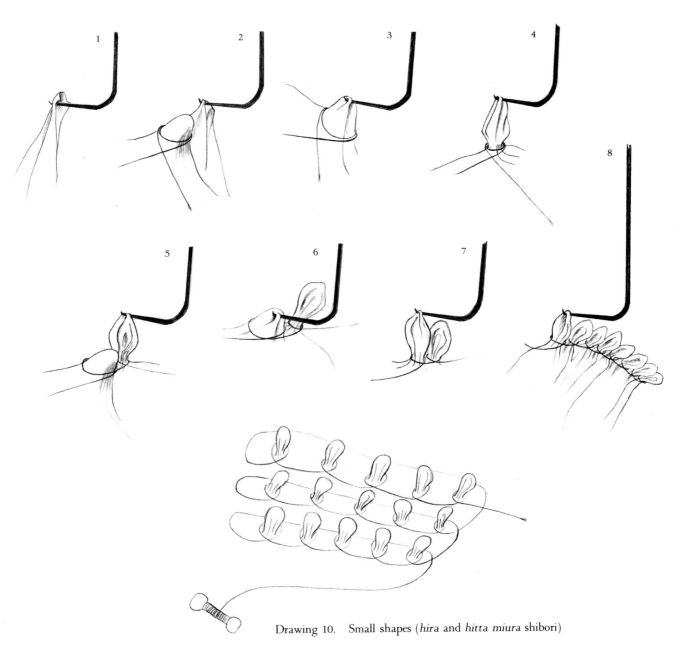

Drawing 10. Small shapes (*hira* and *hitta miura* shibori)

until the next bit of cloth is ready to be caught in it. Unlike the rapid-fire movements used in the binding of resisted dots, the movement here is smooth and gentle.

Plate 55 **Small Shapes Bound on the Bias** (*hitta miura* shibori):   The more regular square shape and small size of the resisted forms, as well as the arrangement of them suggesting a grid, create an allover pattern with some resemblance to *kanoko* shibori. Guide marks are stenciled on the cloth. The shaping and binding of the cloth are as described for the previous technique *(hira miura)* except that the rows are bound on the bias.

CRISSCROSS BINDING (see pages 87, 88)

This fast way of binding involves a special wishbone-shaped loop of wire fastened to a stand. The binding thread is wound on a short wooden dowel, the end is knotted, and the knot is caught in the loop. Tension is maintained on the thread (rather than on the cloth, as is the case with various other hooks), which makes it possible to bind faster with much greater tension on the binding thread and thus to exert greater pressure on the cloth than with the other hook types.

   Crisscross binding may be used to bind cloth drawn up and gathered together with the fingers, but it is most often used to bind cloth that is first shaped by stitching the outline of a motif and drawing up the thread (see pages 86–88). This combination of stitching and binding *(maki-age)* makes it possible to resist almost any design motif.

# Stitching

## CLOTH STITCHED AND GATHERED

Stitching as a way of resisting the dye has been used to a greater extent by the Japanese than by other peoples. They have found, through the flexibility and control that this technique allows, the means with which to create designs of great variety—delicate or bold, simple or complex, pictorial or abstract.

An extant example of a very refined stitch-resisted design on red silk—the lining of a Plate 5 sutra case—which Tetsurō Kitamura, in his book *Shibori*, dates from the Kamakura period (1185–1333), indicates that by the early fourteenth century the use of stitching in creating patterns in cloth with dye was well developed.

In the Muromachi period (1333–1573), stitching came to be used as the means of reproducing stylized natural motifs *(e-moyō)* in cloth by means of·dye. The design possibilities of stitched resist dyeing were extended still further when ways were devised to protect certain portions of cloth from the dye. Stitching delineated design motifs as well as large areas to be dyed or reserved. It was these developments in the use of stitching that made possible the multicolored garments and religious banners—*tsu-jigahana* textiles—of the late Muromachi and Momoyama periods. Extant examples of these precious textiles show how ingenious and imaginative the Japanese textile craftsmen were in the use of stitching to decorate cloth. They give ample evidence of the high level of development to which the Japanese carried resist dyeing during the fifteenth and sixteenth centuries.

The unique effects possible with stitched shibori are created by the type of stitch, whether or not the cloth is folded, and the arrangement (straight, curved, parallel, area enclosing) of the stitches.

After the stitching of a piece is completed, the cloth is drawn into tight gathers along the stitched thread(s) and secured by knotting. It is then dyed. The cloth within the gathers is largely protected from the dye.

The principal stitch used in shibori is the simple running stitch. The stitching thread is inserted into the fabric with even spacing and stitch length and a constant forward movement.

The only other stitch used in Japanese shibori is a type of overstitch, which creates a distinctive pattern in the cloth after it is dyed. This stitch is always made over the edge of a fold of cloth. The stitching proceeds from right to left with a circular motion of the needle. The thread is not drawn up with each stitch, but the cloth is gathered on the needle; as the stitching continues, the gathered cloth is pushed back over the eye of the needle onto the thread.

In stitched shibori, the thread must be of a weight appropriate to the fabric and of a strength that allows it to be tied without breaking. Doubled thread can be easily tied after the stitching is completed and drawn tight.

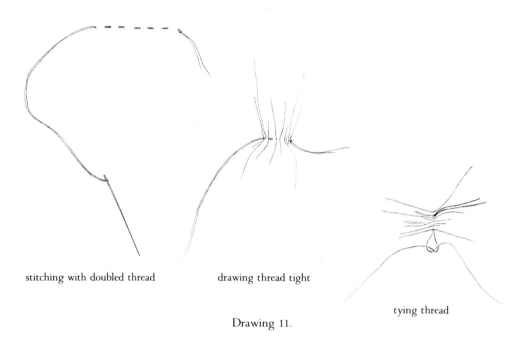

stitching with doubled thread          drawing thread tight

tying thread

Drawing 11.

SINGLE LAYER OF CLOTH

A single line of running stitches made in a single layer of cloth results in a broken line of resisted marks. The name for this type of stitching is *hira-nui* (or *shishige-nui*). This *hira-nui* stitching done in multiple parallel rows in a single layer of cloth creates a textural design effect known as wood grain *(mokume)* shibori.

**Wood Grain** *(mokume* shibori):    The balance of light and dark in this design gives it a textural quality unusual in stitch-resist patterning. The resemblance of this pattern to wood grain is clear enough. The beauty of this type of stitch resist lies in the undulation of the dark lines as they join and break and join again.

Plate 56

This handsome textural effect has long been used in Japan. A Muromachi period example of the classical design of linked circles *(shippō-tsunagi)* is resisted in this way within the elliptical shapes made by the overlapped circles. An example from the Momoyama period shows it in a striking check design in which it is used alternately with blocks of solid color. In a beautiful kimono from the middle Edo period, it is used in certain of the ground areas, dyed in indigo on a brownish gold satin. This versatile type of stitch resist has also been used to create richly textured backgrounds for embroidered designs; to create patterns by filling the entire ground with stitching, leaving only the design areas unfilled (Plate 139; see Plate 105 for a delicate effect with *hon hitta kanoko*); and to create designs with the stitching confined to selected elements of the design.

Plate 7

Plates 139, 105

Different effects are obtained by varying the direction and length of the stitches. One of these variations seen in Arimatsu shibori achieves a herringbone effect by stitching parallel zigzag lines.

Drawing 12

■*Stitching and Gathering*:    Traditionally, the stitching is done parallel to the weft because this allows a shorter thread length, but the stitching may, in fact, be done in any direction; and as long as the repeated rows are parallel to each other, the wood-grain patterning results. The length of the stitches may be the same throughout (traditional),

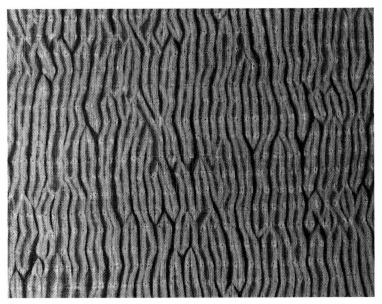

56.  Wood grain (*mokume* shibori)

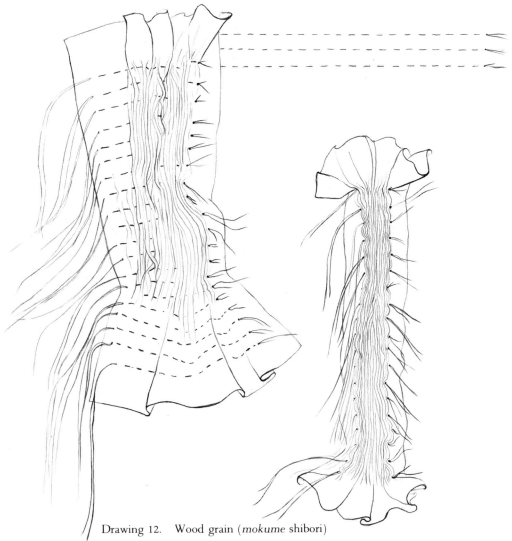

Drawing 12.  Wood grain (*mokume* shibori)

or they may vary in length from row to row. No attempt should be made to rigidly align the individual running stitches with those in other rows; the stitched cloth in Drawing 17, shown with the threads partially drawn up, reveals the discontinuous folds that occur when the stitches are not aligned. These irregular folds create the undulating lines with occasional breaks in them. After the stitching is completed, each thread is drawn up and knotted and the cloth is dyed.

FOLDED CLOTH

The result of stitching through a fold of cloth can best be understood by folding a strip of paper in half lengthwise, making accordion pleats across the folded strip, and, with these folds held compressed, coloring the edges on both sides. When the paper is opened flat, it can be seen that the center fold bisects the design and reverses the arrangement of dark and light—a black line on one side of the center fold will be matched by white on the other.

A single line of running stitches made parallel and close to the edge of a fold results in a line composed of two rows of resisted marks, one row on each side of the fold and alternating as described. This stitching and linear design is called *ori-nui*.

A single line of running stitches made through two layers of cloth along but not parallel to the fold results in a design that is symmetrical along the axis of the fold. Multiple rows (straight or curved) of running stitches made parallel to each other, but not parallel to the fold create patterns that are symmetrical, but display the reversing effect of the fold. In Arimatsu the name for this way of stitching is *hishaki-nui*.

The overstitch, described above, creates a chevronlike stripe, because the fold in the cloth repeats the diagonal slant of the stitch. The stitch is called *maki-nui*.

Plate 57 **Ori-nui Shibori**, undulating lines (*tatewaku* pattern):    This ancient design, of which the piece illustrated is a folk shibori example, appears in woven textiles and lacquerware of the Heian period (794–1185). It can be executed in various types of shibori, such as *kanoko*, *maki-nui*, and *ori-nui*. This design became popular during the Edo period (1615–1868), and during that time a shibori adaptation of it appeared in the folk textiles of Arimatsu.

In this shibori example, the undulating lines of the *tatewaku* pattern run diagonally, whereas the traditional arrangement of the lines is vertical. In textile weaving, the vertical placement of the undulating lines relates to the necessity of building the design

57.   *Ori-nui* shibori, undulating line (*tatewaku*) pattern

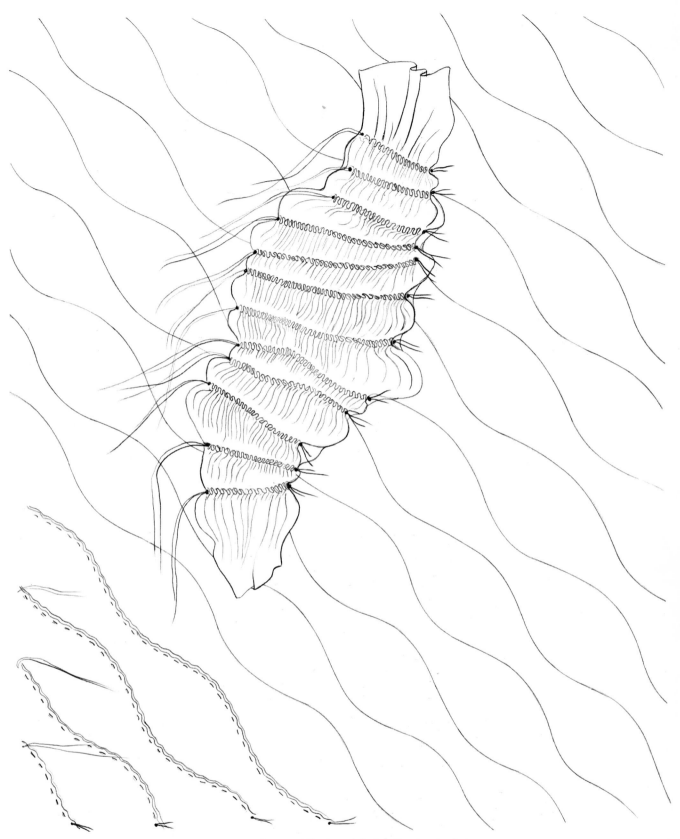

Drawing 13.   *Ori-nui* shibori; undulating line (*tatewaku*) pattern

on the warp threads—*tate* means "warp" as well as "vertical." In shibori, the diagonal alignment of the lines reflects the technical convenience of limiting the length of the thread used to stitch each line of the design. Although it results from a technical consideration, this diagonal alignment enhances the flowing movement of the pattern while preserving the effect of lightness and suppleness. In a garment, this flowing design creates a vibrant effect as the pattern moves and shifts with the movements of the body.   Plates 322, 323

Drawing 13 ▪*Stitching and Gathering*: The *ori-nui* technique is as follows: cloth is pinched with the fingers along the lines of the design marked on the cloth. A single row of running stitches is made close to the edge of the fold, which is pinched as the stitching progresses. When all the stitching is completed, the threads are drawn up tight and knotted and the cloth is dyed.

Plates 5, 58 **Japanese Larch** (*karamatsu* shibori):   The dark radiating lines within this design's circular shape evoke the form of the radiating branches of this deciduous conifer native to Japan. Once a popular design of the Nagoya area, it is now seldom seen. The way the lines break and join shows a relationship to the breaking and joining of the vertical lines in wood-grain shibori. The irregularity of the dark radiating lines within each circle adds variety to the pattern.

▪*Stitching and Gathering*:   Concentric half-circles are marked on the cloth at the fold. The units are in staggered rows. A continuous thread is used to stitch each row of half-circles. Running stitches are made through the two layers of cloth in the fold. When all the stitching is completed, the threads are drawn up tight and knotted. When the cloth is opened flat after dyeing, the rows of full circles are revealed.

A shibori design is often quite sensitive to even seemingly slight changes in how the fabric is manipulated. For example, when the circular motifs are stitched singly instead of in rows with a continuous thread, the resist effect of the knots necessary for each unit is evident as well as a dark band running through the center of each motif, where the fold is. Both effects may be consciously used as design elements. The kimono by the late Plate 328 Motohiko Katano in Plate 328 is illustrative. In Kyoto, these individually stitched units Plates 147, 148, 150 are used alone or in small groups and are called *miru* shibori (sometimes they are diamond shaped), and they may be combined with other shibori effects.

58.   Japanese larch (*karamatsu* shibori)

Drawing 14.   Japanese larch (*karamatsu* shibori)

**Linked Circles** (*shippō-tsunagi* pattern):   This classical design appeared as a textile motif in Japan at least as early as the Nara period (645–794); a shibori example decorated with this pattern is in the Shōsō-in collection. The design, composed of interlocking circles of equal diameter and forming elliptical shapes where the circles overlap, would appear to have been suggested by an old form of Chinese coin. The name for the design, *shippō* (in Japanese), translates as "seven treasures" and is Chinese in origin. *Tsunagi* means "link."

The example illustrated is ingeniously made by stitching along the edge of two adjacent arc-shaped folds of cloth that have been drawn together. Stitching two folded edges together in this manner is known as *awase-nui* and is a variation of *ori-nui* shibori. The elliptical shapes formed by two arcs are also used to suggest the leaves of bamboo or are grouped together to suggest flowers.

In one type of shibori, the areas within the stitch-resisted outlines are completely resisted. This is done by pasting thin paper to the underside of the cloth before it is folded and stitched. This is possible because a "pocket" is formed when the folded lips of the elliptical shape are stitched together. The paper pasted on the back of the pocket stops the dye from penetrating into the area within the stitched lips. This technique is used with indigo and is known as *kamiate* shibori, *kami* meaning "paper," and *ate*, "to apply."

■*Stitching and Gathering*:   The design marked on the cloth indicates the way the cloth is folded before it is stitched. A fold is made along the line of each arc. This fold is matched to the arc adjacent, and a second fold is made, forming two "lips" to the ellipse. The two folds are brought together and held pinched between the thumb and first finger, while the ends of the folds are carefully pinched to meet in points.

Running stitches are made close to the edge of the two folds through four layers of cloth, and one row of designs is stitched continuously across the width of the cloth.

When the stitching is completed, the threads are drawn up and secured and the cloth is dyed.

Plate 2

Plate 59

Drawing 15

Plate 153

Drawings 15, 16

59.   *Awase-nui* shibori, linked circle (*shippō-tsunagi*) pattern

Drawing 15.   *Awase-nui* stitching, linked circles (*shippō-tsunagi*) pattern

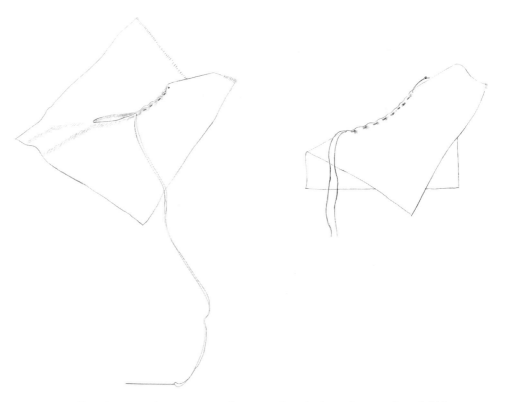

Drawing 16.   *Awase-nui*: stitching together the lips of an arc-shaped fold

Plate 60   **Chevron Stripes** (*maki-nui* shibori):   The lines of chevrons characteristic of *maki-nui* shibori are used here to create a pattern of horizontal stripes.

Drawing 17   ■*Stitching and Gathering*:   The cloth is held on the fold line with the fingers. The stitching is done with a circular motion of the needle; it is inserted at the back of the fold, and the point is brought over the edge of the fold and is inserted again from the back. The thread is not drawn up with each stitch, but the cloth is allowed to gather on the needle, and, as the stitching progresses, the gathered cloth is pushed over the eye of the needle onto the thread. After the stitching is finished, the thread is drawn up and knotted and the cloth is dyed.

60.   Chevron stripes (*maki-nui* shibori)

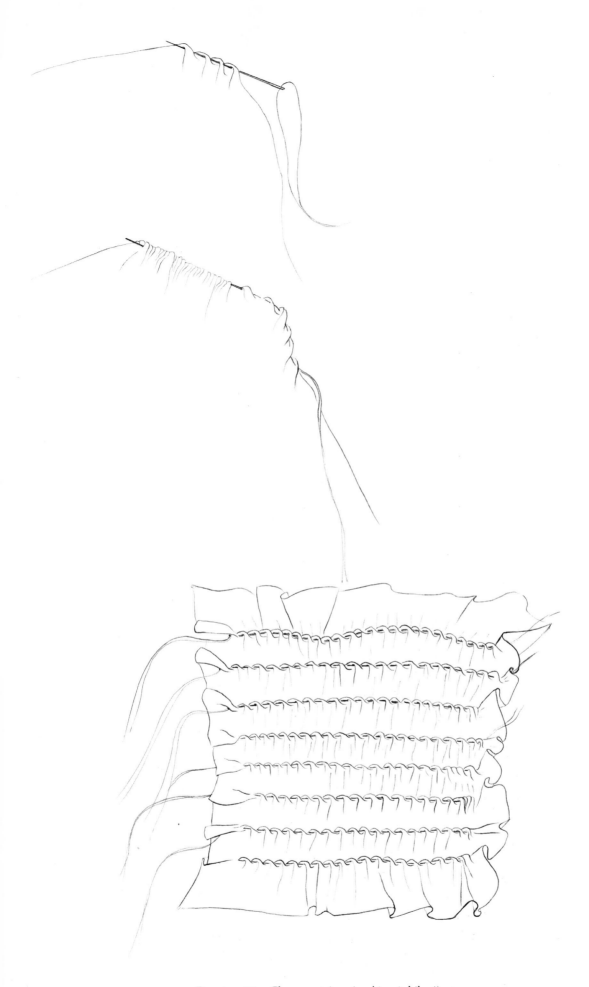

Drawing 17.  Chevron stripes (*maki-nui* shibori)

## CLOTH STITCHED AND BOUND

Many designs and special effects found in Japanese shibori fabrics are the result of combinations of resist processes. Stitching and binding is one such combination. The stitches outline motifs, and the binding thread creates patterns within the outlined forms.

### STITCHING AND OPEN-WOUND BINDING

Plates 28, 38 Open-wound binding and stitching are used to good effect in the bold designs of Hanawa shibori (see Plates 28, 38). These fabrics from the town of Hanawa in the northern part of the island of Honshu are of interest for several reasons: the boldness and simplicity of the patterns, which sets them apart from Kyoto and Arimatsu-Narumi shibori; the beauty of the two natural dye colors—purple and scarlet—that are used exclusively to dye them; and the way the ancient dye process limits the designs to one achieved with a few large stitches and a minimum of binding.

Plates 61, 163 **Squares** *(komasu),* **Hanawa Shibori:**   The simple design of "small" squares in Plate 61 demonstrates how a technical limitation—the stiffening of the textile resulting from a traditional dyeing method—is allowed to contribute to the beauty of the dyed design, rather than attempts being made to overcome or avoid this limitation. When this book was being compiled, this stitching and binding and dyeing was still being used in an isolated area of Japan by one man and his wife, who resolutely carried on an ancient process.

The town of Hanawa, from which this type of shibori takes its name, is located in a mountainous region that was once a great dyeing center. The plants, madder *(akane)* and purple root *(shikon)* that yield scarlet and purple dyes respectively, grew wild and in great abundance in the mountain valleys. The colors, still greatly admired, were in early times so highly prized that their use was regulated by edict. Beginning in the Nara period, these splendid hues were restricted to the garments of the imperial family and the highest ranking courtiers.

Originally silk yarn and textiles were dyed in these two colors. At some later time, shibori-patterned cloth began to be produced around Hanawa. Designs of these fabrics were limited to ones that could be made with cloth temporarily stiffened and rendered coarse by the mordanting process, which is done before the cloth is dyed (see page 278 for a description of the dyeing process).

Drawing 18 ■*Equipment, Cloth, and Thread:*   A special stand is used, consisting of an upright set in a flat wooden base; three strong needles are fixed at an angle of about 60 degrees, 5 millimeters ($\frac{1}{8}$ in) apart near the top of the upright. The cloth, a medium-fine silk, when stiffened with the mordant, is of a thickness comparable to a heavy cotton twill. The designs of Hanawa shibori may be successfully duplicated using any heavy cloth— cotton, silk, or linen—and dyeing with indigo or chemical dyes. The doubled thread used to stitch the cloth must be very strong. Waxed linen thread works well. For the binding thread, 16/3 linen is a good weight.

Drawing 18 ■*Stitching:*   The cloth is folded in half on the warp grain, and the design is indicated with a fugitive blue ink *(aobana).* The stiff cloth is difficult to stitch and gather into folds, so the stitching is done a short length at a time with a long running stitch. In the design of squares *(komasu),* each unit is stitched separately; the thread is drawn up and securely knotted. When the entire length of cloth is stitched, drawn up, and knotted, it is ready to be bound.

Drawing 18 ■*Binding:*   Two shaped portions of cloth (B and C in Drawing 23) are caught on the needles of the tying stand, and the shaped portion of cloth opposite them (A) is bound. All the shaped units on one side of the cloth are bound consecutively in this manner—

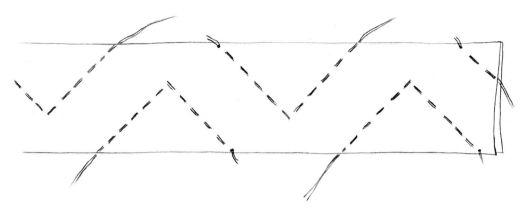

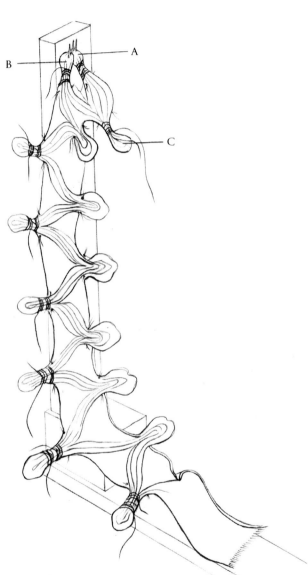

Drawing 18. "Small" squares (*komasu* shibori)

61. "Small" squares (*komasu* shibori)

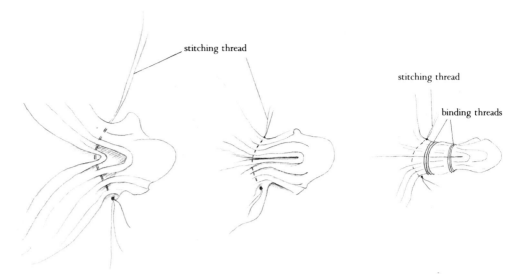

stitching thread

stitching thread

binding threads

Drawing 19. "Small" squares (*komasu* shibori), relationship of stitching and binding threads

Drawing 19

two adjacent shaped units on the opposite side of the cloth are used to anchor the cloth in the hook stand while each shaped unit is bound. (The hook stand makes work precise and efficient but is not necessary. A cord with one end anchored or the hands of a patient friend both suffice to hold the cloth, or binding can be done without these aids.)

The shaped cloth is not bound directly on the stitching but slightly out from it on the neck formed when the stitching is pulled taut. The cloth is bound in two places. Several turns of the thread are made each time, and the thread is securely knotted. When all the units are bound, the cloth is dyed. In Hanawa the stitching and binding are done during the winter, and then the following summer the work of an entire season is dyed.

STITCHING AND CRISSCROSS BINDING

A combination frequently used in Arimatsu shibori, crisscross binding and stitching provides a fast method and a wide range of design possibilities. Any motif of any size may be resisted in this way. The crossed binding thread and the random folds of the cloth create a distinctive patterning within stitch-outlined motifs.

Plate 62

**Patterns within Motifs** (*maki-age* shibori): The distinctive effect, in the typical example illustrated, is one of both narrow and wide dark lines radiating out from the heart of the design motifs; these lines made by the folds are intersected by zigzag resisted lines where the crisscrossing threads bind the shape.

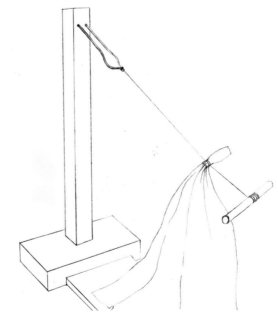

Drawing 20. Wishbone stand, used for crisscross binding

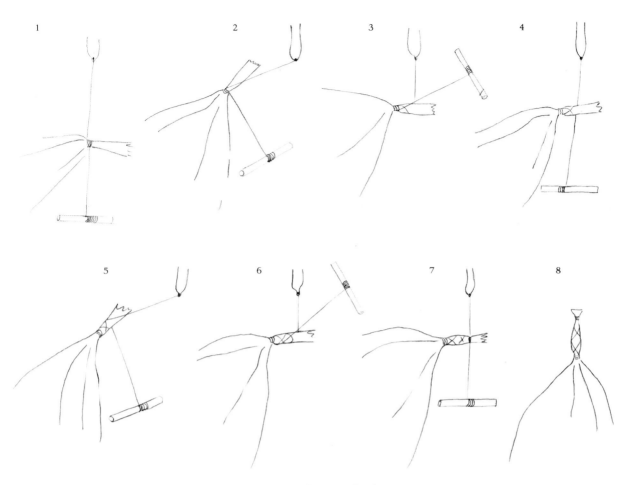

Drawing 21.   Crisscross binding

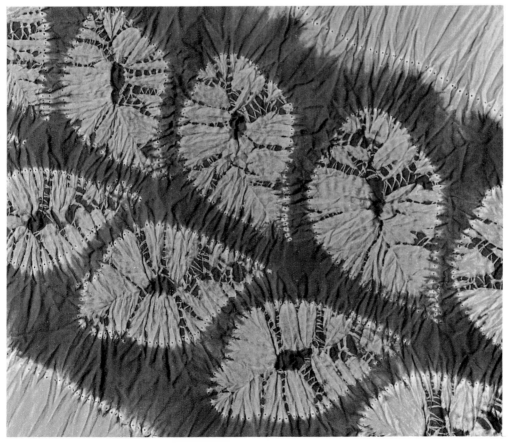

62.   Patterns within motifs (*maki-age* shibori)

Drawings 20, 44

Drawing 43

■*Equipment, Cloth, and Thread*:   The wishbone-shaped wire loop and stand are illustrated in Drawings 20 and 44. The binding thread, which is wound on a wooden dowel approximately 15 centimeters (6 in) long, 2 centimeters ($\frac{3}{4}$ in) in diameter, must be strong.

Drawings 20, 21

■*Shaping and Binding*:   The outline of the design motif is stitched with running stitches, and the thread is drawn tight, forming a neck in the cloth. The binding thread is wound on the dowel, and the end is knotted; this knot is caught in the narrow groove of the wire loop. The thread is held taut with the right hand. Using the left hand, the neck of the shaped cloth is placed on top of the tautly held thread midway between the loop and the dowel. The thread from the dowel is looped once around the neck of cloth. Tension is maintained on the thread by the left hand holding the shaped cloth. The crisscross binding is achieved with a circular motion by using the left hand to turn the shaped cloth down and towards the wire loop, and under the taut thread, and to bring it back over the thread, which is held taut by the right hand. Then the right hand loops one turn of thread *over* the shaped cloth. These two binding actions alternate, bringing the cloth closer and closer to the knotted end of the thread as the thread is wound around the cloth. A single knot (not *kamosage*) secures the thread, and it is cut.

## CLOTH STITCHED AND CAPPED

Design motifs or selected areas of the ground can be completely resisted by covering those portions of the cloth with an impermeable material (capping) or by encasing them in a container of some sort (tub-resist). Both methods have a long history in Japan and are still practiced there.

Stitching has long been used in Japan to create both resisted lines and forms against a dyed ground. When the use of some kind of flexible material to protect areas of cloth was combined with stitch resist, design possibilities were extended greatly.

The reverse, or positive, effect of a dyed image on an undyed ground is achieved by protecting the area surrounding the motif. Containers may be used instead of capping to resist large areas of cloth.

**Dip-Dyeing**:   The same effect is obtained by dipping portions of cloth in one or more dyes after motifs or areas are shaped by stitching or by other shibori techniques. Professor Toshiko Itō in *Tsujigahana, The Flower of Japanese Textile Arts*, calls this method *tsumami zome*, "pinch-dyeing," and dip-dyeing in general is also known as *okkochi zome*. According to Itō, this "pinch-dyeing" was developed to an extraordinary degree of precision in the dyeing of *tsujigahana* textiles during the Momoyama period; the dip-dyeing process exists today in a less refined form and is used occasionally in Arimatsu.

Plate 325

The starfishlike design shown in Plate 325 illustrates the use of dip-dyeing combined with looped binding (see page 71). Only the shaped portions of the cloth are dipped in the dye. The result is a resist design within a somewhat randomly shaped dyed area on an undyed ground. The dyed areas surrounding the resisted motifs take forms reflecting the random nature and large size of the folds of the gathered cloth when it is dipped. Such incidental designs are vigorous, and the free-flowing edges are strong.

The cloth surrounding the design is gathered together to form a neck. Paper is wrapped around the neck to keep that portion undyed, leaving the shaped cloth exposed. The paper is bound firmly in place with heavy string. Holding the shaped cloth by the neck, the shaped portion of the cloth is simply dipped into the dye, immersing the cloth only as far as the neck.

When the design consists of repeated motifs approximately equal in size, the bound necks of the gathered cloth are placed between two pieces of bamboo or wood, which are then bound together. This allows one to dip a number of units at one time.

**Tsujigahana:**   The methods of capping, tub-resist, and dip-dyeing make it possible to separate the ground into differently colored areas. Dyeing the ground in several colors was used extensively in *tsujigahana* textiles, but it is particularly associated with the decorative garments known as Keichō *kosode*, which combine large interlocking, colored ground areas (known as *somewake*, "divided colors") with stitched or bound shibori designs, embroidery, and applied gold leaf. Developed in the Keichō era (1596–1615), it remained popular through the mid-seventeenth century.

Plates 8, 18

Marvelous historical examples of stitch resist combined with the various ways of protecting and dyeing the cloth are the *tsujigahana* textiles seen in Plates 11 and 12. Such lovely designs show several ways in which lines of stitching and stitched and capped areas are used together.

Plates 11, 12

The extremely small size of the stitches used in *tsujigahana* made it possible to recreate the artist's lines, which were freely drawn directly on the silk.

At the present time, capping and container-resist dyeing are still in use in Kyoto, where they are practiced on a highly professional level. Together with *kanoko* shibori, they are the principal silk shibori resist methods employed there. Although both processes were also used in Arimatsu and Narumi for the indigo dyeing of cotton, they have almost disappeared there.

**Small Capped Motifs** (called *kobōshi* in Kyoto, *kawamaki* in Arimatsu):   The Japanese differentiate design motifs that are capped—*bōshi* means "hat"—by their size. The smallest of these *(kobōshi)* are traditionally done by women working in their homes; larger designs are done by professionals who spend ten years learning the craft of capping and tub-resist dyeing and then specialize in one or the other, resist dyeing with the tub being the more demanding of the two. In Kyoto small cap-resisted motifs are frequently combined with resisted dots *(kanoko)*. In Arimatsu a freer use was made of stitching and capping in the patterning of cotton kimono cloth, once a specialty of the area. Resisted dots were used to define the design's linear elements; flower shapes, leaf forms, and other simple motifs predominated in the capped elements. The resisted motifs appear widely and freely spaced on dark indigo, creating designs that are playful and refreshing in their simplicity.

Plates 177, 178

In present-day Kyoto shibori, the small resisted motifs are sharply defined. There, the resist units are bound outside the stitching, and only rarely does the resist effect of the stitching itself show. In capped shibori from Arimatsu, however, binding is done inside the stitching, and it is the line resisted by the stitches that is evident rather than the sharp line made by the thread that binds the cap in place. (Compare Plates 63 and 183.) This is also true of most *tsujigahana* fabrics.

Drawing 22

Plates 63, 183

The typical Kyoto example *(kobōshi)* illustrated shows the small, sharply defined circular forms combined with *kanoko* dots.

Plate 63

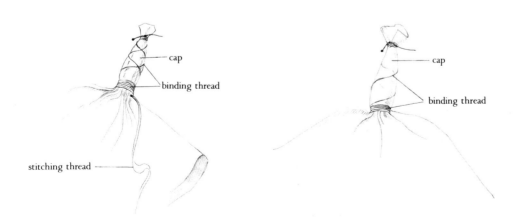

Drawing 22.   Capping, relationship of stitching and binding threads

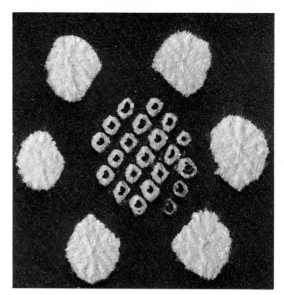

63. Small capped motifs (*koboshi*), circles (with *kanoko* dots)

Plate 36

Drawing 23
In the Arimatsu indigo-dyed example shown in Plate 36 and diagrammed in Drawing 23, the cotton cloth is patterned with simple rectangles, but a sensitivity to let the materials themselves speak has produced a design of quiet subtlety and strength.

This remarkable example is exceptional in a number of ways: the beautifully conceived size, proportion, and spacing of the units; the unusual squareness of the units' corners; the resist "shadow" effect surrounding and between the resisted units; and the attractive dye seepage into the centers, suffusing them with the palest tint of blue. The squareness of the units is achieved by fine and careful capping. The shadow effect and the tinting of some of the resisted areas are the accidental events in shibori dyeing, which are the result of various known causes and of ones unknown. In this case, most likely there was dye seepage under the thread that bound the caps in place and into the center of the units, since no core was used. Or, possibly, the caps were secured a bit above the tightly drawn stitching threads. Or, some unusual condition of the indigo dye played a part. Whatever the cause, this example shows a miraculous harmony of concept, technique, and fortuitous event.

Drawing 44
■*Equipment, Cloth, Thread, and Caps*:   The stand fitted with the wishbone hook, which is used in all types of capping and tub-resist dyeing, is pictured under crisscross binding, page 86. Cloth of light or medium weight is most suitable; in Kyoto, silk is used exclusively. Thread for binding must be strong but not thick.

Bamboo sheath, the outer covering of the plant's new shoots, traditionally is used to cap the small units of cloth *(koboshi)*. Since bamboo grows in most sections of Japan, this natural material was readily available. The leaf-shaped sheath is cut as desired and becomes pliable when soaked in water.

Any flexible and impermeable material can be used for capping. Plastic film or sheeting works well for larger units. It should "give" just a little when stretched between the fingers. Heavy freezer bags, plastic sold for tablecloths, or sheeting sold by the meter are all satisfactory. Lightweight paper is used to line both bamboo sheath and plastic.

Drawing 23
■*Stitching and Capping*:   The design motifs are outlined with stitches, and the stitching threads are drawn up and knotted. A square of paper-lined bamboo sheath or plastic is wrapped around the shaped cloth. The knot in the end of the binding thread is held in the wishbone loop of the stand. The thread is bound two or three times around the capped cloth at the neck, crisscrossed to the top, and bound again, knotted with one or two single knots, and cut. The most experienced worker is able to cap one thousand small units in a day.

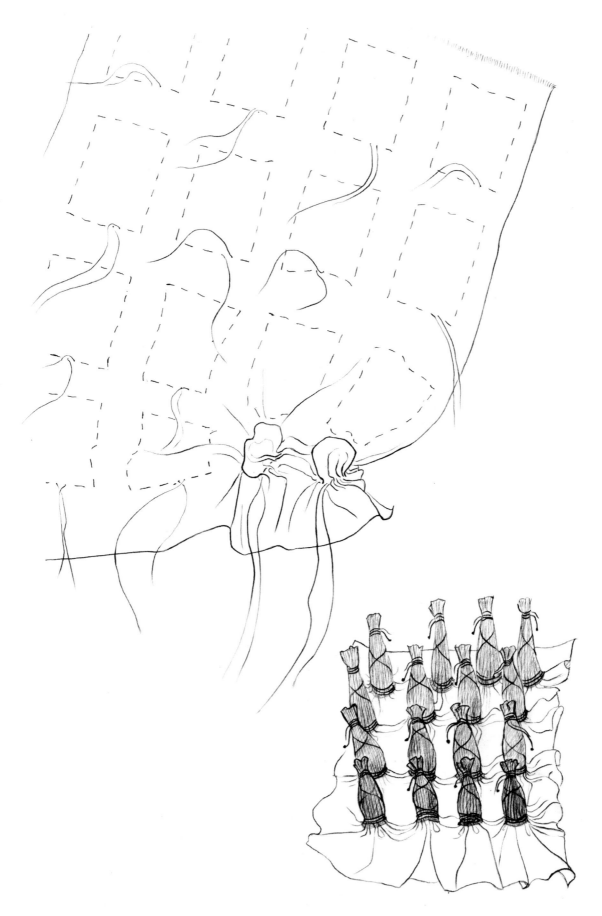

Drawing 23. Small capped motifs (*kobōshi* or *kawamaki*), squares

Plate 64 **Medium and Large Capped Motifs** (*chū-* and *obōshi*):  For motifs larger than about 6 centimeters (2¼ in) in circumference, a core of some material must be inserted into the shaped cloth when it is capped. The reason for this is quite simple and practical—when the gathers that occur after the motif is stitched and the thread pulled tight exceed a certain volume, there will be dye seepage through the gathers into the capped area from behind no matter how tight the thread is pulled. A core to fit into the center of the gathers and against which the binding thread can be drawn very tightly eliminates this seepage and allows a clean resist.

Design motifs with a complex outline cannot be done effectively with this technique. This is the only limitation on the design motifs that can be used.

Drawing 24 ■*Equipment, Cloth, Core, and Caps*:  The stand with the wishbone hook is used; a wooden dowel 15 centimeters (6 in) long holds the binding thread. Light- or medium-weight cloth is the most easily capped. Thread of suitable weight is needed for stitching; and very strong linen cord 16/3–16/5 (in Japan *asa* [hemp] is traditional) for binding caps in place.

Drawing 24 As described above, a core is required in the capping of larger motifs to insure a perfect seal against the dye. Cores were formerly made of wood, but today tightly rolled newspaper is commonly used. Dyers make paper cores of various diameters, in lengths of approximately 30 centimeters (12 in). They are cut with a very sharp knife into suitable lengths as needed. Large *bōshi* require cores of 4 to 8 centimeters (1½–3 in) in diameter, medium *bōshi*, 2 to 4 centimeters (¾–1½ in). Cores can easily be cut from balsa wood available in an assortment of sizes at hobby supply stores.

Plastic sheeting serves as capping material, replacing the bamboo sheath or kelp used formerly.

■*Stitching and Shaping the Cloth; Inserting the Core*:  The outline of the design is stitched with medium-sized stitches. The two ends of the thread are drawn up and knotted, and both knots are caught in the wire loop of the stand. With controlled tension on the thread, the gathers are arranged evenly. The core is covered with plastic kitchen wrap and fitted into the opening in the cloth. It extends 0.5 centimeter (⅛ in) out of the opening and need only be long enough to allow thread to be bound around it in two places about 1 centimeter (⅜ in) apart.

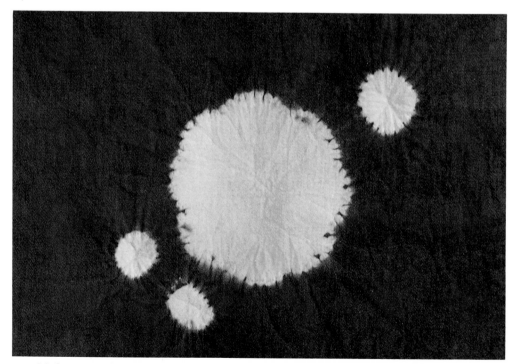

64.   Medium capped motifs (*chūbōshi*)

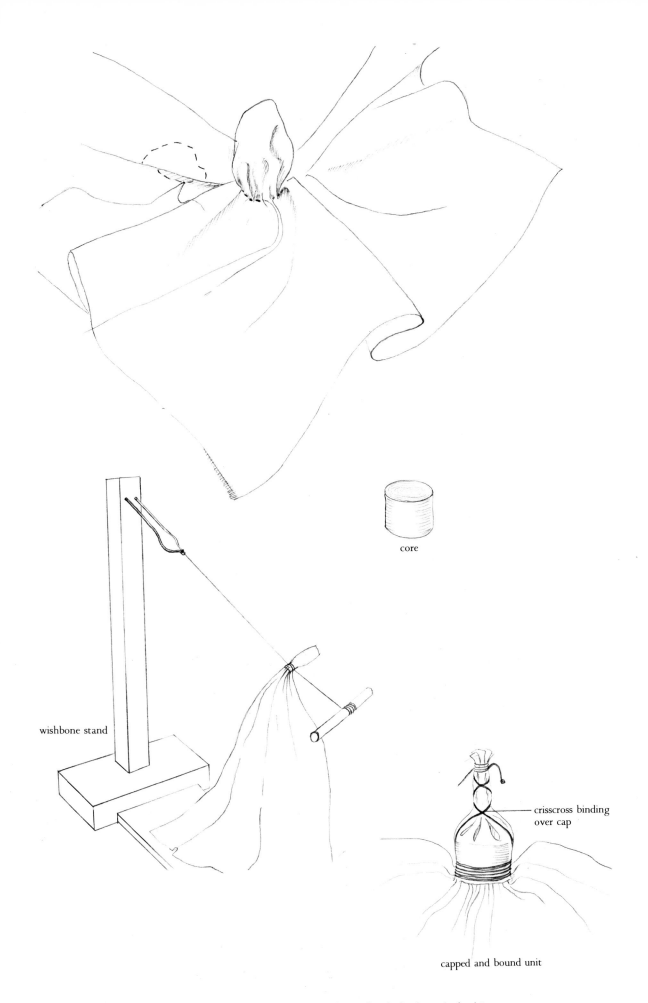

core

wishbone stand

crisscross binding
over cap

capped and bound unit

Drawing 24.   Medium and large capped motifs (*chūbōshi* and *ōbōshi*)

One end of the thread is removed from the wire loop and wound firmly around the core on the stitch line of the gathered cloth. Two or three turns of the thread are made to hold the core securely in place. The thread is fastened with two half hitches, tied with one end still held in the wire loop, and then is cut.

The cloth that is to be covered is brushed lightly with water and gathered into a neat bundle.

■*Capping; Binding the Cap:*    Heavy binding thread is wound on the wooden dowel and soaked in water. The free end is knotted, and the knot is caught and held in the

Drawing 24 wishbone hook. In some workshops the hooks are fastened to low benches of heavy construction instead of to a wooden stand; the worker sits on the floor with legs extended under the bench.

A piece of plastic, measuring about three to five times the length of the core, is wrapped two and one-half times around the shaped cloth. The lower edge of the plastic comes just a bit $(2-3 \text{ mm}/\frac{1}{16} \text{ in})$ below the drawn-up stitching.

With the thread from the hook pulled taut, the capped unit is placed on top of the thread (at the edge of the plastic), and then it is wound just inside (or outside, if you like the edge of the plastic cap with four turns of thread from the dowel. Thereafter the crisscross binding method described on page 87 is used to bind the cap three or four times up to a short distance from the top of the plastic, where the thread from the dowel is wound a few times around the cap, fastened with two half hitches, and cut. The knot is slipped free of the hook, and the plastic is neatly trimmed off at the top of the cap.

**Capped Ground** *(tako-bōshi):*    The ground can be protected from dye by placing that portion of the cloth in a container, or the process of capping can be used. The latter method is chosen if the design motifs are few and "float" in large areas of background.

This capped ground method is perhaps a recent innovation. The shaped segments of cloth are pulled through slits cut in a large sheet of plastic. Each slit in the plastic is bound, sealing off the exposed cloth segment. The plastic sheet is drawn together into a sphere so that all of the cloth to form the ground is inside it, and the neck of the sphere is bound very tightly with strong cord. This plastic-covered cloth resembles an octopus, hence the name *tako*, which means just that. It floats in the dye bath but is moved around to bring the exposed cloth in contact with the dye. The temperature of the dye bath must be controlled because too hot a bath will cause the air inside the plastic to expand, bursting the plastic.

**Tub-Resist** *(oke zome):*    The use of a container or tub to protect certain portions of cloth while dying other portions may have originated in a practice of protecting cloth with sections of bamboo, suggests Mr. Yamagishi, a Kyoto tub-resist craftsman. Toshiko Itō mentions the use of bamboo in *Tsujigahana, The Flower of Japanese Textile Arts* but does not speculate on the way it was utilized.

A section of bamboo cut below two joints or nodes becomes a natural container. If the portion of cloth to be reserved was stuffed very tightly into it, that portion would be protected from the dye, especially if indigo, which depends on oxygen, was used. Conceivably a section of bamboo with both joints left intact and split in half could also be used to protect portions of cloth if the cloth was stuffed into the split tube and the two halves were bound tightly together. This is speculation, of course, but it appears likely that, although the development cannot be traced, the lidded tub used in Kyoto at the present time evolved from bamboo used in some such way.

Drawing 25 There are two types of designs that can be successfully resist dyed by means of the lidded tub: designs that contain colored motifs that "float" in an uncolored ground *(rindashi)* and designs composed of colored and uncolored bands extending from selvage to selvage of the cloth *(dan mono).*

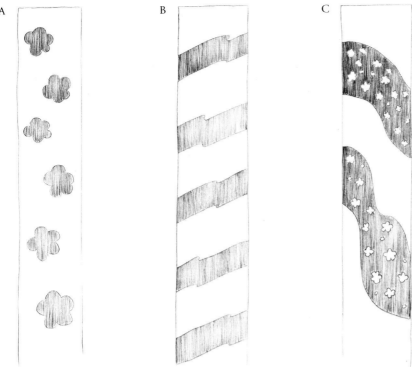

Drawing 25. Designs that can be tub-resisted float in a plain ground (A) or extend across the weft (B, C).

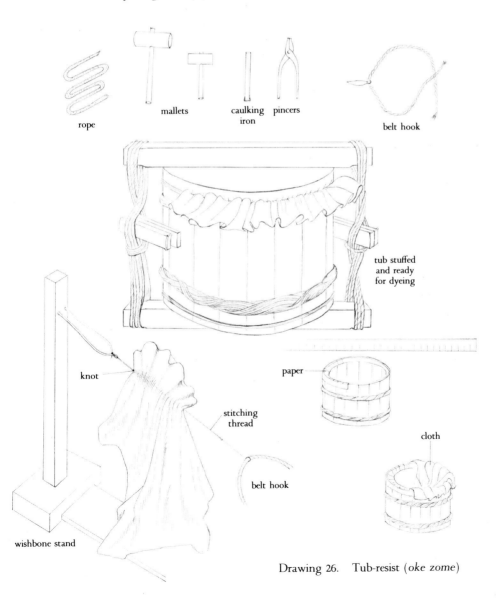

rope

mallets

caulking iron

pincers

belt hook

tub stuffed and ready for dyeing

knot

stitching thread

paper

cloth

belt hook

wishbone stand

Drawing 26. Tub-resist (*oke zome*)

■*Tub, Equipment, and Materials*:    The heavy wooden tub, open at both ends, is sturdily constructed with close-fitting covers or lids that are held in place by two heavy bars of wood placed at top and bottom and secured by rope.

A stand fitted with a wishbone hook is used. Flexible headless pins *(oke bari)* hold the cloth in place on the tub's flat rim. A wooden mallet is used to secure them in place, and special pincers to remove them. A chisellike tool is used to insert cotton roving between the rim and the lid of the tub.

■*Marking the Design, Stitching the Cloth*:    The design is drawn on the cloth with a fugitive blue ink *(aobana)*. Women working at home stitch the outlines of the areas to be dyed or reserved, and the cloth is sent to the tub dyer. Calling him a dyer is a misnomer; he is a specialist in shaping the cloth and arranging it in the tub—a tub stuffer. He gets the tub ready and sends it to yet another specialist who does the dyeing.

■*Shaping the Cloth*:    The worker sits facing the wishbone hook of the stand. The stitches outlining the motif area are not yet drawn up; the two ends of the stitching thread are knotted together, and this knot is caught in the loop of the hook. Before the knotted ends of the thread are inserted in the hook, however, a second knot is made in the doubled thread several centimeters from the first. The stitching thread, which is now a loop, is drawn up just a bit at the point opposite the knot and caught in a hook attached to the waistband worn by the worker. The thread is now held between the wishbone hook and the waistband. The worker keeps the thread taut by simply leaning backward.

The gathers of cloth are moistened by brushing water along the stitch line and are arranged evenly on the taut thread. This is done by pushing the cloth towards the wishbone hook against that second knot made in the thread. When the gathers are evenly lined up, the thread is unhooked from the waistband and wrapped several times around the shaped cloth to hold it together temporarily.

■*Preparing the Tub*:    The tub is soaked in water for two hours before the cloth is placed in it. Strips of paper are cut to fit the lid and the tub's rim and put in place. The paper protects the cloth from wood stains.

■*Arranging the Cloth in the Tub*:    The cloth is placed in the tub with the stitch line of the shaped cloth laid on the tub's rim. The portion of cloth to be dyed extends over the rim outside the tub, and the portion to be protected is inside the container.

The evenly arranged gathers are pinned in place with special headless, flexible pins *(oke bari)* pounded 1 centimeter ($\frac{3}{8}$ in) apart through the cloth into the tub's flat rim. Both tub rims may be used, utilizing the tub fully. After the lids are fastened securely in place, the flexible pins, which extend outside the tub, are pulled out with pincers. Tub rims must be sanded smooth after every third stuffing. When the tub is reduced in height to 15 centimeters (6 in) it is discarded.

■*Closing and Sealing the Tub*:    The heavy wooden lids are placed on the rims of the tub. A sturdy wooden bar is put in place at the top and the bottom, and thick cotton
rope is bound over the ends, connecting the bars and holding down the lids. Short, flat pieces of wood are inserted into each loop of the rope and twisted to tighten the rope and increase the tension on the lids. They are held in place against the side of the tub by the pressure of the twisted rope and, after dyeing, must be freed from the rope with a hammer blow.

After the pins are removed, cotton roving is inserted between the cloth remaining outside the tub and the lid. A blunt-edged chisellike tool and small wooden mallet are used for this most difficult and critical operation. Even the most experienced craftsman may lose two or three bolts of silk a year because of dye leakage due to faulty insertion of the roving.

■*Dyeing*:   The tub (it holds three lengths of kimono cloth when filled to capacity) is sent to a professional dyeing specialist. The cloth is dyed by immersing the tub completely in the dye bath.

## CLOTH STITCHED AND CORE-RESISTED

The Japanese use a core to protect the ground areas of stitch-resisted designs. This creates an effect unusual in resist dyeing, that of stitch-resisted patterning on an undyed ground. Both rigid and flexible cores are used.

In the mid-nineteenth century a method was devised using a pole as a rigid core to produce this unusual effect in indigo-dyed cotton. It is not known when flexible cores were first used with stitch resists, but in the early part of the seventeenth century a pattern of stripes and bands was made in Arimatsu; presumably this was made by binding pleated cloth to a flexible core of rope. The two types of core require different handling and present different design opportunities.

The rigid core is used to reserve ground areas of linear designs created by stitching. While it is possible to include small motifs as accents, the nature of the process restricts the patterns to linear ones. However, with a flexible core it is possible to reserve the background of many other types of stitch-resisted designs and to create these designs with patterned backgrounds.

Plate 188

Plates 68, 168–74

### RIGID CORE

The use of a short wooden pole as a core was developed in Arimatsu about 1850 by Suzuki Kanezō. He called the process *shirokage*, "white shadow" shibori, a name as lovely as the designs it produced—lines of indigo blue traced on white. The light, cool appearance of these *shirokage* fabrics probably accounted for their great popularity for summer kimono during the Meiji (1868–1912) and Taishō (1912–26) periods.

The *ori-nui* stitching (page 76) that is always used raises ridges in the cloth when the threads are drawn up, making it possible to expose and dye only the stitched parts when the cloth is wound around the pole (see Drawing 28). The unstitched ground areas of the cloth, protected from the dye by the pole on one side and the close arrangement of the stitches on the other, remain undyed. This shibori type involves more labor and skill than is practical in today's economy and is no longer produced.

Drawing 28

**Squares**:   The effectiveness of this simple grid arrangement of lines that divides the white ground into squares can best be seen in the kimono of Plate 303. The same design is illustrated here in a detail to show the stitching. Plates 187–92 are illustrative of other *shirokage* designs.

Plate 65
Plate 303
Plates 187–92

■*Equipment, Cloth, and Thread*:   The pole traditionally used is of wood, 60 centimeters (2 ft) long, 12 centimeters (4¾ in) in diameter, fitted into an octagonal base. A stand, consisting of a horizontal wooden base with a heavy vertical at one end that has a semicircular notch cut out of the top, supports the pole at an angle while the cloth is being wrapped around it. The end of the pole rests in this curved notch, while the octagonal base rests on the horizontal piece of the stand. A small rigid spatula is used to arramge the cloth on the pole. The plastic cylinder described on page 124 may be substituted for the wooden pole, and the supporting base and stand can be easily constructed of plywood. Traditionally *shirokage* shibori was made exclusively of cotton, a limitation imposed by the fabrics' use as light kimono (*yukata*), rather than by the process itself. Thread for stitching must be strong, with enough twist to prevent it from breaking and fraying.

■*Marking the Design*:   *Ori-nui* is the type of stitch used, and the stitching is always done in the direction of the warp, though detours to right or left are possible. Lines of stitching must begin and end at the same point along the warp—that is, both the

Drawing 27

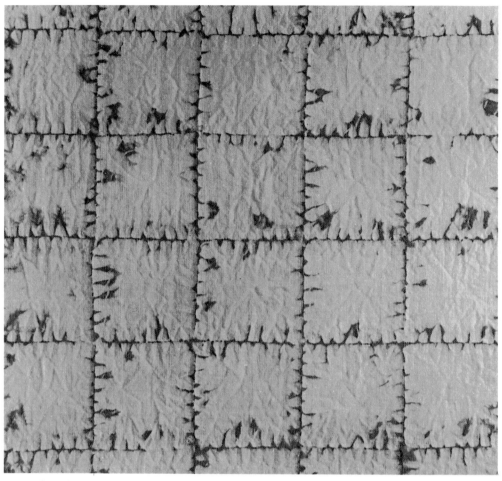

65. White shadow (*shirokage* shibori), squares

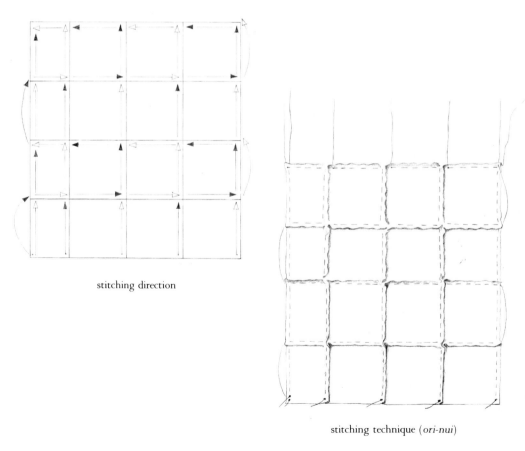

stitching direction

stitching technique (*ori-nui*)

Drawing 27. White shadow (*shirokage* shibori), squares pattern

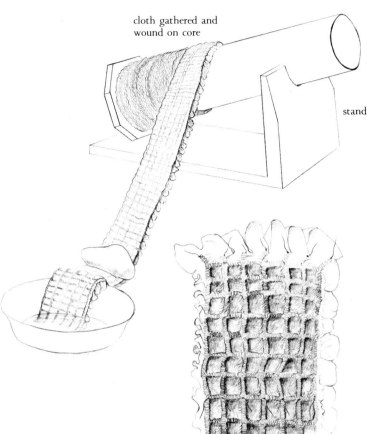

cloth gathered and
wound on core

stand and core

Drawing 28.   White shadow (*shirokage* shibori),
squares pattern

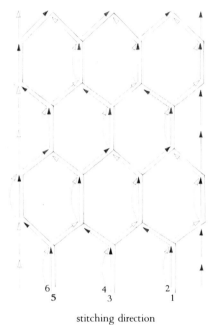

Drawing 29.   White shadow (*shirokage*
shibori), tortoiseshell pattern

6
5   4
3   2
1

stitching direction

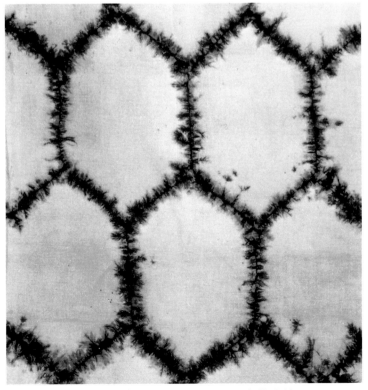

66.   White shadow (*shirokage* shibori), tortoiseshell (*kikkō*) pattern

beginning and the end of each "line" of stitching must be the same distance from the selvage or cloth edge.

The design is marked on the cloth, and the way each line is to be stitched determined in advance. Drawings 27 and 29 schematically show the stitching plan for two *shirokage* patterns.

■*Stitching and Gathering the Cloth*: Each line of the design is stitched with a separate thread (the thread is not doubled) until all the lines are completed. To insure that all the threads are drawn up equally, one of the threads at the approximate center of the width of cloth is drawn up the desired amount and secured. This serves as a guide, and the other threads are drawn up an equal amount and each is fastened. Unlike other stitch resists, the thread is not drawn up to its limit, but only enough to arrange the gathers evenly.

Drawing up the stitching threads dramatically reduces the length and width of the cloth. Naturally the amount varies with each pattern; the tortoiseshell *(kikkō)* pattern in Plate 66, a design of hexagons, provides an example. A two-meter length of cloth 36 centimeters (14 in) wide stitched in this design is reduced to a strip 33 centimeters (13 in) in length by 10 centimeters (4 in) in width. The pole, 60 centimeters (2 ft) long, holds one kimono length (11 m/36 ft) of stitched and gathered cloth.

■*Wrapping the Cloth on the Pole*: One end of the pole is fitted into the curved notch of the stand. The other end rests on one of the flat sides of the octagonal base. The pole is given a turn as the cloth is wound on it.

The strip of stitched cloth is first sprayed lightly with water to dampen it slightly and is then placed on the pole at the base end. The end of the strip is fastened with nails to the wooden pole (masking tape serves to hold cloth on a plastic cylinder). The cloth is kept flat on the pole, and for the first turn (in a clockwise direction) around it, it is pressed firmly against the base. It is important to wrap the cloth firmly enough against the base to prevent dye from seeping under the cloth. Light tension is maintained on the cloth strip with a weight of some kind—a stone or heavy book will do. The cloth is kept slightly damp, which makes it easier to compress.

The ridges of the stitched cloth are carefully brought up to the surface with the spatula; the cloth between them is pushed in towards the surface of the pole. Space between the ridges is eliminated by pressing them together. It is easier to eliminate these spaces with some designs than with others, and they cannot always be completely eliminated. To insure an absolutely white ground, cotton wadding is stuffed into spaces that cannot be eliminated.

When all of the cloth is wound on the pole, a heavy rope is bound around the end opposite the base to hold the cloth in place, and cotton wadding is inserted between the cloth and the rope to prevent seepage of dye to the underside of the cloth.

The pole is lifted out of the stand and immersed in the dye bath.

FLEXIBLE CORE

Rough rope made of rice straw is still used in Arimatsu for flexible core shibori processes. Rope core is also used with stitch resists to reserve or to pattern the ground portions of the designs. The core *(shin)* was in earlier times covered with paper to prevent the straw from staining the cloth; now it is sealed in plastic.

The process, called *shin ire*, "to insert core," requires that the stitching be done in rows that extend from selvage to selvage on the weft grain or bias of the cloth. Either *ori-nui* or *hishaki-nui* (pages 76ff), or combinations of the two types of stitching, may be used. The cloth is stitched, the threads are drawn up, and the narrow strip of cloth is placed around the core with the selvages touching, then the cloth is bound.

The cloth may be bound in one of two ways, depending on the effect desired. To

Plate 66

reserve the ground, close-wound binding is used, and the areas between the raised rows of stitched units are completely covered by the binding material. Open-wound binding is used to achieve a patterned ground. The patterning results from the way the thread binds the casual folds between the rows of raised, stitched portions of cloth.

Formerly the *shin ire* process was a means of decorating cotton cloth, and the dye used was indigo. At the present time multicolored silks dyed with chemical dyes are being produced by this method in Arimatsu.

**Sunrise** (*hinode* pattern):   The pattern illustrated is a very simple one composed of small repeated shapes suggesting rising suns. Plates 167–74 illustrate a variety of *shin ire* shibori designs.

■*Equipment, Rope, Cloth, and Thread*:   A stand, consisting of a flat wooden base with an upright of bamboo fixed at one end is used to hold the rope and stitched cloth. The bamboo, about 72 centimeters (28 in) long and 5 centimeters (2 in) in diameter, has a long notch cut in the top. The cloth-wrapped rope fits down into the notch, where it is held fast.

A rope with a circumference equal to the width of the stitched cloth is used as a core. Heavy nylon or hemp rope or plastic tubing (all are available from hardware or surplus stores) may be substituted for the straw rope used in Japan.

Plate 67
Plate 68

Plates 67, 68
Plates 167–74

Drawings 30, 44

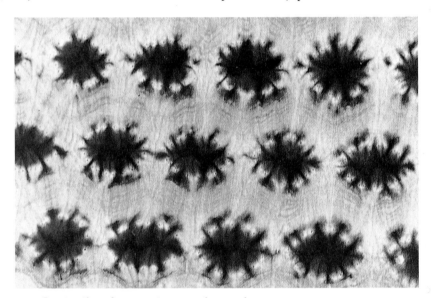

67.   Sunrise (*hinode* pattern), reserved ground

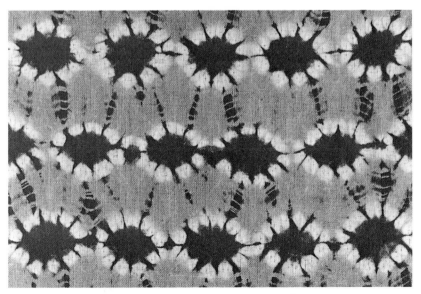

68.   Sunrise (*hinode* pattern), patterned ground

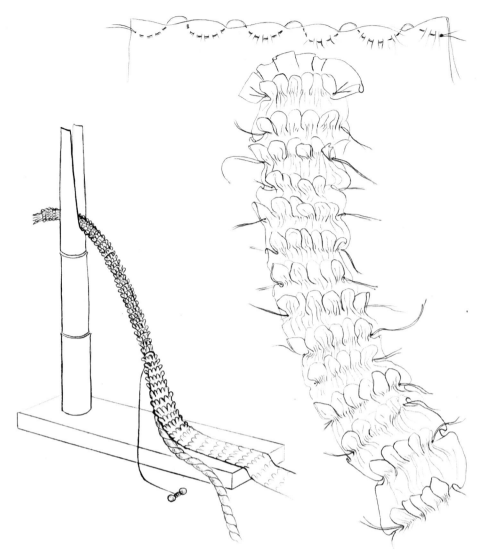

Drawing 30.   Flexible core (*shin ire*) shibori, sunrise (*hinode* pattern)

Light- or medium-weight cloth is most suitable. Thread for stitching should be related in weight to the type of cloth that is used. Binding thread must be strong. If the ground areas are to be completely resisted, a very thick, soft cotton may be used. The Japanese use rubber innertubes cut into 0.5-centimeter ($\frac{1}{8}$-in) strips to bind, instead of thread. It is convenient to wind the long binding material on a wooden dowel.

Drawing 30   ■ *Stitching and Gathering:*   Half-circles to indicate the stitching are marked along the fold lines made on the weft grain. The cloth is folded and stitched (*hishaki-nui*; page 76). Each row of half-circles is stitched with a continuous thread. When all have been stitched, each thread is drawn up tight and secured with a square knot.

■ *Binding:*   One end of the stitched cloth is fitted around the rope with the selvages touching and fastened to it and placed in the notch of the bamboo stand. The worker sits on the base of the stand and keeps the cloth and rope taut by sitting on them. The cloth-covered rope is bound: close-wound binding is used to resist the ground areas; open-wound binding to pattern them.

The same small device used to bind pleated cloth (page 105) may also be used to hold and turn the cloth-covered rope. The cloth is first fastened around the rope with thread, but in this case the tension and number of turns of the thread need be only just enough to hold the cloth in place. After the cloth is fastened to the rope, it is tightly bound, using the turning device.

# Folding

## CLOTH PLEATED AND BOUND

Binding and dyeing lengths of pleated cloth is a resist method used in Japan for at least three hundred years. Early records at Arimatsu tell of a gift of silk horse reins, decorated in this way, that was presented in 1680 to the fifth Tokugawa shogun by the daimyo of Owari, the feudal lord of the fief that included Arimatsu. The design of this important gift, a combination of vertical stripes and horizontal bands, has been called *tazuna*, "horse rein," shibori ever since and, on occasion, is still made in Arimatsu.

Vertical stripes are made by the simple process of pleating the cloth along the warp, then binding the pleated cloth either by itself or around a core. The size of the pleats is dictated by the design effect desired. Since only the edge of each pleat is exposed when the cloth is bound and dyed, a pattern of stripes results. The resisting effect of the binding thread results in fine resist lines crossing the dark stripes, adding interest and variety to very simple patterns.

The Japanese have devised ingenious ways of manipulating cloth when it is pleated to create designs other than stripes. By covering sections of the pleated cloth with paper or strips of cloth before it is bound, by pleating and dyeing the cloth more than once, and by binding the pleated cloth on a flexible core, the design possibilities of this relatively simple resist process have been increased. The pleating types discussed below provide means of exploiting the possibilities of folding and binding cloth to create designs.

## CONTINUOUS PLEATING

Forming the cloth into continuous pleats—by hand, machine, or stitching—then binding it results in simple designs of vertical stripes. Repeating the process, folding the cloth differently each time, adds variety, depth, and subtlety to the patterns.

If the cloth is pleated continuously in the regular way but is bound intermittently, patterns of vertical stripes and plain horizontal bands result. To create yet another effect, plain bands may be resisted by covering portions of the pleated cloth with paper before it is bound.

The cloth is folded into uniform vertical pleats, the folds of which are extended a few centimeters at a time. The first pleated length is held together with thread, and the thread is wound around it as the pleating progresses. This thread *(kake-ito)* is not wound with enough tension or at close enough intervals (the turns of the thread are about 4 cm/1½ in apart) to bind the cloth; it merely holds the pleats together in a ropelike shape. The cloth is then bound when all of it is pleated and secured in this way.

69.   Stripes, hand pleating (*tesuji*)

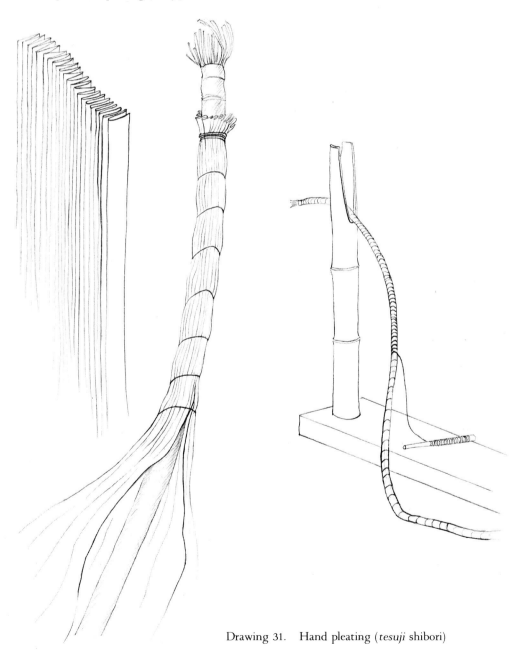

Drawing 31.   Hand pleating (*tesuji* shibori)

The binding may be done by hand, with the cloth held taut in a special stand, or with a device that rotates the "rope" of pleats. In either case the thread is stout, the tension is strong, and the turns of the thread are 1 centimeter ($\frac{3}{8}$ in) apart.

The process of hand pleating and the resulting designs are called *te* ("hand") *suji* ("stripe") shibori.

**Stripes** (hand pleating; *tesuji* shibori):    In the typical example illustrated, variations in the width of the stripes and the resist effect of the binding thread add interest to the patterning.

■*Equipment, Cloth, and Thread*:    A stand *(tesuji dai)*, consisting of a length of bamboo approximately 7 centimeters ($2\frac{3}{4}$ in) in diameter, with a deep V-shaped cut in the top and fitted upright in a flat wooden base, is used to hold the cloth while it is pleated.

A tapered wooden dowel, about 18 centimeters long, 2 centimeters in diameter at one end, and 5 centimeters at the other ($7 \times \frac{3}{4} \times \frac{1}{2}$ in), holds the thread.

Any light- or medium-weight cloth may be used. A stout thread is needed for binding; linen 16/2 is satisfactory. The *kake-ito* thread that is used to merely hold the pleats together should be fine but need not be especially strong, since little tension is exerted on it.

■*Pleating and Holding the Pleats Together*:    The worker sits on the base of the stand facing the V-notch in the bamboo upright. The cloth is lightly sprinkled with water from time to time to keep it damp.

The cloth is first pleated from selvage to selvage. Typically twenty-five to thirty pleats are made in one 36-centimeter (14-in) width of kimono cloth. Thread is wound around these guide pleats for a few inches and fastened with one or two *kamosage* knots. When a flexible core of rope is used, as in this example, the guide pleats are arranged evenly around it and secured to it with thread.

The pleated cloth and the rope (if one is used) are fitted down into the notch in the bamboo upright. The worker holds the cloth taut by sitting on it. Fifteen to 20 centimeters (6–8 in) of cloth are pleated at one time. The pleats are held together in the left hand, the thread-wrapped wooden dowel in the right. With a kind of flicking motion, the dowel is carried clockwise end over end, under and over the tautly held pleated cloth. The tapered dowel, being heavier at one end, facilitates this quick, sure movement. The thread is wound at intervals of about 4 centimeters ($1\frac{1}{2}$ in). The actions of pleating and winding alternate.

The dowel is never allowed to drop to the floor. When both hands are needed to pleat the cloth, the dowel is shifted to the left hand and the small end is held between the third and fourth fingers, leaving the other fingers free. The weight of the large end of the dowel maintains tension on the thread until the winding action begins again.

From time to time the pleated cloth is lifted free of the notch in the bamboo, moved forward, and refitted into it. When all the cloth is pleated and wound with thread, it is ready to be bound.

■*Binding*:    The binding process is called *tatsumaki*, "tornado." The cloth may be bound with the aid of a turning device or entirely by hand with the cloth held in the bamboo stand. The hand-binding process is the same as the method described above used to hold the pleated cloth together with the *kake-ito* thread. However, for binding, strong thread is used, and it is bound around the cloth with greater tension. The turns of the binding thread are the same—1 centimeter ($\frac{3}{8}$ in) apart—whether the binding is done by hand or with the turning device.

The turning device consists of two rotating hooks fastened to fixed supports some distance apart. The ends of the "rope" of pleated cloth are caught in the hooks, and the

Plate 69

Drawings 31, 44

Drawings 31, 43

Drawing 31

cloth is stretched horizontally between them. Once, turning was done with a hand crank; the device is now motor driven.

The speed with which the cloth rotates is controlled by one worker. A second worker steadies the "rope" of pleated cloth by placing the left hand around it, as if to grasp it, with the first finger and thumb touching. With the right hand the worker controls the binding thread—it is under tension—and spaces the turns of thread at regular intervals by sight and with a sure hand while walking along the length of the turning cloth.

The coil of pleated and bound cloth is immersed in the dye bath.

**Stripes** (machine pleating; *fukuzō suji* shibori):    Several small pleating machines were invented in the Arimatsu-Narumi area during the Meiji period (1868–1912). They were devised to pleat two bolts of kimono cloth vertically (American pleating machines create horizontal pleats) and at the same time to secure the pleats with thread. This type of

Plate 223    machine pleating—one machine was patented by a shop named Yama-shū—is called *fukuzō suji* or *Yama-shū-suji*.

Patterns made with Japanese machine-pleated cloth are distinguished from those using cloth that is hand pleated by the narrow width of the stripes, the small amount of space left between them, and a mechanical uniformity. The different effects created by

Plates 197, 223    hand- and machine-pleated cloth may be seen by comparing Plates 197 and 223.

**Stripes** (stitched pleating; *nui yōrō* shibori):    Pleats may be made by stitching the cloth and drawing up the stitching threads. The cloth is held under tension, and parallel rows of stitches are made on the weft grain of the cloth, extending from selvage to selvage. The stitches in all of the rows must be precisely aligned with those made in the first row. This careful alignment insures that the cloth will be shaped into regular vertical folds when the threads are drawn up. The cloth is brushed with starch to set the pleats, dried, and bound.

Plate 70    Stitch-pleated patterns resemble those made of machine-pleated cloth, but the stripes are not as uniform and the effect is finer.

■*Equipment, Cloth, and Thread:*    A wooden bar suspended at a convenient height above and in front of the worker holds the cloth. Two pieces of split bamboo (flat pieces of smooth wood do as well) are used to press the pleats after the stitching thread is drawn up. Lightweight cotton or silk cloth may be used. Sewing thread is a medium-weight cotton; binding thread is of linen 16/2.

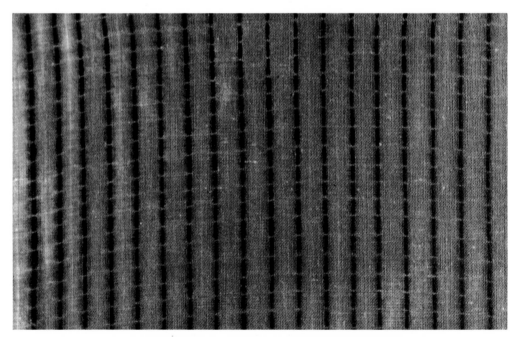

70.   Stripes, stitched pleating (*nui yōrō*)

■*Stitching and Forming the Pleats:* One end of the cloth is fastened in place around the wooden bar. The worker sits on the floor facing the bar and draws the cloth taut and keeps it that way by sitting on it.

Alternate rows of short (1 mm/$\frac{1}{32}$ in) and long (5 mm/$\frac{1}{8}$ in) stitches are used. After each row of stitches is made across the width, the cloth is turned over and the next row of stitches is completed. Thus the stitching always procedes from right to left. The short stitches form the "top" of the pleats; the long stitches create the intervals of space between pleats. These measurements produce fifty-four pleats in one standard width (36 cm/14 in) of cloth.

Drawing 32

When the thread is drawn up, pleats are formed. Each pleat is sharply creased on the warp grain with the fingers for several centimeters, then the cloth is reversed, and another row of stitches is made about 1.5 to 2 centimeters ($\frac{1}{2}-\frac{3}{4}$ in) from the first row. This process is repeated, reversing the cloth for each row of stitches, for the length of the cloth. The sharp creases made in the cloth serve as a stitching guide. Thus the stitches made in this second row and in all of the subsequent ones are precisely aligned with those made in the first row.

When the stitching thread is drawn up, the width of the cloth is reduced to a strip approximately 4 centimeters (1$\frac{1}{2}$ in) wide. When about ten rows are stitched and drawn into pleats, the tautly held strip of cloth is pressed between the two pieces of bamboo (or wood). This is done by grasping the ends of the bamboo that extend beyond the width of the cloth strip, holding them tightly together, and moving them up and down over the cloth, pressing it between them.

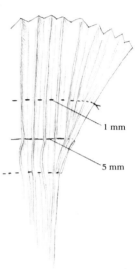

When the entire length of cloth is pleated and pressed in this way, it is brushed with starch and dried. The application of starch sets the pleats.

■*Binding:* The cloth strip is fitted around a flexible core of rope and secured with the *kake-ito* thread, then bound using the turning device (see page 105). If the design calls for alternate striped and plain bands, one of the methods described under *tazuna shibori* is used.

Drawing 32. Stitched pleating (*nui yōrō*); placement and length of stitches

**Stripes** (double pleating; *nido suji* shibori): Repeating the pleating and dyeing process makes it possible to create patterns of stripes having a depth and subtlety lacking in those that are made by pleating and dyeing the cloth once. One thing to note in these examples and in the example illustrated in Plate 71 is the soft-edged quality of one set of

Plates 200–02

Plate 71

71. Stripes, double pleating (*nido suji*)

the stripes, invariably those that were dyed first. How the soft edges were achieved is unclear. Is it something that is unknown to us about the way the natural indigo worked; or could it be that the binding of the first set of pleats was done with less tension, permitting more oxygen to enter into the folds; or was the cloth dry when it was immersed in the dye? The usual practice is to eliminate any accumulation of air from the cloth by first soaking it in water. Whatever the explanation, the contrast of hard and soft edges gives these textiles a special quality.

The equipment, materials, and method of pleating and binding are described above under *tesuji* shibori (page 105).

After the cloth is dyed the first time, it is unbound, rinsed, and pressed flat and pleated again using a different width and spacing of the pleats.

Other very interesting "interwoven" effects are made by partially covering one or both sets of pleats with bands of paper *(kami maki)* or strips of cloth *(nuno maki)*, a process called *kantera maki*.

Paper bands may be fitted at intervals around the pleated cloth after the *kake-ito* thread is wound. They are temporarily held in place and then secured by the binding thread. The cloth strip is long and is handled somewhat differently. Open-wound binding (page 67) is used to wind the strip around the pleated cloth after the *kake-ito* thread is in place. The resisting cloth strip creates a slightly different effect from the paper bands. Compare Plates 208 (cloth strip) and 209 (paper bands).

**Stripes and Dyed Bands** (*tazuna* shibori): Patterns composed of striped and plain bands of color were an early creation of Arimatsu shibori craft workers. It was this type of design, dyed on silk and made into splendid ceremonial horse reins, that the lord of Owari presented to the fifth shogun on the occasion of his investiture in 1680.

The example illustrated is too small to convey the strength and bold effect the design must have created when made up into the wide flowing reins favored by the horsemen of the seventeenth century.

The bands of solid color are achieved by intermittent binding of the pleated cloth. There are three methods of binding.

■*First method*: The cloth is pleated, wound with the *kake-ito* thread, and bound with thread at intervals. Portions of cloth left unbound create the dyed bands. The binding may be done by hand or with the turning device.

Plates 203–05, 207–10

Plates 208, 209

Plate 72

Drawing 33

72. Stripes and bands (*tazuna* shibori)

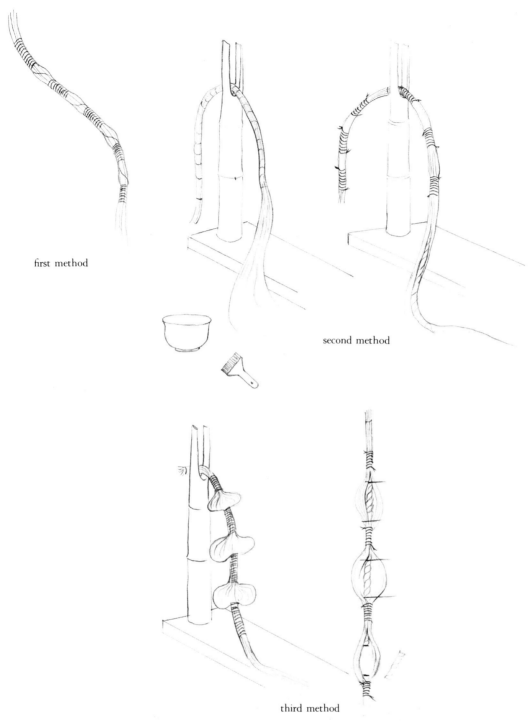

first method

second method

third method

Drawing 33.   Stripes and bands (*tazuna* shibori)—three methods

■*Second method*:   A rope whose circumference is the same as the width of the pleated cloth is used as a core. The cloth is pleated, wound with the *kake-ito* thread, then brushed lightly with water and dried to set the pleats. The *kake-ito* thread is removed. A small length of pleated cloth is fitted around the rope so that the two selvages meet, and this section is fitted into the notch of the bamboo stand. The cloth is bound onto the rope core the desired width of one striped band, and the binding thread is fastened but not cut. A section of the pleated cloth, the desired width of the plain dyed band, is pushed up along the rope. This opens the pleats, ballooning the cloth out free of the rope, and the cloth is held in that position by the next portion of cloth, which is bound tightly to the rope. This is carried on alternately until all the cloth is bound.

Naturally when the coil of pleated cloth is dyed, the unbound areas readily receive the dye, assuring an even distribution of dye in the plain bands.

Drawing 33

Drawing 33 ■*Third method:* The cloth is pleated for a distance of several centimeters, the pleats are arranged around a rope core, fitted into the notch of the bamboo stand, and wound with *kake-ito* thread as the pleating progresses. When all the cloth is wound, it is refitted into the notch of the stand and bound. Thread is bound around the portion of cloth that is to form each striped band. The thread is securely fastened and cut at each band. The pleated cloth between the bound sections lies flat on the rope core. When all the sections are bound, these portions of rope are cut and removed, allowing the cloth between the bound sections to be freely exposed to the dye, creating the bands of solid color.

Plates 203–05 **Stripes and Undyed Bands:** Paper wrapped and secured around sections of pleated cloth *(kantera maki)* create resisted bands when the cloth is dyed. If the pleats between the wrapped sections are closely bound, patterns of alternating stripe-dyed and undyed bands result.

Plate 302 The handsome garment in Plate 302 shows a striking checkered design created in this way.

REVERSED PLEATING

The cloth is folded across its width into uniform pleats, with the folds extended a few centimeters at a time, until the point is reached at which the pleating is to be reversed. The pleats are held together with the *kake-ito* thread. In the next step the cloth is pleated so that the knife-edge folds of pleats in the first section are succeeded by depressed folds, and the depressed folds of that section become knife-edge folds. When this process of pleating and reversed pleating has been completed, the cloth is bound to a rope core. This type of pleating, called *midori*, results in patterns of tapered leaflike forms.

Plate 73
Plate 215
Plates 216,221
Plate 212 **Willow Leaf** (*midori* shibori): The tapered forms of *midori* shibori suggest the willow's slender leaves. This is often combined with vertical stripes (*tesuji;* Plates 215 and 216) and rarely with stitched motifs (Plate 221). An exceptional example is shown in Plate 212, in which the triple pleats create a striking positive-negative effect. This is the most difficult way of pleating and is no longer done.

Equipment, cloth, and thread are described on page 105. In addition a flexible core of rope is needed.

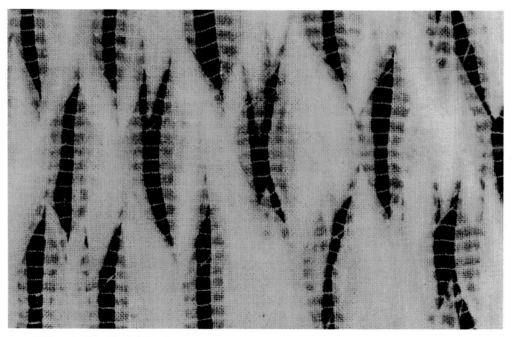

73. Willow leaf (*midori* shibori)

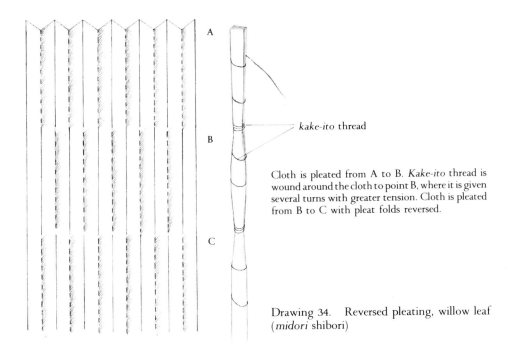

kake-ito thread

Cloth is pleated from A to B. *Kake-ito* thread is wound around the cloth to point B, where it is given several turns with greater tension. Cloth is pleated from B to C with pleat folds reversed.

Drawing 34.   Reversed pleating, willow leaf (*midori* shibori)

Traditionally the pleating is done without any marks on the cloth to indicate the reversing of the folds, however, anyone attempting to use the process would be well advised to mark the desired length of the pleats and to indicate which are knife folds and which are depressed ones.

The cloth is pleated across the width, several turns of *kake-ito* thread are made, holding it to the rope core, and the cloth is pleated again with the folds reversed. The *kake-ito* thread is wound for several turns at intervals determined by the desired length of the leaflike form. After the cloth is pleated, it is bound in the usual way.

VARIEGATED PLEATING

■*Hand method*:   The pleats are usually but not invariably extensions of the tiny folds made by small bound units scattered throughout the cloth and bound before the cloth is pleated. Unlike the uniform stripes of *suji* shibori, which are regularly spaced and continuous, the patterns resulting from this way of pleating are ones in which the lines, created by the pleats, flow in a generally warpwise direction without being uniform, regularly spaced, or continuous.

The pleating process, unique to Japan, and the patterning it creates are called *yanagi* ("willow") shibori.

*Machine method*:   The Matsuoka family, specialists in pleated shibori, devised a machine that pleats the cloth discontinuously. The patterning produced with cloth pleated on this machine is one of irregular warpwise stripes that divide in random fashion. It should not be confused with *yanagi* shibori. Variegated machine pleating is called *Matsubun suji*.

**Willow** (*yanagi* shibori):   Graceful, flowing lines, created by irregular pleating of the cloth, strongly suggest the supple cascading effect of the weeping willow. These designs are immediately identifiable, yet no two are ever alike. No guiding marks are made on the cloth to indicate the lines or to locate the small motifs that are often included.

In traditional *yanagi* shibori, small circular *kumo* motifs are included, but other small designs may be used. This is seen in the lovely pale red underkimono in which various motifs appear. In this exceptional example, the motifs rather than the lines are the dominant design elements—a consequence of the dyed ground.

Another example, a marvelous one, of variegated pleating is the festival kimono in Plate 317. The design is created by extending all the pleats from one point (the center

Drawing 34

Plate 224

Plate 74

Plate 29

Plate 317

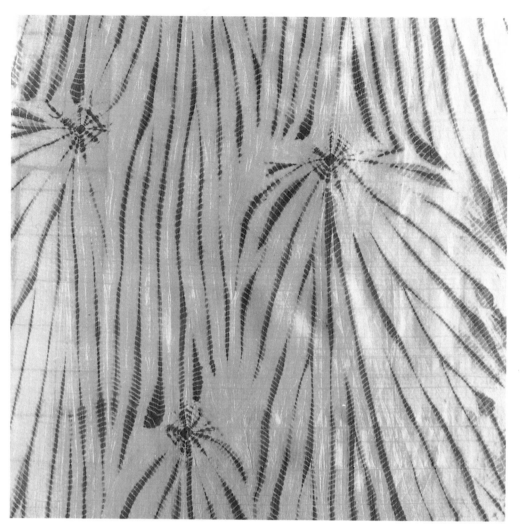

74. Willow (*yanagi* shibori)

back of the neckband) instead of from many scattered motifs. The delightful concept that it conveys so successfully—that of the straw raincape worn by fishermen and farmers—is brilliantly executed. The lines made by the pleats suggest the straw as well as the construction of these picturesque garments; the harmony of concept and process is notable.

Plate 74      The lovely traditional willow shibori patterning is shown in Plate 74. The design, here dyed red on white silk, was favored in the past for the underkimono. For summer

Plate 316      wear, willow shibori's graceful lines were dyed with indigo on white cotton.

The equipment, thread, and cloth, as well as the general process are described under continuous pleating, pages 103ff.

The small *kumo* motifs (page 68) are bound first; their size and placement in the length of cloth determine the scale of the design and the direction and flow of the lines. The tiny folds made by the bound units are extended into the folds of the pleats, which widen as they curve away from the bound units.

The use of a flexible rope core to produce a clearly resisted ground and sharply defined lines is optional; a much softer effect results without it.

SWITCHBACK PLEATING

Plate 75      **Mountain Path** (*yamamichi* shibori):     The pleating of the cloth is done in bands only a few centimeters wide. The bands change direction as they zigzag across the width of cloth. Naturally, in order to bind the pleats, the bands must extend from selvage to selvage even though the route they follow is not a direct one. Each section of pleated cloth is bound separately.

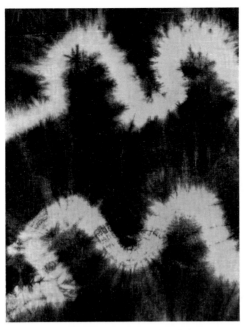

75.   Mountain path (*yamamichi* shibori)

The resisted bands created in this way meander across the cloth with switchback turns suggesting a mountain path. The pleating process is called *age-sage* shibori, meaning "up and down," which describes the way the cloth is manipulated as it is being pleated. The designs are called *yamamichi* ("mountain path") shibori. A variation in which the pleated band simulates a bolt of lightning is called just that, *inazuma*.

The resisted bands that meander across the cloth in these shibori designs provide a strong contrast to the orderly, rhythmic patterns of *suji* shibori.

Equipment, materials, and thread are described on page 105. The pleating is done in a very free way that is easier to do than to describe.

The end of the cloth is caught in the notch of the bamboo stand and held in both hands. The left hand is used to pleat the cloth, beginning at the right-hand selvage. As each pleat is made, the right thumb holds it against the fingers of the right hand. The pleats are made without regard to the grain of the cloth, and their direction changes frequently according to the whim of the worker. The change in direction is accomplished by pulling the unpleated portion of cloth away from (up) or towards (down) the worker. Hence the name *age-sage* ("up-down") shibori.

When the cloth is pleated across the width, it is bound several times, and the thread is fastened and cut. See Plate 214 for detail of pleats and an exceptional example of the incidental patterning that may occur when shaped cloth is dyed with indigo.

Plate 214

## CLOTH PLEATED AND STITCHED

In mid career the Japanese batik artist Motohito Katano became interested in shibori, which had been ignored by his peers and dismissed, no doubt, as a village industry. Encouraged and urged on by Sōetsu Yanagi, the founder of the folkcraft movement, he devoted the remaining twenty years of his life to exploring shibori's possibilities, using his discoveries and rediscoveries of this ancient craft as the vehicle for his creative expression.

Katano viewed shibori from a different perspective than that of a village craftsman and brought new insights to bear on the traditional methods. One of the most ingenious resist processes he devised, and one he used extensively, combines pleating, covering, and stitching in a way as brilliant as it is simple. It seems fitting that it should bear his name. Katano died in 1975. The example of his work created with this process in Plate 332 shows its depth and luminosity.

Plate 332

Plate 76

**Katano Shibori** (an adaptation):   The cloth is folded into vertical pleats, which are held between protective strips made of folded cloth. Stitching is then done through all of the layers. The pressure exerted on the cloth by the stitches and protective strips serves to define the elements of the design by directing, channeling, and controlling the dye penetration.

The influence on the design of the folds is clear enough; the precise relationship of the stitching to the forms that result may require study of Drawing 35.

■*Equipment, Cloth, and Thread*:   The bamboo stand described on page 105 may be used to hold the cloth taut while it is being stitched. It is convenient when long lengths of cloth are stitched, but is not essential.

A light- or medium-weight cloth is most suitable, but cloth of any weight may be used as long as it is possible to stitch through the multiple layers of the pleats as well as those of the protecting cloth strips. The greater the number of pleats made in the cloth, the lighter the cloth must be.

Thread used for stitching must be strong; whether it is used singly or doubled is optional.

Cloth for the protecting strips is folded several times to provide sufficient thickness to prevent dye from seeping through the needle holes. Clearly, a sturdy needle and considerable strength are needed to stitch many layers of cloth.

■*Pleating and Stitching*:   The cloth is folded into vertical pleats, and the protecting strips are folded the same width as the pleated cloth. Guidelines for the stitching are marked on one of these strips. The strips are placed on both sides of the pleated cloth and may be temporarily held in place with long basting stitches or pins. The stitching needle should be inserted at a right angle to the cloth.

The pleated and stitched strip of cloth is immersed in the dye. This is a resist process ideally suited to indigo and the other natural dyes that Katano used exclusively; it awaits experimentation with chemical dyes.

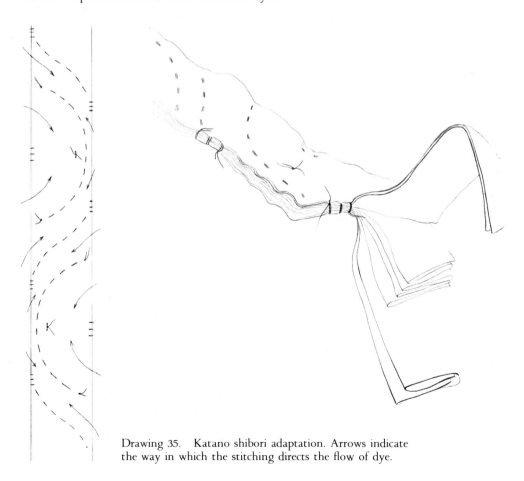

Drawing 35.   Katano shibori adaptation. Arrows indicate the way in which the stitching directs the flow of dye.

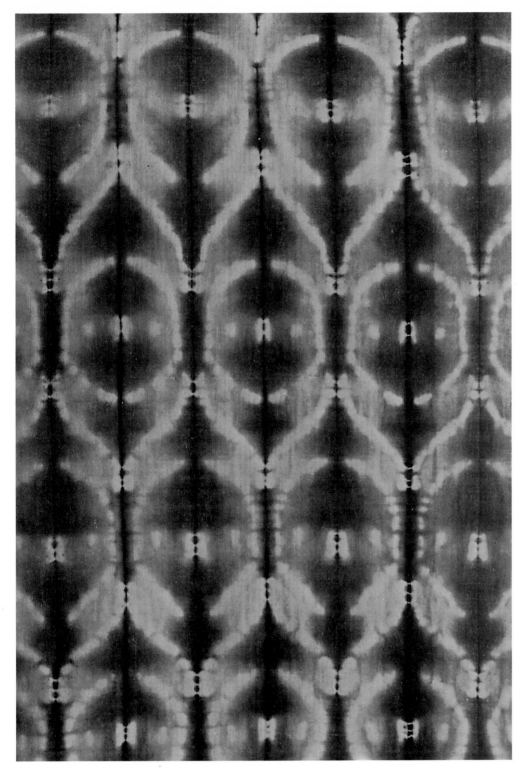

76. Katano shibori adaptation

## CLOTH FOLDED AND CLAMPED

Dyeing cloth that is folded in two or more directions into a neatly shaped bundle and held clamped between boards or sticks is an art historian's enigma. There are eighth century examples in the Shōsō-in, but subsequent examples are so scarce until the nineteenth century that doubt is cast on this technique existing in Japan before the latter date. Chemical blues bleed into beautiful, soft effects with this technique, whereas indigo does not penetrate deeply into the many layers of cloth. It does seem to indicate that board-clamping of folded cloth may have developed from or appeared with the introduction of chemical dyes.

Plate 11

Cloth decorated by folding and clamping until relatively recently was used to line simple garments or for baby diapers. The latter were often homemade and given as gifts for the newborn infant. Anything so commonplace was unlikely to be recorded or preserved. The cloth was used until worn out; few examples remain. Although cloth dyed in this way is rarely seen today, decorative paper is made by folding and dyeing in a similar fashion. The technique is also employed in nontraditional ways by Japanese artist-craftsmen.

The process is simple enough. Cloth is folded into wide vertical pleats. The pleated cloth strip is then repeatedly reverse folded, either horizontally or diagonally, into a square, rectangular, or triangular form. This creates a neat bundle of folded cloth that is fitted between boards or sticks, held in place with cord, and dipped selectively in the dye. The multiple folds create simple geometric patterns, and the dye is drawn into the folds, creating a distinctive soft-edged effect. In Arimatsu-Narumi, the general name for both patterns and process is *sekka* shibori, snow crystals (literally, "snow flowers"). The term in more general use is *itajime*. This word stands alone; the term *itajime* shibori is not used.

The shape of the folded cloth, the amount of pressure exerted on it by the clamping device, the areas that are dipped in the dye (it is never completely immersed), and the length of time the cloth remains in contact with the dye all affect the outcome.

The action of the dye often creates totally unexpected effects—perhaps it is the element of surprise, as well as the quick results that makes the process an immediately rewarding one. The traditional designs that are reproduced in the examples here will suggest many possibilities to the creative reader.

■*Board Clamps*:    Flat pieces of wood cut to the appropriate size and shape are the most usual type of clamp. If the cloth bundles are small, balsa wood works very well, since it is easy to cut with a sharp knife or fine coping saw. Masonite or other hard board or foam board used for architectural models may also be used. When the placement of the binding cords is determined, matching notches are cut into the two pieces of wood or other material. The notches prevent the cord from slipping. The term *itajime* literally means "board clamping."

■*Stick Clamps*:    Flat smooth sticks are also used as clamps (balsa wood, readily available in a variety of sizes is easy to cut and split). These are placed on both sides of the cloth bundle and bound around with cord. In some cases the sticks are not cut all the way through but resemble a pair of Japanese disposable chopsticks before they have been split apart. Several folds of the cloth are laid between them, and the open ends are bound together. Clamping between sticks is called *bōjime*.

The process described below is the same regardless of design. The variables that determine the design are the shape into which the cloth is initially folded and the size, shape, and placement of the boards or sticks.

■*Folding*:    The cloth is thoroughly dampened, laid flat on the work surface, and accordion-folded into uniform, vertical pleats that extend the length of the cloth.

Drawings 36–38    The strip of pleated cloth is then folded into a square, rectangle, or triangle, the choice of which is dictated by the design desired. The first fold remains in place on the work surface, and all subsequent folds are made by moving the strip of cloth back and forth. The cloth is precisely folded so that the layers are arranged in a stack, each exactly above the other.

Drawings 36, 38    ■*Clamping*:    The boards or sticks are cut to the desired size and shape and notched to hold the cords. The cloth is protected from possible stains by cloth or paper next to the wood. The boards (sticks) are placed as desired and bound together with stout cord.

■*Dyeing*:    The clamped cloth is dipped into dye. Very little dye is needed, for the exposed edges of the folds are just barely submerged in the dye, and capillary action does the rest. Some colors move more quickly into the cloth than others, so different design effects occur when the same type of fold is dyed in different colors.

The cloth may be dipped in several colors either selectively or successively. The clamps may be removed after one dipping and the cloth dipped again with a different set of clamps or with the same clamps placed differently. The process is fast, at least for small amounts of cloth, and allows one to experiment freely.

The cloth must be unfolded immediately after dyeing in order to allow it to dry. Care must be taken when unfolding the cloth that undyed areas are not stained by the damp dyed portions.

**Triangles** (*sankaku* pattern): In the example illustrated, the structure of the design is Plate 77 that of a grid, reflecting the square shape into which the cloth was folded when it was clamped and dyed. The circular design elements, however, are one of the surprise results mentioned above. A pattern composed of triangular forms was expected, but the action of the dye transformed straight lines into curves. Why the dye seeped into the cloth in this way is unclear. It just did.

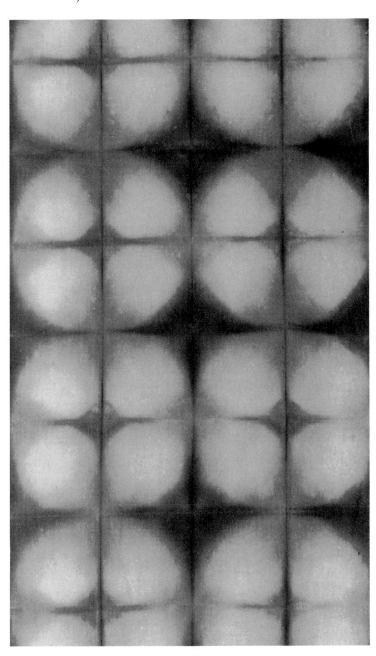

77. Board clamping (*itajime*), triangles

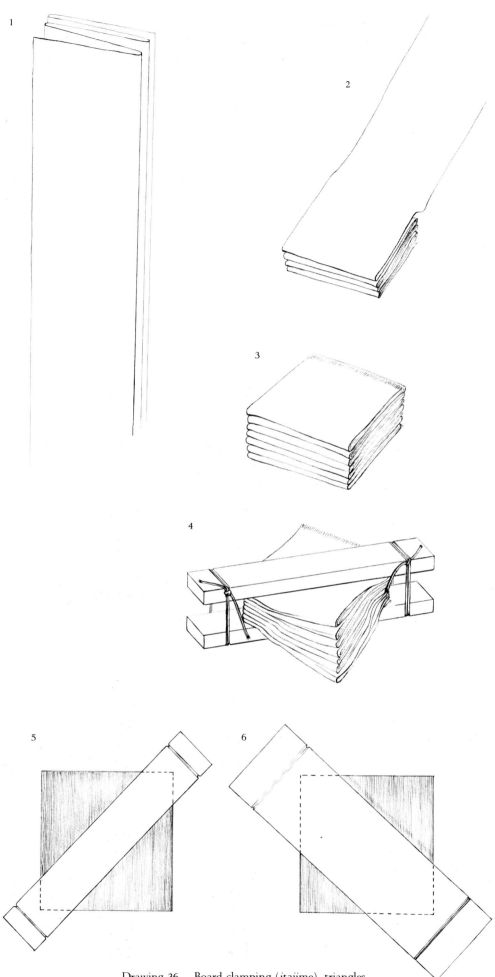

Drawing 36.   Board clamping (*itajime*), triangles

■*Folding and Clamping*:    The cloth is folded lengthwise in four accordion pleats. The Drawing 36
end of the pleated cloth is folded over once on the weft grain to form a square, and the
cloth is turned over so this square rests on the work surface. Subsequent folds are made
by moving the pleated length of cloth back and forth. If the cloth is too long to be
handled easily, the free end may be rolled up.

Each fold is carefully lined up with the previous ones and is sharply creased. When all
of the cloth is folded into a neat stack, the clamps are put in place.

The first set of clamps—narrow boards—are placed diagonally on the folded cloth Drawing 36
and fastened in place with cords.

■*Dyeing*:    The two exposed portions of the cloth are dipped in the dye. The boards are
removed, and the stack of cloth is left undisturbed. Then a second set of board clamps,
wider than the first, are secured in place, and the cloth is dipped a second time. The
second set of boards is clamped diagonally across the cloth, covering the corners left Drawing 36
exposed by the first clamps. The boards are removed, and the cloth is carefully opened
flat and dried.

An entirely different design results if the cloth is folded as described above but is Plate 78
clamped with square boards that are the same size as the folded cloth. In this case all
four exposed edges of the folds are dipped in the dye.

78.   Board clamping (*itajime*), grid

**Tortoiseshell** (*kikkō* pattern):    The traditional oriental tortoiseshell pattern of hexagons appears frequently in Japanese textiles. In the *sekka* shibori example illustrated in Plate 79, the soft-edged quality that the dye seepage imparts to the lines creates an effect reminiscent of frost-patterned windowpanes. The triangular structure of the design is clear.

Plate 79

■*Folding and Clamping*:    The cloth is folded lengthwise into four accordion pleats. To establish the triangular form, the cloth is first folded to form half an equilateral triangle and is turned over so this fold faces the work surface, as shown in Drawing 37. The second fold forms a full equilateral triangle, which is again turned over to face the work surface. It does not move from this position; the subsequent folds are made by moving the pleated cloth back and forth.

Drawing 37

The cloth is folded into a neat triangular stack, and rectangular board clamps are put in place and secured with cord.

■*Dyeing*:    The exposed tip and base of the triangular cloth shape are dipped in the dye (indicated by shading in Drawing 37.7).

Drawing 37.7

79.   Board clamping (*itajime*), tortoiseshell (*kikkō*)

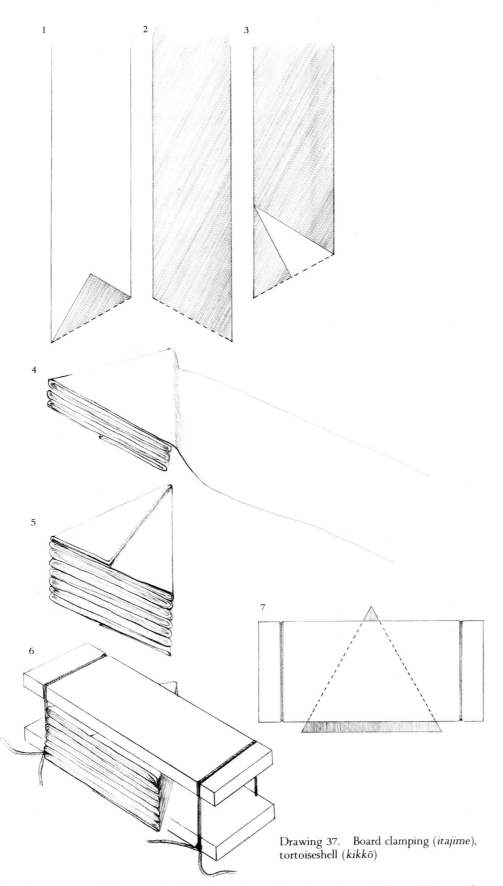

Drawing 37.   Board clamping (*itajime*),
tortoiseshell (*kikkō*)

**Lattice** (*naname gōshi* pattern):    The interplay of horizontal, vertical, and diagonal
lines creates a strong patterning of dark and light. The triangular structure is obvious.

Plate 80

■*Folding and Clamping*:    The cloth is folded lengthwise into four accordion pleats. To
establish the triangular form, one diagonal fold is made in the pleated cloth strip,
aligning the bottom edge of the cloth with the left-hand edge. The cloth is turned over

Drawing 38

and remains with this first fold facing the work surface. All subsequent folds are made by moving the strip of cloth in the order shown in Drawing 38.

When all the cloth is folded into a neat stack, triangular boards the same size as the cloth or slightly smaller are put in place and secured with cord.

Each of the three sides of the stacked cloth is dipped in the dye.

80.   Board clamping (*itajime*), lattice

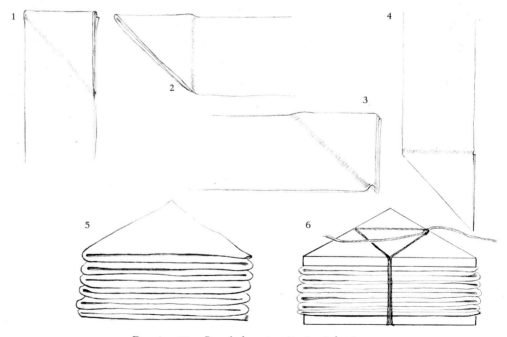

Drawing 38.   Board clamping (*itajime*), lattice

# Pole-Wrapping

## CLOTH POLE-WRAPPED AND COMPRESSED

*Arashi*, "storm," is the name the Japanese have given patterns resist-dyed by an ingenious process of wrapping cloth around a pole, compressing it into folds, and dyeing it. Indeed, many of the diagonal patterns suggest rain driven by a strong wind. The particular quality and subtlety of the patterns are fully revealed only in a length of cloth. Small samples are insufficient. These patterns are by no means haphazardly achieved, but not even the most skillful worker has complete control over the process, making slight irregularities of pattern inevitable. To be sure, if complete control were possible, the results could hardly be called *arashi*, for it is precisely the irregularities, like those in the changing patterns of wind-driven rain, that give these fabrics their special beauty.

This unusual process was invented in 1880 by Kanezō Suzuki in Arimatsu expressly for the production of indigo-dyed cotton. Today cloth is no longer dyed on 4-meter-long (about 13-ft) wooden poles in special troughlike vats, as was done in the original process. However, cotton and silk dyed with chemical dyes are now produced in Arimatsu using an adaptation of the process—one that changes the design effect somewhat. It, too, is likely to die out there—only one man, Reiichi Suzuki, working with his wife, produces *tatsumaki arashi*, and when this book was being written, he had no successor.

Recently several American textile artists have made a successful adaptation of the original process. A short length of plastic pipe is substituted for the long wooden pole, making it possible for one person to rotate it manually while controling the thread winding—the original process required two workers—and to dye the cloth on the plastic cylinder in either an ordinary indigo vat or a hot dye bath.

**Original Process:**   Following its invention in 1880 (Meiji 12), five years were spent perfecting the process. By the late Meiji period, *arashi*-patterned cloth had gained great popularity. During its relatively short history, more than one hundred different patterns were created.

While shibori is traditionally, although not exclusively, done by women working in their homes, *arashi* shibori was always produced by men in small workshops, where there was space to accommodate the large dye vats and the stands to wind the long poles. At the peak period of production, there were fourteen producers in the Nagoya area, each using from thirty to one hundred fifty poles. Each pole held four lengths of kimono cloth (approximately 44 m/144 ft), so that it is easy to estimate that thousands of meters were produced.

The term *bōmaki*, literally "pole-wound," is used in shibori to describe any process in which a pole is used as a core to protect one side of the cloth from the dye. Although it is descriptive of the process used in *arashi* shibori, it is also correctly applied to rigid core shibori (*shirokage*; pages 97ff) and cloth shaped around a pole (*mura kumo*; see below, page 137). It is a general term, not a specific name for one process.

Drawing 45

In the original *arashi* process, the cloth is wrapped around a slightly tapered wooden pole set in a horizontal position in a device that allows the pole to be rotated with a hand-turned crank or small motor. Thread is then wound on the cloth-covered pole. One worker, the *arashi* craftsman, controls the thread as it winds onto the rotating pole, which is rotated by his assistant. Together, the two workers periodically push the thread-wound cloth along the pole into compressed folds. The slight taper of the pole makes this easier. When the pole can hold no more cloth, it is removed from the supporting beams and immersed in troughlike indigo vats. To dip the heavy poles into the dye bath required at least two workers. The high cost of labor and indigo, the introduction of chemical dyes, and competition from machine-printed cloth finally made the original process of dyeing on a long pole obsolete.

**Japanese Adaptation** *(tatsumaki arashi)*:   The process presently being used in Arimatsu to produce a very limited quantity of silk and cotton involves wrapping and compressing the cloth folds on the pole, but instead of dyeing it on the pole, cloth is brushed with sizing, dried, removed from the pole, fastened around a rope that serves as a core, and bound to it using the same process *(tatsumaki)* that is used in pleated shibori (see pages 105ff). The coil of cloth-covered rope fits easily in conventional dye pots. *Arashi* patterns dyed in this way are limited to those in which the cloth becomes sufficiently constricted to fit around a rope.

Plates 90, 271–74

*Tatsumaki arashi* fabrics are distinguished from those dyed on the pole or plastic cylinder by a pattern of very fine resisted lines running diagonally on the cloth. These lines result from the resist effect of the binding thread on the compressed folds of the cloth when it is bound to the rope.

Plates 293–300

**American Adaptation**:   The plastic cylinders used in this latest adaptation are either lightweight drainage pipe obtained from suppliers of building materials or plastic plumbing pipe; the latter is heavier and more expensive but is more durable. It does not crack if dropped or become distorted when repeatedly subjected to the heat required in some types of dyeing. The drainage pipe in various diameters is available in 12-foot lengths and is easily cut with a hacksaw. Lengths of 3 to 5 feet are convenient to handle.

Cloth is wrapped around the plastic cylinder and held in place temporarily with masking tape. To wind the thread, the cylinder is held in an almost vertical position with one end resting on the floor. It is held at the top and rotated with the left hand, while the right hand controls thread tension and placement.

Unlike the pole used in the original process, the cylinder is not tapered, making it somewhat difficult to push the cloth along it. This is overcome by winding the thread over a small portion of the wrapped cloth at a time and then pushing the cloth into folds. To compress the cloth, the cylinder is grasped with both hands, and, with the top braced against a wall or fixed object, the cloth is pushed towards the top of the cylinder. The steps are repeated until all the cloth is in tightly compressed folds. The thread is securely fastened, and the cloth is ready to be dyed. The cylinder may be set upright in an indigo vat or in a heated dye pot.

BASIC PROCESS

*Arashi* shibori patterns may be divided into two general types: those composed of lines and those of small, diamondlike forms. Innumerable variations and combinations are possible. Each one of the four steps of the process—wrapping the cloth; winding the thread; compressing the cloth; and dyeing—may be carried out in different ways. Each change affects the final design. The four-step process may be repeated once or several times. Each time it is repeated, additions are introduced or the design is subtly altered.

This process is tricky at first. More detailed directions for the dyer are given in the Appendix, page 288.

■*Step One—Wrapping the cloth around the cylinder*:  Cloth wrapped around the cylinder with the selvages or edges (the fabric may be cut to fit the cylinder) parallel along the length of the cylinder results in a design on the weft grain of the cloth. However, when the cloth is wrapped spirally around it, a design on the diagonal of the cloth is the result. Diagonal designs run from lower left to upper right when the cloth is wrapped in a clockwise direction, from lower right to upper left when it is wrapped counterclockwise.

The cloth may be stitched together at the selvages into a tube. If the tube fits snugly on the cylinder, the cloth can be compressed—thread is not needed—into controlled but discontinuous folds, creating patterns of undulating lines that join and break. If the cloth tube fits loosely on the cylinder, a different process is required (see page 137).

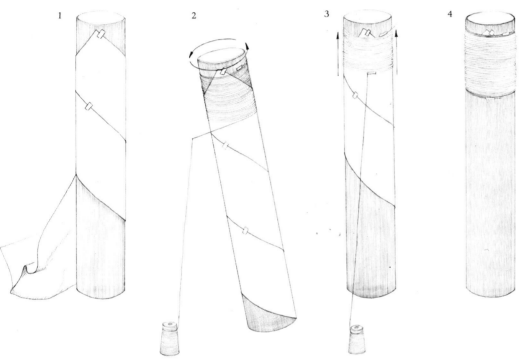

1.  Cloth is wrapped around cylinder and secured with masking tape.
2.  Thread is secured with masking tape then held a short distance from rotating cylinder to control tension as it is wound over cloth.
3.  Thread is secured to cloth with tape while portion of cloth is pushed to top of cylinder.
4.  All the cloth has been compressed; thread is secured with masking tape.

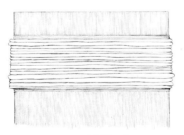

diagram of folds when
cloth is pushed straight

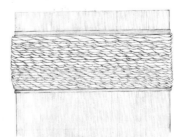

diagram of folds when cloth
is twisted as it is pushed

Drawing 39.  *Arashi* shibori basic technique

Drawing 39.1

Plate 83

Plate 82
Plate 81
Drawing 41

Plate 87

Drawing 39.2　■*Step Two—Winding the thread*:　The thread (20/4 cotton is used in Japan) is secured with masking tape and is wound onto the cylinder by rotating the cylinder with the left hand while controling the tension on the thread with the right. The right amount of thread tension is a matter of "feel" and experience (see Arashi Notes, page 288). The thread has two functions: to hold the cloth on the cylinder and to regulate the size of

Drawing 40　the folds. The width of the intervals between each turn of thread determines the amount of cloth there will be in each fold when it is compressed. If the intervals are narrow, the resulting design will be small in scale. The thread must be secured when winding is finished.

Drawing 39.3–4　■*Step Three—Compressing the cloth into folds*:　The cylinder, functioning as a core, protects one side of the cloth from the dye, but unlike other types of core-resisted shibori, the core is used to shape the cloth as well. It is the folds of cloth compressed on the cylinder that create the design in *arashi* shibori.

Drawing 39.5–6　　Cloth pushed straight along the cylinder into folds results in patterns composed of
Plates 83, 91　lines. However, when the cloth is twisted as it is pushed, patterns of diamondlike motifs are formed.

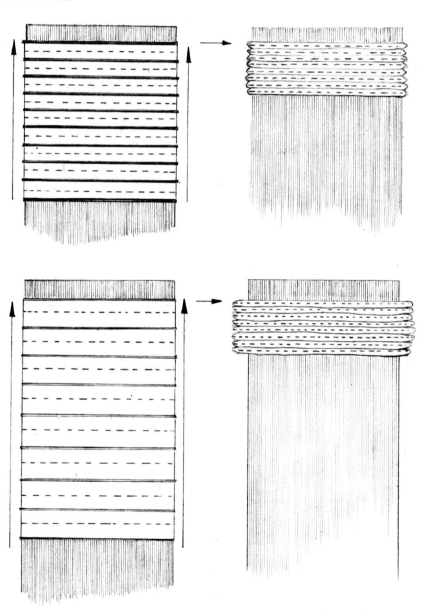

Drawing 40.　*Arashi* shibori; effects of small and large intervals
between winds of thread upon compressed folds of cloth

■*Step Four—Dyeing or sizing the cloth*:   The cloth may be dyed as the final step each time the process is repeated, or it may be brushed with water or a sizing made of the seaweed glue called *funori* and dried on the cylinder. This is called *karadori* ("empty process"), because the cloth has been carried to the point of dyeing, but the dye is omitted. The sizing stiffens the folds, making it possible to remove the cloth without disturbing their arrangement. Depending on the pattern desired, the cloth is opened out a bit or reversed on the pole. The opening out is not extreme enough to eliminate the folds but only modifies their shape. The cloth is wrapped again around the cylinder, with appropriate modification of the folds or wrapping, and finally dyed.

The cylinder now is usually immersed in water to thoroughly wet the cloth before dyeing. This step is especially important when indigo is used because it not only assures a more even dye penetration but prevents bubbles from being caught in the folds and thus inhibiting the dyeing process. Also, when water is in the folds, the dye does not penetrate as far, and the final effect is sharper than with dry cloth.

Different types of dye and, indeed, different colors of the same type have different rates of penetration, a fact that may be utilized to obtain beautiful effects.

PROCESS VARIATIONS

By varying the four basic steps described above, different *arashi* effects may be achieved. For example, surface resists applied to the compressed cloth, cylinders of different diameters, fine and heavy winding thread, and discharge dyeing all may be used to further expand the design possibilities of the process.

■*Surface Resists*:   Portions of the compressed cloth may be resisted by covering it with strips of cloth or plastic to create patterns within patterns, or the winding thread may be used as a surface resist. In this case certain areas of the cloth are left without being compressed into folds; the winding thread lying on the surface of flat cloth will resist the dye, creating fine, undyed lines within bands of color.   Plates 96, 255

■*Cylinders of Different Diameters*:   The basic process may be repeated on a pole or cylinder of diameter different from the original. This results in the crossing of two sets of lines.   Plates 96, 258

■*Different Thread Weights*:   Number 20/4 cotton is normally used for *arashi* shibori. When heavy thread is used, it increases the intervals of space between the folds into which the cloth is compressed.   Plate 97

■*Discharge Dyeing*:   *Arashi* patterns of great delicacy may be achieved by compressing dyed cloth on the pole and discharging (removing or lightening) the dye.   Plates 295, 296, 298, 386–92

■*Different Pole Types*:   The work of Yoshizō Aoki, an Arimatsu craftsman, is presented in Plates 275 to 292. The only clue to the way he obtained certain effects is in the poles he used.   Plates 275–92

The exact date of Yoshizō Aoki's death is not known, and all that remains of a lifetime's work is the sample book illustrated in these plates. Glimpsed even in such small pieces, the work is impressive. The designs, strikingly different from other *arashi* fabrics, give ample evidence of his creative use of the process. Just how he achieved the effects he did is not known. The clue lies in the wooden poles that are stored unused above the rafters of his grandson's shed in the village where he worked—the poles are grooved throughout their length. Perhaps some future craftsman will experiment and rediscover his secret.

In the following pages are examples of the work of another *arashi* shibori craftsman, Gintarō Yamaguchi, who died in the late 1960s. He was the last to use the original process. During the last few years before his death he produced one kimono length of cloth in each of the forty or more designs he knew how to make and dictated directions for making them. The following pattern processes indicated by an *asterisk are based on Yamaguchi's directions and have been reproduced successfully using a hand-turned plastic cylinder, 15.5 centimeters (6 in) in diameter. Additional examples are included to show the possibilities of the *arashi* technique. The directions accompanying the latter are translations of Yamaguchi's notes taken from *Nihon no shibori-zome* by Kahei Takeda and have not been tested. They provide clues for experimentation.

**Stripes:**   Lines, uniform in width and precisely spaced at equal intervals, create either clean, crisp, somewhat static effects or bold patterns of bands, depending on the stripes' width and arrangement. When the lines show variation in width—expanding and contracting along their length—the results are more dynamic.

81.   Thin diagonal stripes (*hosoito ichido kairyō*)

82.   Medium diagonal stripes (*chūito ichido kairyō*)

Plate 81   ■*Diagonal Stripes (hosoito ichido kairyō)*
1.   Cloth is placed on the cylinder at a 45° angle and wrapped counterclockwise around it. Masking tape is used to fasten selvage to selvage.
2.   Cylinder is rotated counterclockwise to wind the thread.
3.   Cloth is pushed straight to compress it into folds. Steps 1–3 are repeated until all the cloth is compressed into folds on the cylinder.
4.   Cloth is dyed.

Plate 82   If the cloth is wrapped clockwise instead of counterclockwise, the lines of the design will run from lower left to upper right on the cloth.

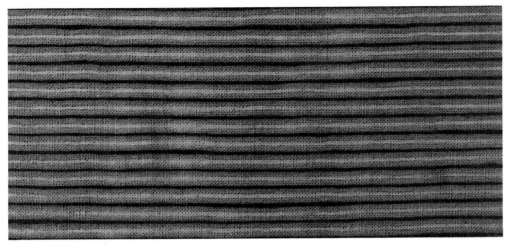

83. Horizontal stripes (*hosoito yoko kairyō*)

■\**Horizontal Stripes (hosoito yoko kairyō)*
    1.  Cloth is wrapped around the cylinder with the selvages parallel along the length of the cylinder. Masking tape is used to temporarily hold the cloth in place.
    2.  Cylinder is rotated clockwise to wind the thread. The tape is removed.
    3.  Cloth is pushed straight to compress it into folds.
    4.  Steps 1–3 are repeated until all of the cloth is compressed into folds on the cylinder.
    5.  Cloth is dyed.

Plate 83

Drawing 41. Parallel selvages aligned along length of cylinder

84. Wind in the pines (*matsukaze*)

85. Pine winds crossing (*matsukaze koshi*)

Plate 84

■\**Wind in the Pines (matsukaze arashi):*   Random changes in the width of the lines in this example result from the way the thread is wound.

1.   Cloth is placed on the pole at a 45° angle and wrapped counterclockwise.
2.   Cylinder is rotated counterclockwise to wind the thread. It is wound from the top of the cylinder towards the bottom for a few inches and then back again to the top. This reversal of the winding operation is called "return-trip thread" *(ōfuku kake-ito)*. The crossing of the threads results in variation in the width of the lines.
3.   Cloth is pushed straight to compress it into folds.
4.   Steps 1–3 are repeated until all the cloth is compressed on the cylinder.
5.   Cloth is dyed.

   If the process is then repeated with the cloth wrapped clockwise instead of counterclockwise, the two sets of stripes cross—a pattern called Pine Winds Crossing

Plate 85

*(matsukaze koshi;* Plate 85).

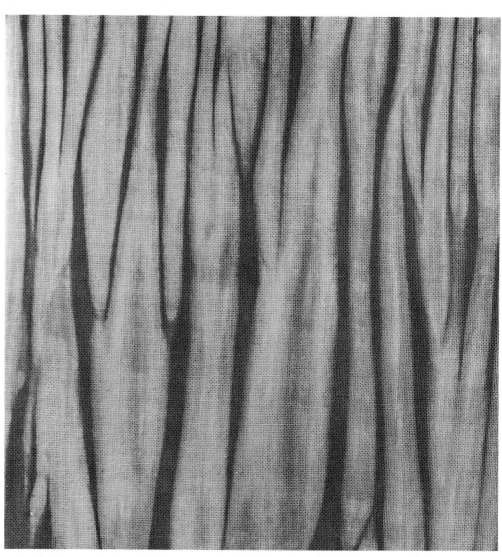

86.   Vertical wood grain *(tate ōmokume)*

**Irregular Lines:**   Irregular lines that join and separate randomly create strong, dynamic designs, suggesting the patterning of wood. The direction of the lines may be vertical or horizontal.

Plate 86

■\**Vertical Wood Grain (tate ōmokume)*
1.   Cloth is fastened with masking tape at the top of the cylinder and wrapped clockwise around it.

2. Thread is omitted, this allows the cloth to form into large unrestricted folds when it is compressed.
3. Cloth is twisted *hard* clockwise as it is pushed along the pole to compress it into folds. The compressed cloth must be held in place with tape or string at top and bottom of the cylinder.
4. Cloth is dyed.

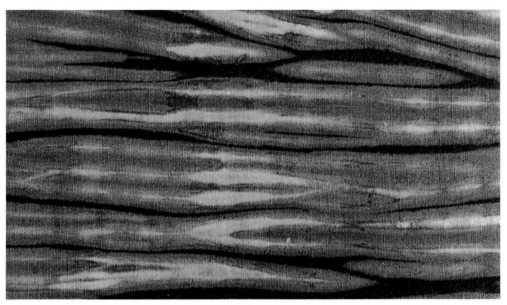

87. Horizontal wood grain (*yoko ōmokume*)

■\**Horizontal Wood Grain (yoko ōmokume)*  Plate 87

*Note*:  Yamaguchi's directions are unclear about the way the cloth is placed on the pole, but his sample has been successfully duplicated using the method described below. This is similar to *mura kumo* shibori, page 137, but in this case the cloth fits snugly on the cylinder.

1. Cloth is stitched together at the selvages into a tube that fits snugly on the cylinder.
2. Thread is omitted.
3. Cloth is pushed straight to compress it into folds.
4. Cloth is dyed.

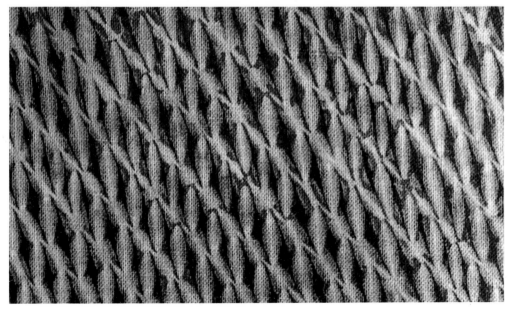

88. Vertical diamonds (*ōchiri*)

**Diamondlike Motifs:** The diamondlike motifs of these designs result from twisting the cloth as it is compressed on the cylinder, making broken folds.

Plate 88 ■*Vertical Diamond (ōchiri)

1. Cloth is wrapped counterclockwise around the cylinder.
2. Pole is rotated counterclockwise to wind the thread.
3. Cloth is twisted counterclockwise to compress it into folds.
4. Steps 1–3 are repeated until all the cloth is compressed on the cylinder.
5. Cloth is dyed.

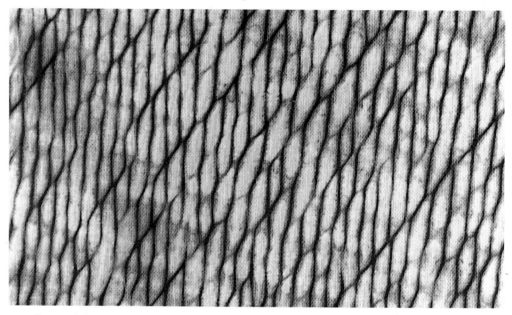

89. Diagonal diamond net (hasu ami)

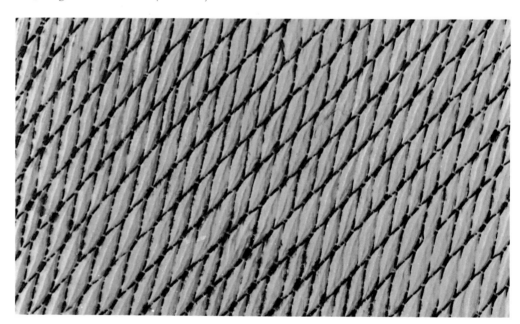

90. Diagonal diamond net, tatsumaki arashi process (note fine diagnonal resist lines)

Plate 89 ■*Diagonal Diamond Net (hasu ami): Surprisingly, this design is the negative reverse of the vertical diamond pattern—the motifs are undyed, and the lines dyed (compare Plates 88, 89 Plates 88 and 89). To achieve this result, the cloth is wound on the cylinder twice.
Plate 90 *Note:* Plate 90 illustrates the different effect that results when the cloth is dyed on a rope core (tatsumaki arashi; see page 124).

   1–3. Same as vertical diamond pattern, above.
    4. Cloth is brushed with *funori* sizing, dried, and removed from the cylinder.

5. The compressed and sized cloth is reversed and replaced on the cylinder (what had been the outside surface now faces the cylinder); without stretching it, it is wrapped counterclockwise.

6–8. Same as Steps 2–3 in the vertical diamond pattern, above.

9. Cloth is dyed.

91. Horizontal diamond (*yoko chiri*)

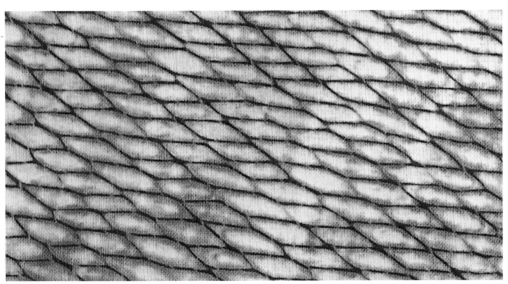

92. Horizontal diamond net (*yoko ami*)

■*Horizontal Diamond (yoko chiri)*                                     Plate 91
1. Cloth is wrapped clockwise around the cylinder.
2. Cylinder is rotated counterclockwise to wind the thread.
3. Cloth is twisted counterclockwise to compress it into folds.
4. Steps 1–3 are repeated until all the cloth is compressed on the cylinder.
5. Cloth is dyed.

■*Horizontal Diamond Net (yoko ami)*                                   Plate 92
1–3. Same as the horizontal diamond pattern, above.
4. Cloth is brushed with *funori* sizing, dried, and removed from the cylinder.
5. The compressed and sized cloth is reversed and replaced on the cylinder (what had been the outside surface now faces the cylinder) and, without stretching it, it is wrapped clockwise around the cylinder.
6–9. Same as Steps 2–5 in the horizontal diamond pattern, above.

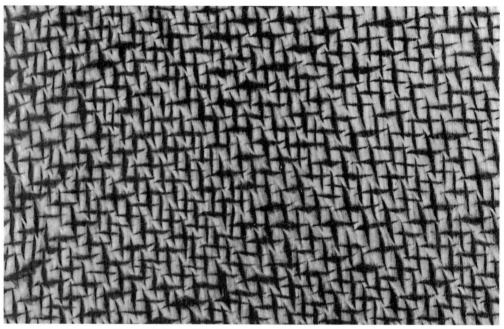

93.  Crossed diamonds (*tate yoko chiri*)

Plate 93  ■*Crossed Diamonds (tate yoko chiri):*  When the two diamond patterns, vertical *(ōchiri)* and horizontal *(yoko chiri)* are combined, the effect is of short brushstrokes made in two directions. First the process for horizontal diamond *(yoko chiri)* is completed, then the process for vertical diamond *(ōchiri)* is applied to the same cloth.

## Patterns Created by Altering the Basic Process

### SURFACE RESISTS

Plate 94  ■*Diamond Stripe with Surface Resists (nuno maki gōten sakura):*  The total effect of the surface resists is difficult to see in the small sample illustrated. It is possible, however, to see that the areas resisted are neither sharply defined nor uniform in width. In some
Plate 255  places the stripes have been covered, in others the diamond motifs. (See Plate 255 for a similar pattern made with surface resists.) Any *arashi* pattern may be treated in this way.

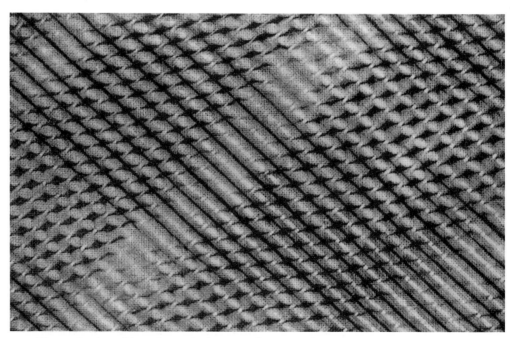

94.  Diamond stripe with surface resist (*nuno maki goten sakura*)

1. Cloth is placed on the pole at a 45° angle and wrapped counterclockwise.
2. Pole is rotated clockwise to wind the thread.
3. Cloth is pushed straight to compress it into folds. Strips of cloth are wound on top of the compressed cloth.
4. Cloth is pole-dyed, dried without rinsing it, and removed from the pole.
5. The compressed cloth is opened out a bit but not stretched, then wrapped counterclockwise around the pole.
6. Pole is rotated clockwise to wind the thread.
7. Cloth is twisted clockwise to compress it into folds. Strips of cloth are wound on top of the compressed cloth.
8. Cloth is pole-dyed.

95. Ripples ( *sazanami*)

## POLES OF DIFFERENT DIAMETERS

■*Ripples (sazanami)*                                                     Plate 95

1. Cloth is wrapped clockwise on a pole 9 centimeters ($3\frac{1}{2}$ in) in diameter.
2. Pole is rotated clockwise to wind the thread.
3. Cloth is pushed straight to compress it into folds.
4. Cloth is brushed with water, dried, and removed.
5. The compressed cloth is opened out a bit but not stretched and wrapped clockwise around a pole 6 centimeters ($2\frac{3}{8}$ in) in diameter.
6. Pole is rotated clockwise to wind the thread.
7. Cloth is twisted clockwise to compress it into folds.
8. Cloth is pole-dyed.

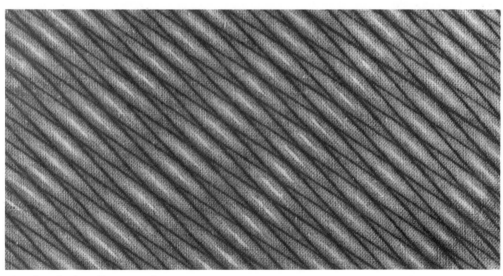

96. Angel wings (*hagoromo*)

Plate 96    ■ *Angel Wings (hagoromo)*

1.  Cloth is wrapped clockwise on a pole 12 centimeters (4½ in) in diameter.
2.  Pole is rotated clockwise to wind the thread.
3.  Cloth is pushed straight to compress it into folds.
4.  Cloth is dyed, rinsed, and dried.
5–8.  Repeat steps 1–4, using a pole 6 centimeters (2⅜ in) in diameter.

97.  Tiger (*kairyō tora*)

## DIFFERENT WEIGHT THREADS

Plate 97    ■ *Tiger (kairyō tora)*

1.  Cloth is wrapped clockwise around a pole 9 centimeters (3½ in) in diameter.
2.  Pole is rotated clockwise to wind the thread (20/4 cotton).
3.  Cloth is pushed straight to compress it into folds. An assistant is needed to help push the cloth. Four hands and strength are required.
4.  Cloth is brushed with *funori* sizing, dried, and removed.
5.  The compressed and sized cloth is placed on the pole without turning or stretching it and wrapped clockwise.
6.  Pole is rotated clockwise to wind the thread (10/4 cotton).
7.  Cloth is twisted clockwise with a very strong twist.
8.  Cloth is pole-dyed.

98.  Tiger stripes (*ami tora*)

Plate 98

■*Tiger Stripes (ami tora)*

1. Cloth is wrapped counterclockwise around a pole 9 centimeters ($3\frac{1}{2}$ in) in diameter.
2. Pole is rotated clockwise to wind the thread (20/4 cotton).
3. Cloth is twisted clockwise to compress it into folds.
4. Cloth is brushed with water, dried, and removed.
5. Compressed and dried cloth is reversed and replaced on the pole (what had been the outside surface now faces the pole), wrapping it counterclockwise.
6. Pole is rotated clockwise while winding with extraheavy thread (20/11 cotton).
7. Cloth is pushed straight to compress it into folds.
8. Cloth is pole-dyed.

## CLOTH SHAPED AROUND A POLE (*MURA KUMO* SHIBORI)

Although a pole *(bō)* is used in *mura kumo* shibori and the cloth is shaped around it and dyed in place, it is not considered an *arashi* process, since both process and result differ. To what extent *mura kumo* shibori was produced in Arimatsu is not known; however, half a century ago this method of decorating cloth was popular with Japanese hobbyists, and at that time kits consisting of pole, base, clamping ring, and wedges were readily available.

The process is a simple one. The cloth is stitched together at the selvages into a tube that is slipped down over a short pole or cylinder fitted upright into a base. The loose fitting cloth, slightly dampened, is arranged in folds with the fingers or a spatulalike tool. If the diameter of the cloth tube is much larger than the diameter of the pole, it is necessary to use a wooden ring that fits down over the pole and holds the cloth against the base. Wedges inserted between ring and pole hold the ring in place. The ring acts as a clamp compressing the loose folds of cloth between it and the base. The cloth is dyed by immersing the pole in the dye bath.

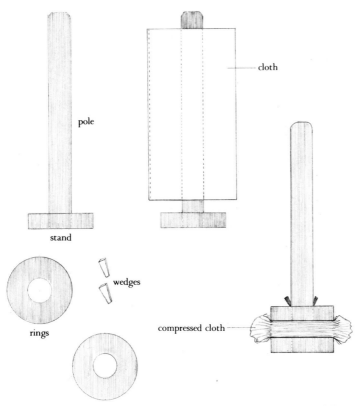

Drawing 42. *Mura kumo* shibori

A wooden pole or cylinder of metal or plastic may be used. Sixty centimeters is a convenient length. The base into which the pole is fixed prevents the cloth from slipping free of the pole, and when the ring is used, the base provides a surface to clamp against. Without this base, a heavy rope bound around the end of the pole can be used to prevent the cloth from slipping.

Cloth resist-dyed in this way is patterned with random dark and light areas suggesting scattered clouds and accounting for the name—*mura*, "splotched," and *kumo*, "cloud"—given to both method and designs. The process is sometimes referred to as *en chu* (pillar) shibori or *bō* (pole) *mura kumo*.

# Gallery of Shibori Examples

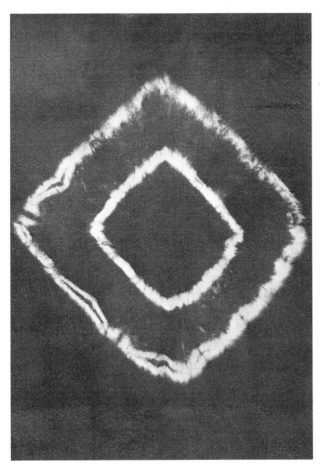

99. Thread-resisted rings (*ne-maki shibori*; p. 55)

100. Bamboo-resisted rings (*chikuwa shibori*; p. 58)

101.

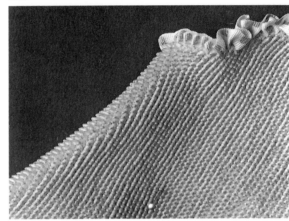

102.

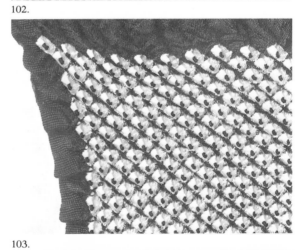

103.

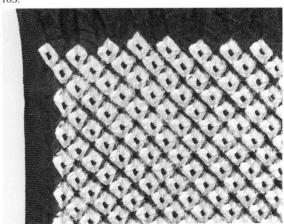

101–04. Dots within squares (*hon hitta kanoko*; p. 58), four aspects of one example. 101. Detail of bound units. 102. Texture of unpressed cloth. 103. Partially opened cloth. 104. Cloth pressed flat.

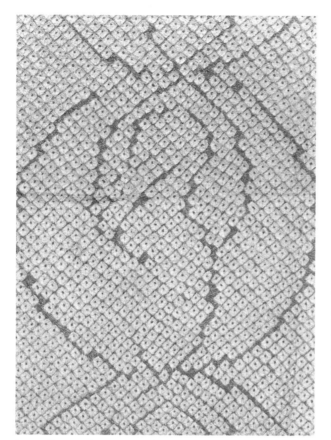

105. Dots within squares (*hon hitta kanoko*; p. 58); design formed by negative space where *kanoko* units are omitted.

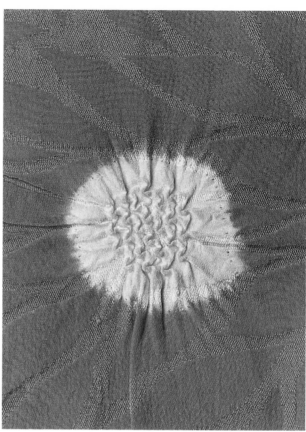

106. Unpressed *hitta kanoko* dots create a textured center for a round motif resisted by capping; figured silk crepe, red dye.

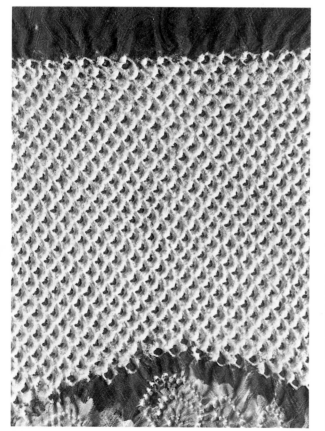

107. Medium dots within squares (*chū hitta kanoko*; p. 62); figured satin, red dye. Compare size, shape, and repeat of dots with Plate 105.

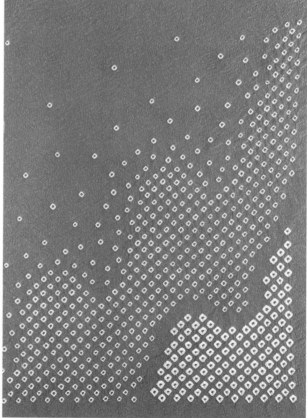

108. Square ring dots (*yokobiki kanoko*; p. 62); this contemporary design, executed with great skill, uses *kanoko* in a lively way both en masse and as individual units.

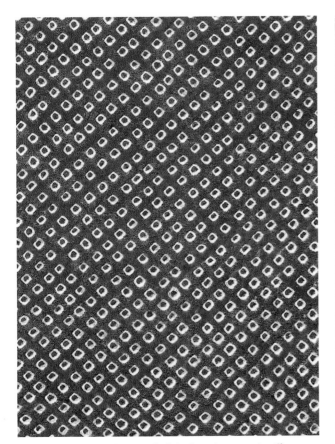

109. Square ring dots (*yokobiki kanoko*; p. 62); silk crepe, purple dye

110. Square ring dots; silk crepe, blue dye. Design defined by negative space and direction of lines of dots.

111, 112. Square ring dots; silk, yellow and brown dye, undulating line (*tatewaku*) and linked circles (*shippō-tsunagi*) patterns

112.

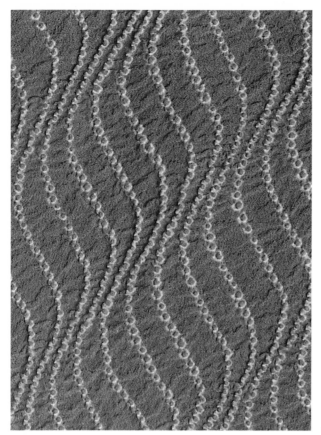

113. Linked dots (*tatebiki kanoko*; p. 64); silk crepe, green dye, undulating line pattern

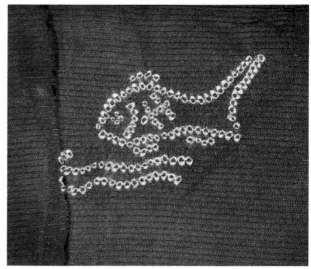

114. Half dots (*te-hitome kanoko*; p. 64); silk, blue dye. This tiny swimming carp is on the back of boy baby's garment.

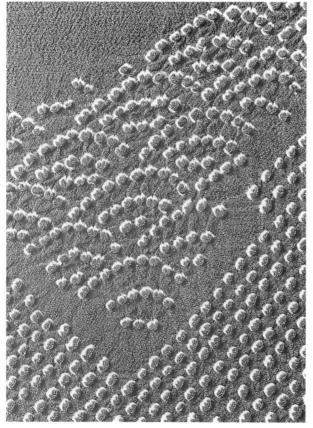

115. Spaced dots (*tsukidashi kanoko*; p. 65); silk crepe, black dye

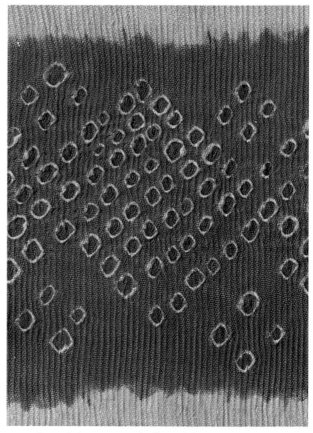

116. Spaced dots; textured silk, red dye

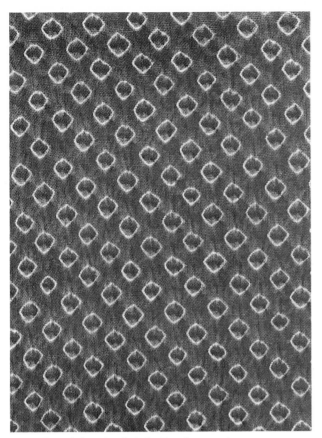

117. Spaced dots (*tsukidashi kanoko*; p. 65)

118. Square ring dots (*yokobiki kanoko*; p. 62); silk, gauze weave, purple dye

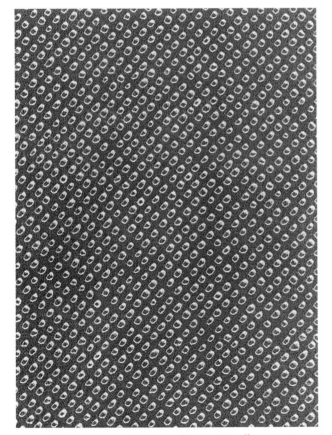

119. Linked dots (*tatebiki kanoko*; p. 64); silk crepe, gray-brown dye

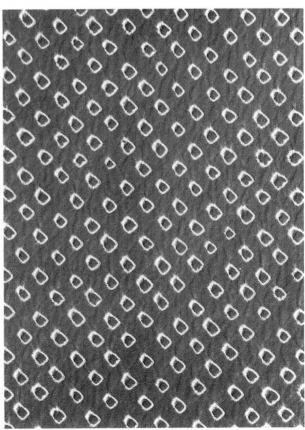

120. Linked dots (*tatebiki kanoko*). Note the difference in effect when these dots are bound in cotton (this example) and silk (left).

121. Shell (*bai* shibori; p. 68). Small bound units are combined with a variant of wood-grain (*mokume*) shibori.

122. Shell (*bai* shibori); silk, red dye. This Kyoto style example shows the shell units combined with *yokobiki kanoko* (p. 62).

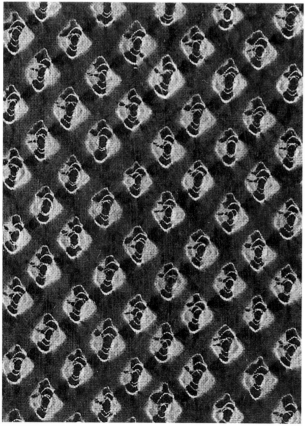

123. Spiral (*rasen* shibori; p. 67). Note clarity of the lines resisted by the binding thread.

124. Machine-bound spiderweb (*kikai kumo*). Uniformity is the characteristic of cloth shaped by a mechanical device.

125. Spiderweb (*kumo* shibori; p. 68)

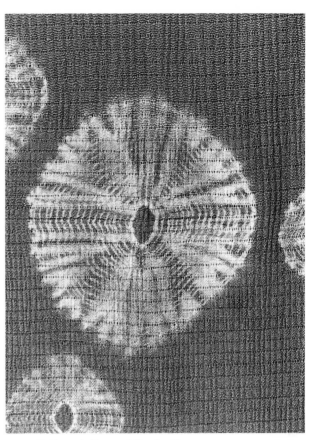

126. Spiderweb (*kumo* shibori); silk, gauze weave, purple dye

127. Spiderweb variation (*kikkō kumo*). The large dark centers of these motifs resemble the markings on a turtle's back, hence the name tortoiseshell (*kikkō*).

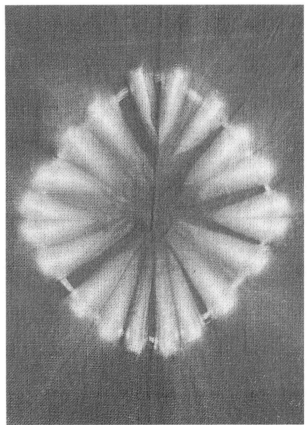

128. Tortoiseshell (*kikkō* shibori). Resembles spiderweb, but made by a different technique. Cloth is folded once, held in a hook, pleated, and a toothpick is bound against it.

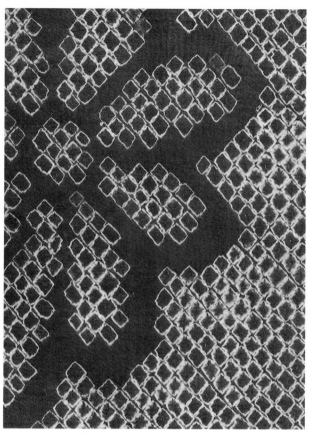

129.  Looped binding (*hira miura* shibori; p. 70) combined with wood grain and capping. Negative areas define the design.

130.  Looped binding (*hitta miura* shibori; p. 72), silk, purple dye. The large, square units evidence much skill. Similar square motifs are seen in early seventeenth century paintings.

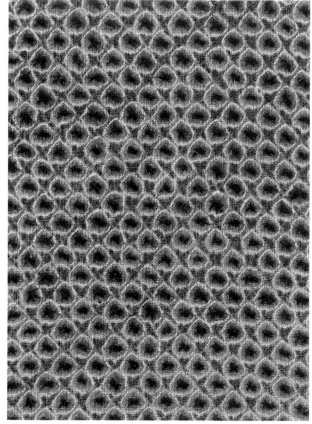

131.  Looped binding (*suji miura*; p. 70)

132.  Looped binding (*hitta miura*). No two examples of *miura* shibori are ever the same. Compare with *hitta miura* example above.

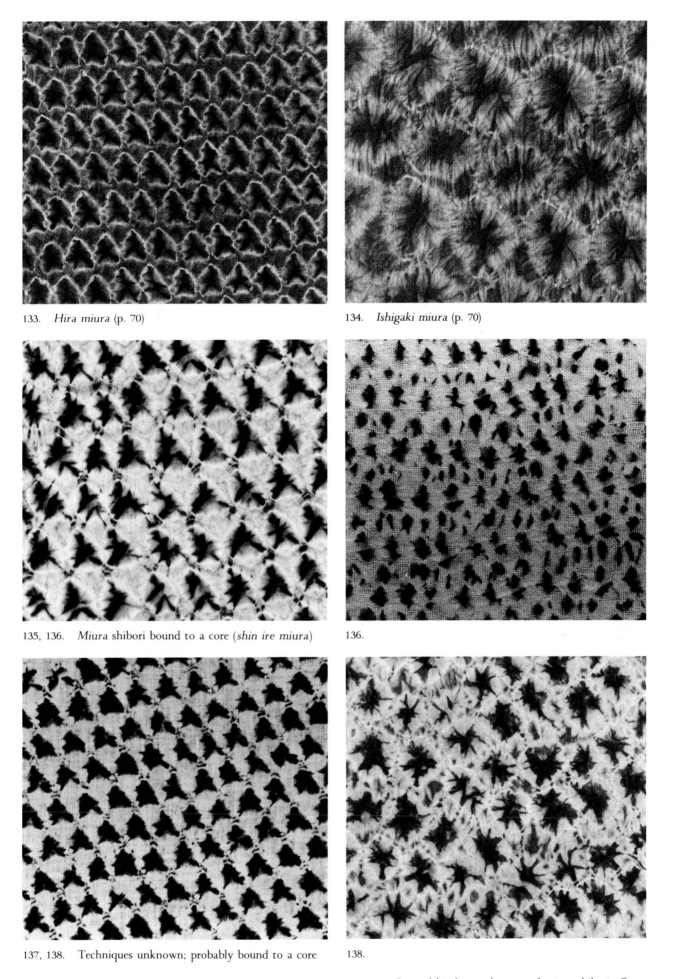

133.  *Hira miura* (p. 70)

134.  *Ishigaki miura* (p. 70)

135, 136.  *Miura* shibori bound to a core (*shin ire miura*)

136.

137, 138.  Techniques unknown; probably bound to a core

138.

133–38.  Looped binding; a harvest of *miura* shibori effects

139. Wood grain (*mokume* shibori; p. 74); hemp-leaf (*asa-no-ha*) pattern formed by negative ground

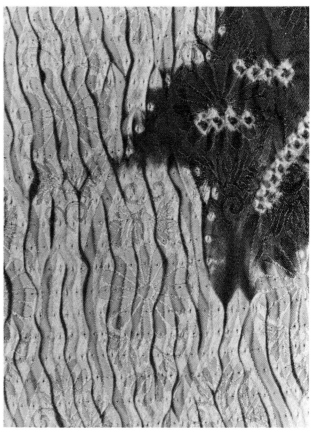

140. Wood grain (*mokume* shibori), negative ground design; figured satin (*rinzu*), red dye

141. Wood grain (*mokume* shibori), open-weave silk, black dye. Note the way the shibori breaks the negative areas.

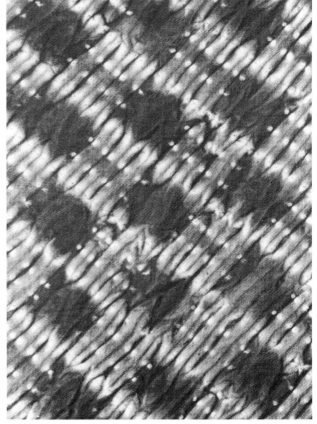

142. Wood-grain (*mokume*) check pattern. Note that continuous stitching rows separate the checks and that each wood-grain check contains two rows of stitching.

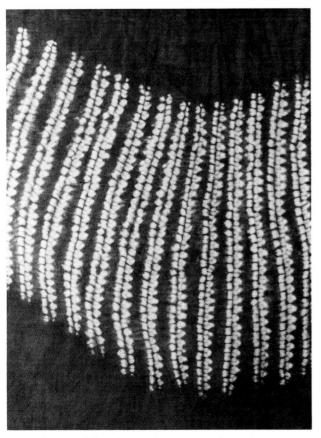

143. *Ori-nui* shibori (p. 76), lines in undulating band

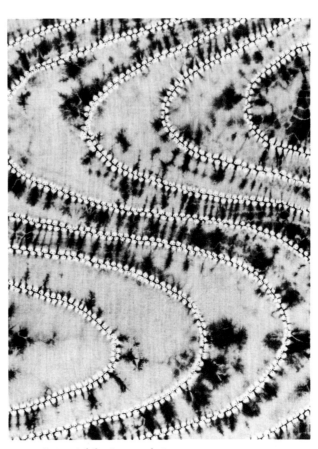

144. *Ori-nui* shibori, meandering stream pattern

145. *Ori-nui* shibori, pine motif. Very likely made by a farmer's wife rather than a specialist craftsman.

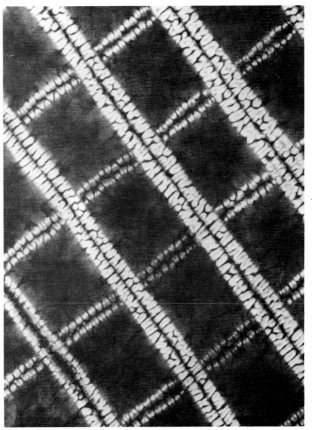

146. *Ori-nui* shibori, lattice pattern

147. *Miru* shibori (p. 78), large and small circles stitched on vertical folds; small circles were drawn up after cloth was dyed once.

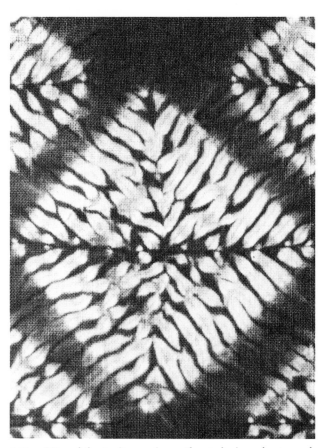

148. *Miru* shibori, diamond motifs stitched on horizontal folds

149. Japanese larch (*karamatsu* shibori; p. 78); stitching with continuous thread on horizontal folds creates circles without a dark line on the fold.

150. *Miru* shibori; size and layout of individually stitched circles is the same as in Plate 149, but note the different effect.

151. *Awase-nui* shibori (p. 80) variation

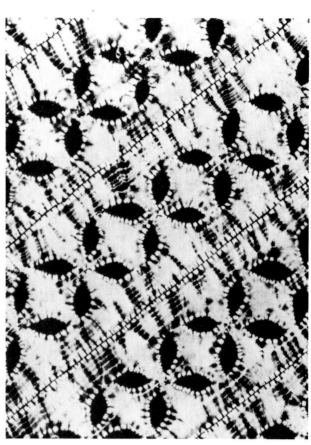

152. Mixed techniques: *hishaku-nui* and *ori-nui* (both p. 76). Cloth was stitched, dyed gray, bound to a flexible core, and overdyed in indigo.

153. *Awase-nui* shibori, bamboo leaf design. Leaves are completely resisted by pasting paper to underside of cloth before stitching (*kamiate*).

154. *Ori-nui* shibori and capping, maple leaf motif. The leaf's outline was stitched and threads drawn up; cloth was dyed palest indigo, then motif was capped and ground dyed.

155. Chevron stripe pattern (*maki-nui* shibori; p. 82)

156. Allover chevron stripe pattern

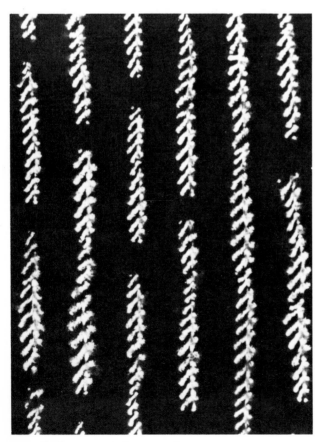

157. Broken vertical chevron stripes

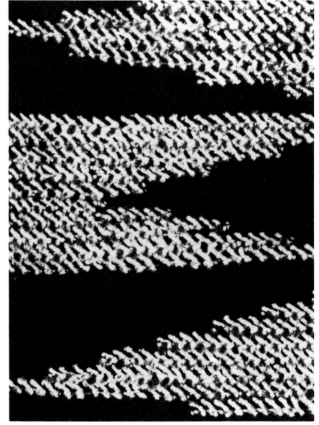

158. Chevron stripes used to create rhythmic positive and negative areas

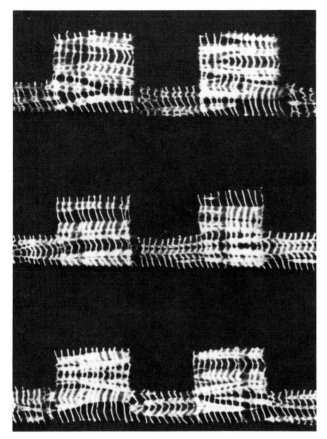

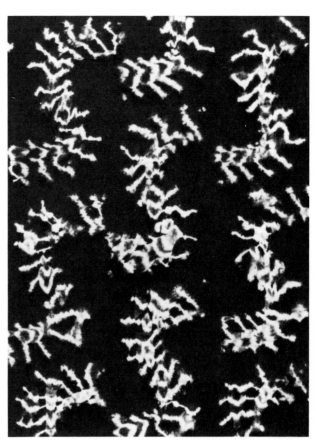

159–62.   Variations of *maki-nui* shibori (p. 82) designed by
Motohiko Katano

160.

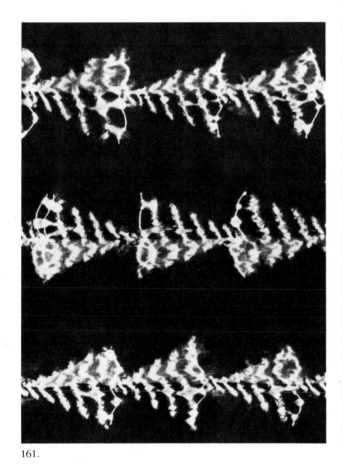

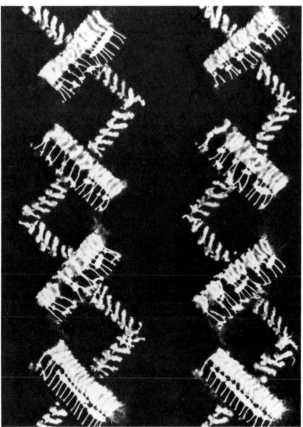

161.

162.

163. "Large" squares (*ōmasu*), Hanawa shibori (p. 84)

164. "Small" squares (*komasu*; p. 84), Hanawa shibori (detail of Plate 61)

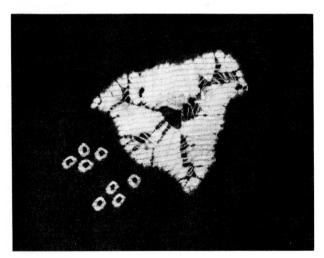

165. Patterns within motifs (*maki-age* shibori; p. 86), plover, silk, blue dye. This charming *maki-age* example is found on the same infant's garment as the *te-hitome kanoko* fish in Plate 114.

166. Patterns within motifs (*maki-age* shibori), leaf motifs. Note the effect created by crisscross binding within the motifs.

167. Mixed techniques: stitching and flexible core binding (*shin ire*; p. 100). Motifs outlined with stitching, cloth bound to a flexible core. Designed by Motohiko Katano.

168. Mixed techniques: *hishaku nui* (p. 76), spiderweb (p. 68), and flexible core binding (p. 100)

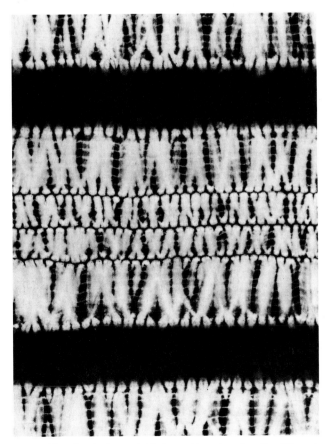

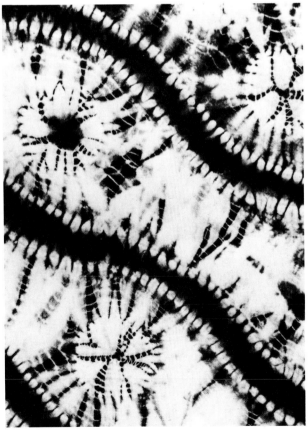

169. Mixed techniques: *hishaku nui* (p. 76), *ori-nui* (p. 76), and flexible core binding (p. 100)

170. Mixed techniques: *hishaku nui* (p. 76), spiderweb (p. 68), and flexible core binding (p. 100). In all examples on this page, the cloth was bound to a flexible core before dyeing.

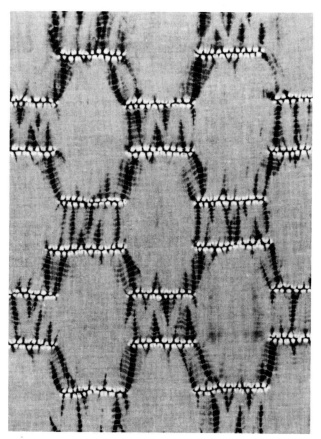

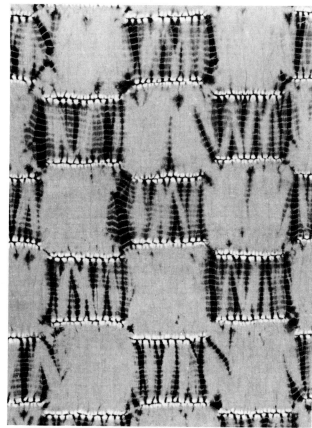

171–74.    Patterns formed with *ori-nui* (p. 76) shibori. Cloth was stitched, dyed gray, bound to a flexible core (*shin ire*; p. 100), and overdyed in indigo.

172.

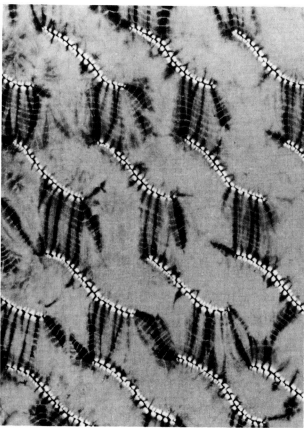

173.

174.

175. Capping (*bōshi*; p. 88) and half dots (*te-hitome kanoko*; p. 64). Compare the linear elements done by *te-hitome kanoko* here and by *ori-nui* stitching in Plate 176.

176. Capping (*bōshi*) and *ori-nui* shibori (p. 76)

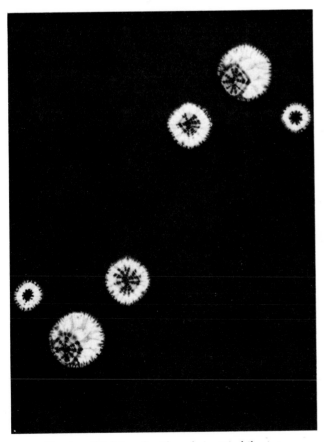

177. Capping (*bōshi*) and spiderweb (p. 86) shibori

178. Capping (*bōshi*) and spiderweb shibori

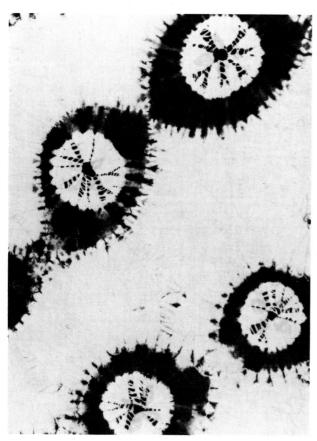

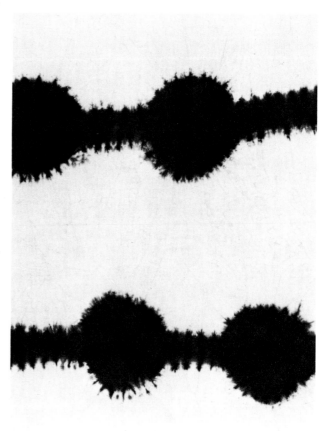

179. Mixed techniques: stitching (p. 74), *maki-age* (p. 86), and resist-wrapped ground (*kantera maki*; p. 108). The examples in Plates 179–81 were designed by Motohiko Katano.

180. Stitching and resist-wrapped ground (*kantera maki*)

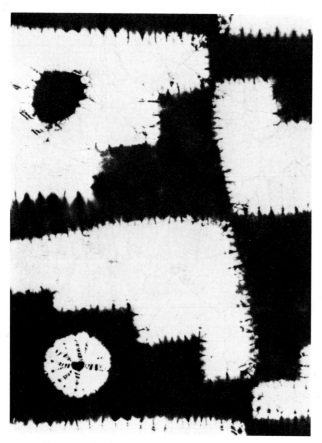

181. Capping (*bōshi*; p. 88) and *maki-age* shibori

182. Process unknown

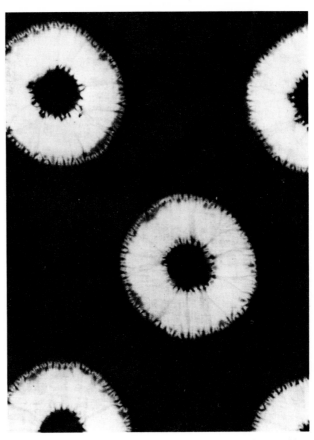

183. Capping (*bōshi*; p. 88). Note the soft-edged outlines that result when the cap is bound in place with the drawn-up stitches left exposed.

184. Capping (*bōshi*; p. 88). Plates 184–86 were designed by Motohiko Katano.

185. Capping (*bōshi*)

186. Stitching and resist-wrapped ground (*kantera maki*; p. 108)

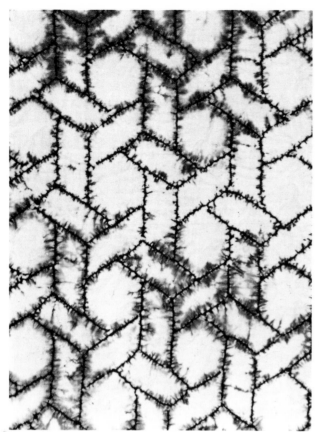

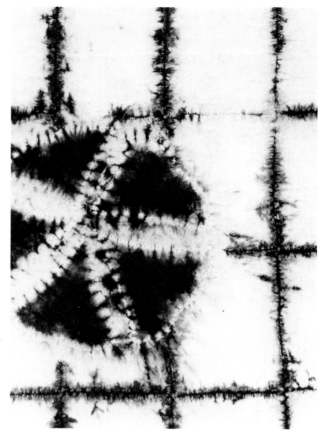

187. White shadow (*shirokage* shibori; p. 97)

188. White shadow and stitched motif

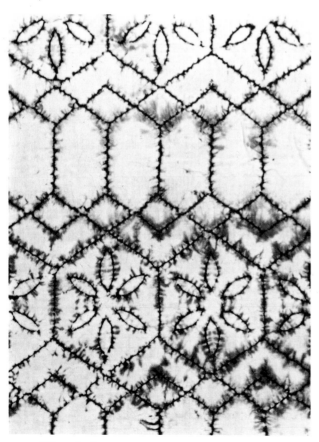

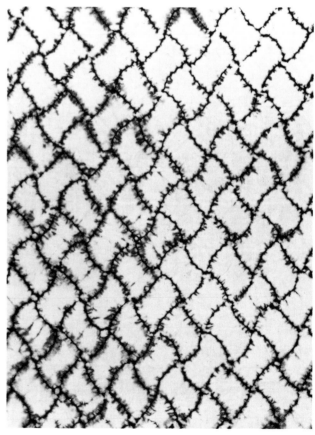

189. White shadow

190. White shadow

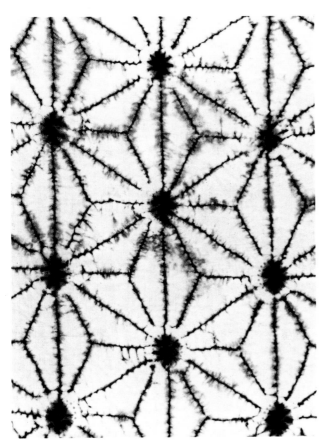

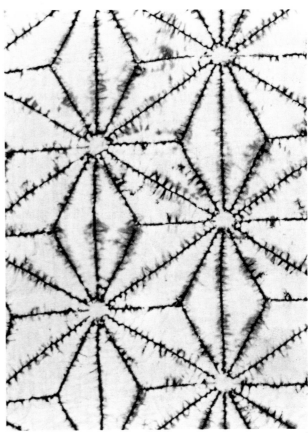

191, 192.   White shadow (*shirokage* shibori), two types of hemp leaf pattern (*asa-no-ha*)

192.

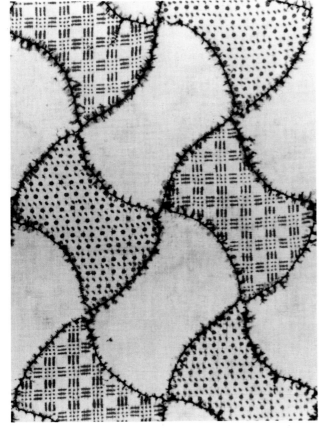

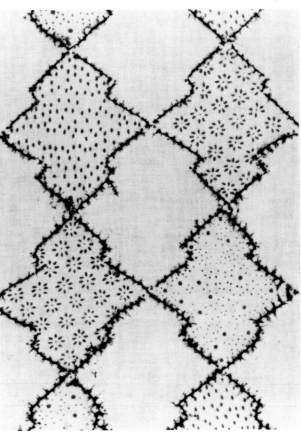

193, 194.   White shadow (*shirokage* shibori) and stenciled patterns within the shibori outlines. The effect of these two pieces is reminiscent of American patchwork.

194.

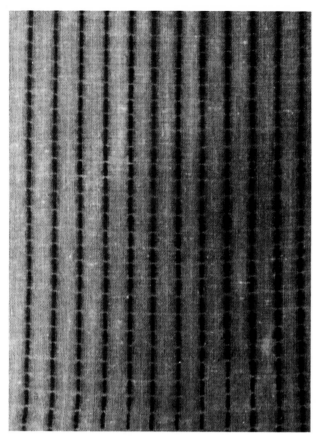

195. Stripes, hand pleating (*tesuji*; p. 105)

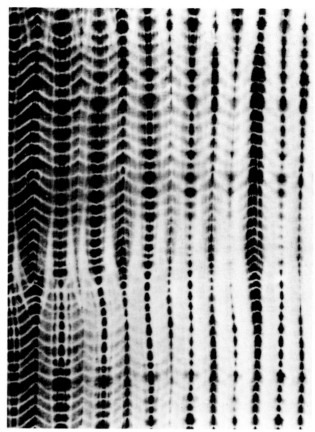

196. Stripes, hand pleating (*tesuji*)

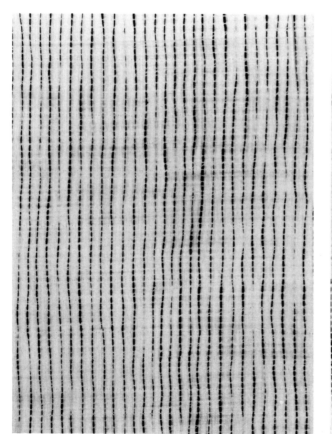

197. Stripes, stitched pleating (*nui yōrō*; p. 106). Example made by Shizu Ozeki, one of the few workers doing this fine pleating. Pleated cloth is bound without a core.

198. Stripes, stitched pleating (*nui yōrō*). Pleated cloth is bound on a flexible core (*shin ire*; p. 100).

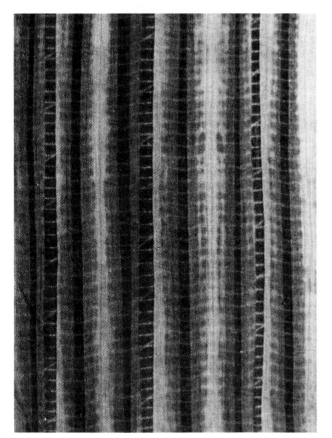

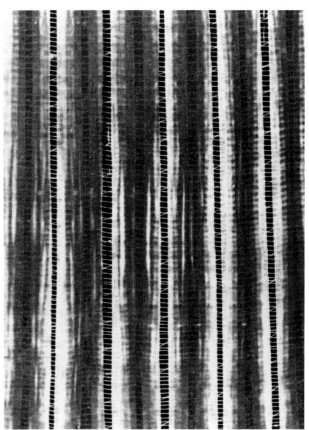

199.   Stripes, double pleating (*nido suji*; p. 107). Subtle effects are created by pleating and dyeing the cloth twice. Note the soft edges of one set of stripes.

200.   Stripes, double pleating

201.   Stripes, double pleating

202.   Stripes, double pleating

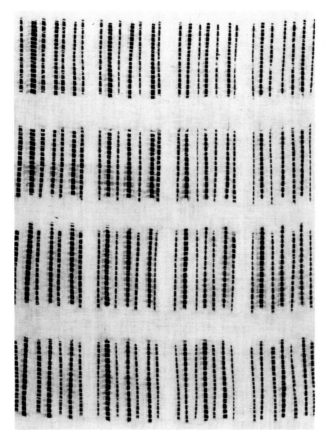

203.    Broken stripes, double pleating (*nido suji*; p. 107) and resist wrapping (*kantera maki*; p. 108)

204.    Broken stripes, double pleating and resist wrapping (*kantera maki*)

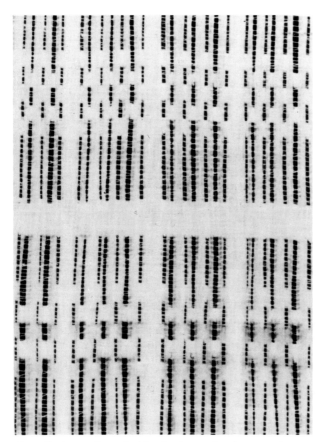

205.    Broken stripes, double pleating and resist wrapping

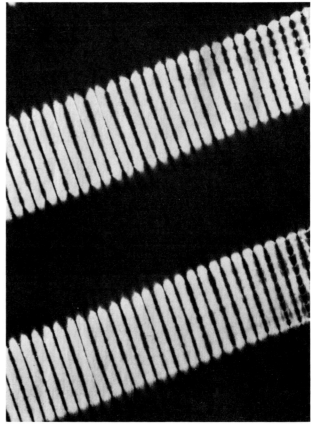

206.    *Tatsumaki arashi* (p. 124) variation. Only the striped bands were bound, creating an effect similar to stripes and dyed bands (*tazuna* shibori; p. 108).

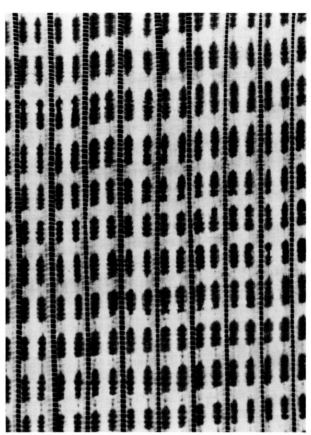

207.   Broken stripes, double pleating (*nido suji*; p. 107) and resist wrapping (*kantera maki*; p. 108). A continuous cloth strip is wound around the pleats each time the cloth is pleated.

208.   Broken stripes, double pleating and resist wrapping. A continuous cloth strip is wound around the cloth the first time it is pleated.

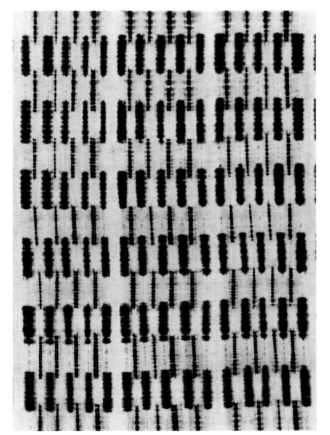

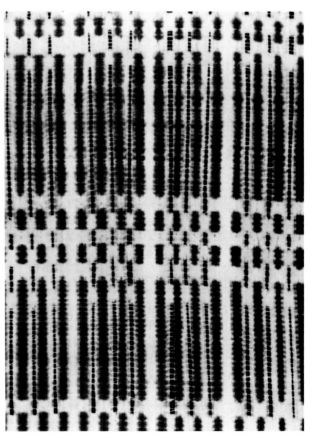

209.   Broken stripes, double pleating and resist wrapping. Paper strips are wrapped around the cloth each time it is pleated.

210.   Broken stripes, double pleating and resist wrapping. Paper strips are wrapped around the cloth each time it is pleated.

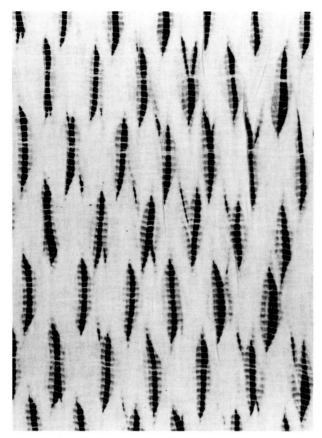

211. Reversed pleating, willow leaf (*midori* shibori; p. 110)

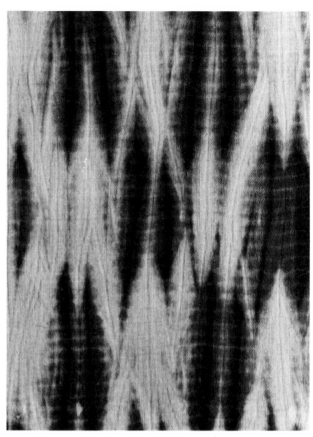

212. Reversed pleating. This difficult type of reversed pleating is no longer done.

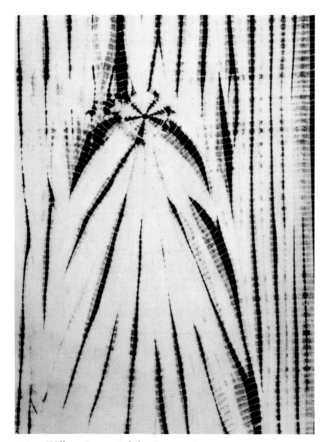

213. Willow (*yanagi* shibori; p. 111)

214. Mountain path (*yamamichi* shibori; p. 112)

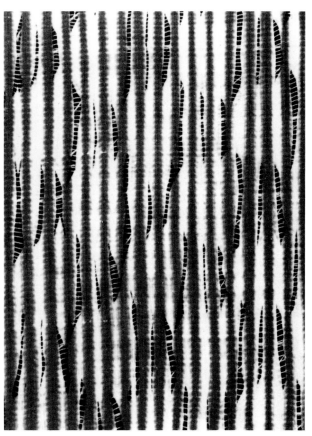

215. Mixed techniques: double pleating (*nido suji*; p. 107) and willow leaf (*midori*; p. 110)

216. Mixed techniques: hand pleating (*tesuji*; p. 105) and willow leaf (*midori*)

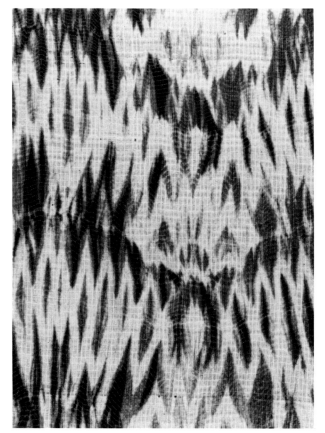

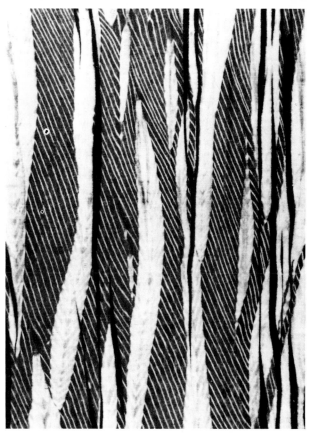

217. Process unknown

218. Exact process unknown. The nature of the stripes suggests that the cloth was bunched and tightly bound. The resist effect of the thread is clear.

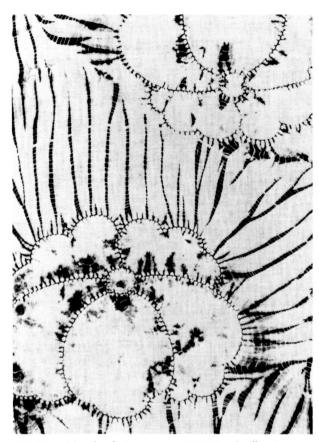

219, 220.  Mixed techniques: *ori-nui* (p. 76) and willow (*yanagi shibori*; p. 111) ground

220.

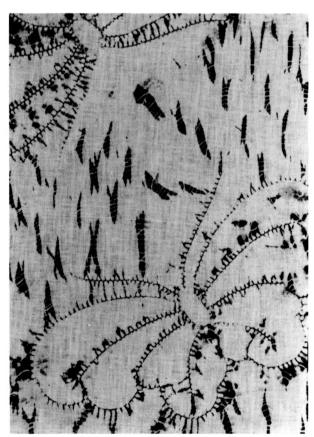
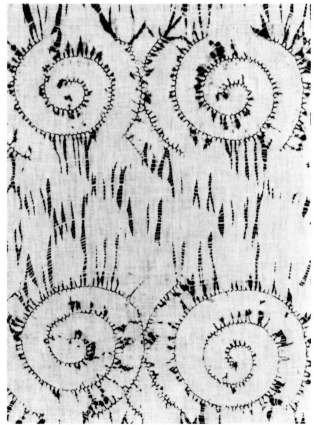

221, 222.  Mixed techniques: *ori-nui* and willow leaf (*midori shibori*; p. 110) ground

222.

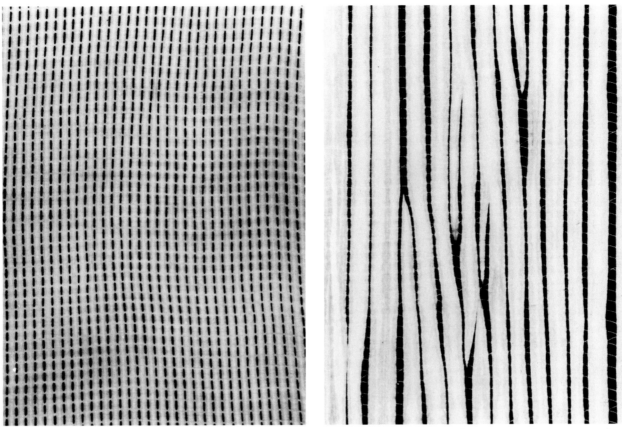

223. Machine pleating (*fukuzō suji*; p. 106)

224. Machine variegated pleating (*Matsubun suji*; p. 111)

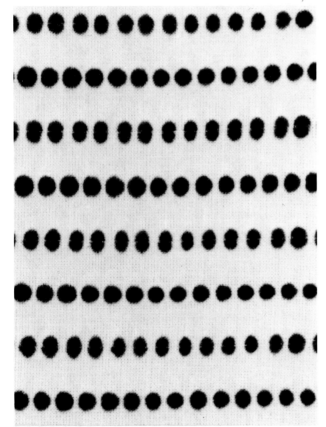

225. "Bean" pattern (*mame* shibori; made with a special device). This old and popular pattern is usually seen on small towels (*tenugui*; see Plates 9, 301).

226. Sunrise (*hinode* pattern; p. 101)

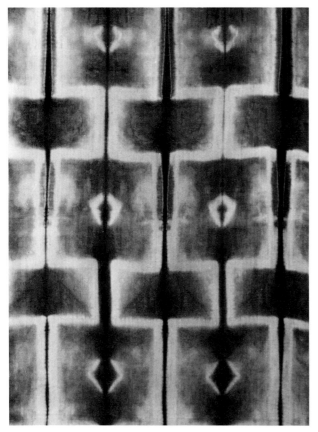

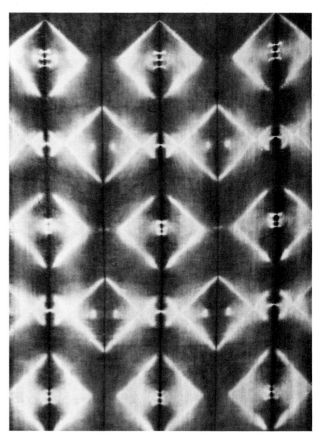

227. Katano shibori (p. 114). Plates 227–29 demonstrate the luminous effects possible with this process; all are indigo on cotton batiste.

228. Katano shibori

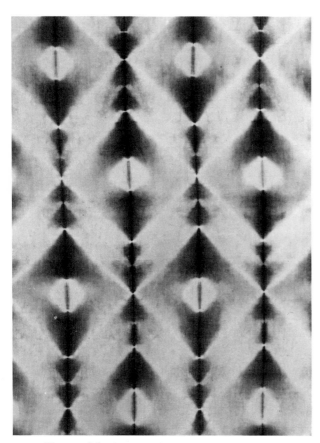

229. Katano shibori

230. Board clamping (*itajime*; p. 116), lattice pattern (p. 122)

231.   Board clamping (*itajime*; p. 116), tortoiseshell (*kikkō*) pattern (p. 120)

232–34.   Board clamping (*itajime*, also called *sekka shibori*; pp. 116ff). These three examples were folded in the same way, but dye seepage created different pattern effects.

233.

234.

235, 236.  *Arashi* shibori, thin diagonal stripes (*hosoito ichido kairyō*; p. 128)

236.

237, 238.  *Arashi* shibori, medium diagonal stripes (*chūito ichido kairyō*; p. 128)

238.

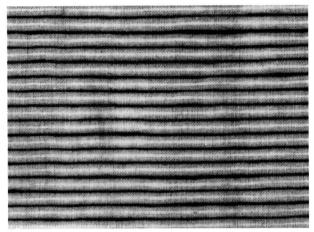

240. *Arashi* shibori, medium horizontal stripes (*chūito yoko kairyō*)

239. *Arashi* shibori, thin horizontal stripes (*hosoito yoko kairyō*; p. 129). This page shows effects obtained by different sizes of winding thread and intervals between turns of thread.

241. *Arashi* shibori, bands (*yoko ōdan*)

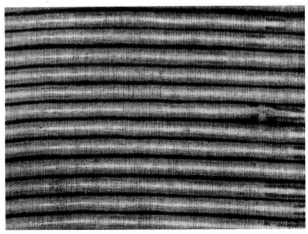

242. *Arashi* shibori, medium horizontal stripes (*chūito yoko kairyō*)

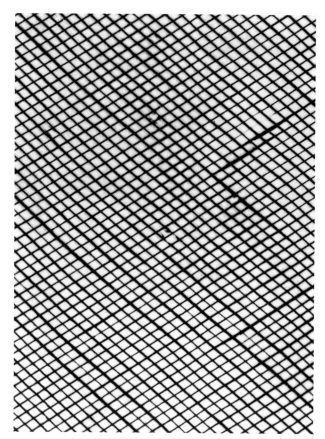

243. *Arashi* shibori, crossed diagonal lines (*koshi kairyō*). This and the next plate show the subtle variations that occur in *arashi* patterns.

244. *Arashi* shibori, crossed diagonal lines (*koshi kairyō*)

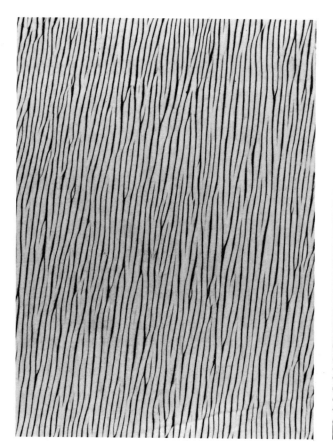

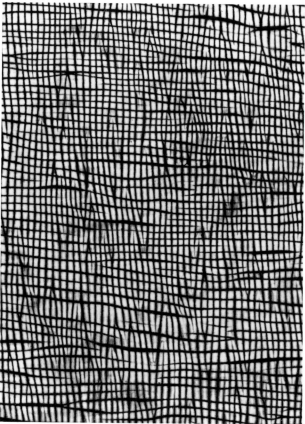

245. *Arashi* shibori, vertical fine wood grain (*tate komokume*; p. 130). Compare with stitched wood grain shibori, Plate 56.

246. *Arashi* shibori, crossed fine wood grain (*tate yoko komokume*)

247–50.  *Arashi* shibori. These examples are made by combining the diamond pattern with diagonal stripes, but the exact process is not known.

248.

249.

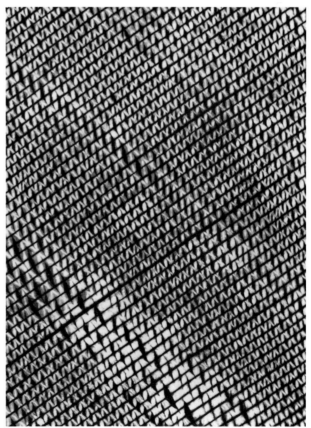

250.

251. *Arashi* shibori, small horizontal diamonds (*ichido sakura*; see *yoko chiri*, p. 133)

252. *Arashi* shibori, small vertical diamonds (*tate chiri*; see ōchiri, p. 131)

253. *Arashi* shibori, crossed diamonds (*tate yoko chiri*; p. 134)

254. *Arashi* shibori, crossed diamonds (*tate yoko chiri*) variation

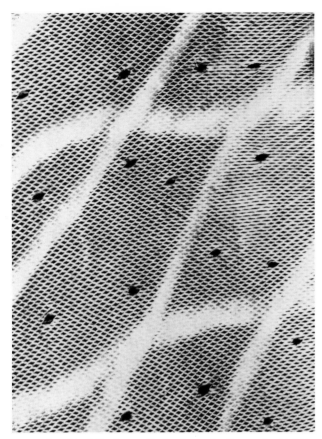

255. *Arashi* shibori, small horizontal diamonds (*ichido sakura*; see *yoko chiri*, p. 133) and resist wrapping (*kantera maki*; p. 108)

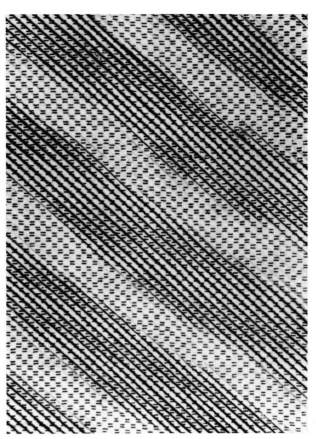

256. *Arashi* shibori, tiny squares and stripes. Stencil-printed cloth was used; *arashi* diagonal stripes and resist wrapping (*kantera maki*, p. 108) were applied.

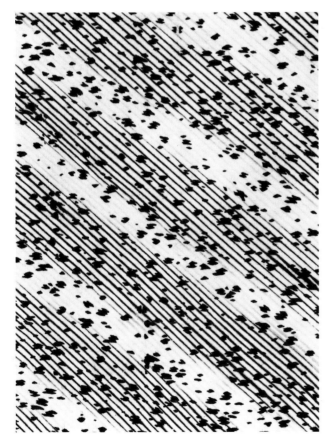

257. *Arashi* shibori, flecks and stripes. The process is the same as in Plate 256.

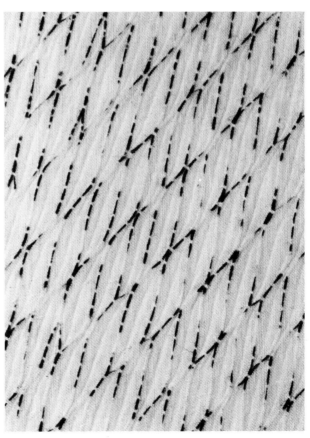

258. *Tatsumaki arashi* shibori (p. 124), diagonal diamond net (*hasu ami*; p. 132), and resist wrapping (*kantera maki*; p. 108)

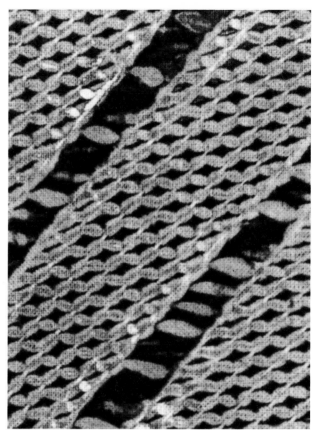

259. *Arashi* shibori, spaced diagonal stripes (*nishiki kairyō*). The threads are moved after winding to create the uneven spacing.

260. *Arashi* shibori, diamond brocade (*nishiki sakura*)

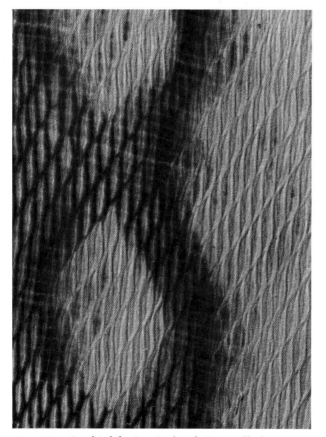

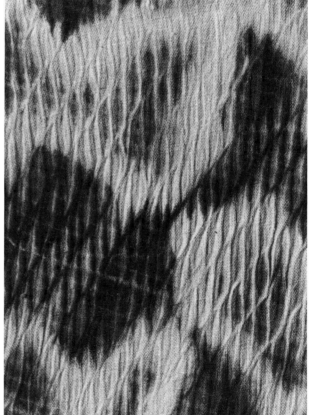

261, 262. *Arashi* shibori, mixed techniques. Cloth is compressed into diamond net pattern (*hasu ami*; p. 132), sized, pleated, bound to a flexible core, and dyed.

262.

263. *Arashi* shibori, stripes and diamonds. Japanese name and process unknown.

264. *Arashi* shibori, diamond variation. Japanese name and process unknown.

265. *Arashi* shibori, diamond variation (*tatsu ichi raku*). Process unknown.

266. *Arashi* shibori, diamond variation (*yoko ichi raku*). Process unknown.

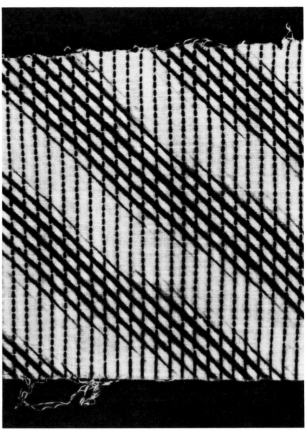

267.   Mixed techniques: machine pleating (*fukuzō suji*; p. 106) and *arashi* wood grain (*mokume*; p. 130). Exact process unknown.

268.   Mixed techniques: machine pleating (*fukuzō suji*), *arashi* diagonal stripes (*hosoito ichido kairyō*; p. 128), and resist wrapping (*kantera maki*; p. 108)

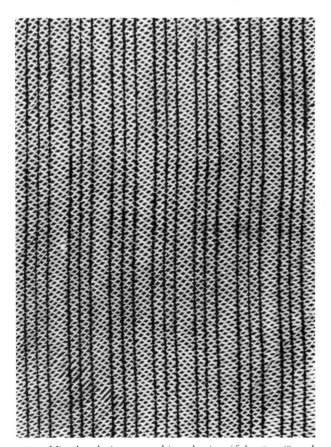

269.   Mixed techniques: machine pleating (*fukuzō suji*) and *arashi* small diamonds (see *yoko chiri*, p. 133)

270.   Mixed techniques: machine pleating (*fukuzō suji*) and *arashi* diamond brocade (*nishiki sakura*)

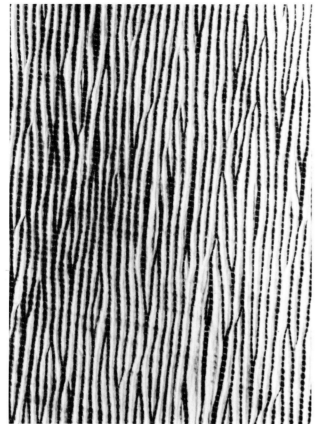 

271–74.  *Tatsumaki arashi* (p. 124)

272.

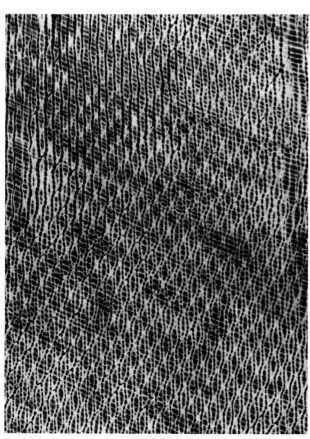 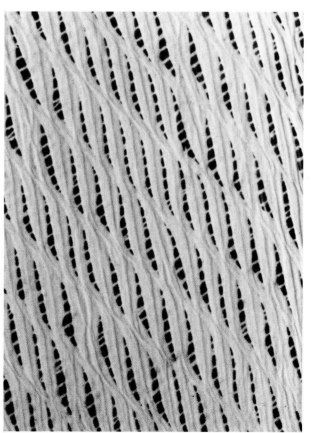

273.

274.

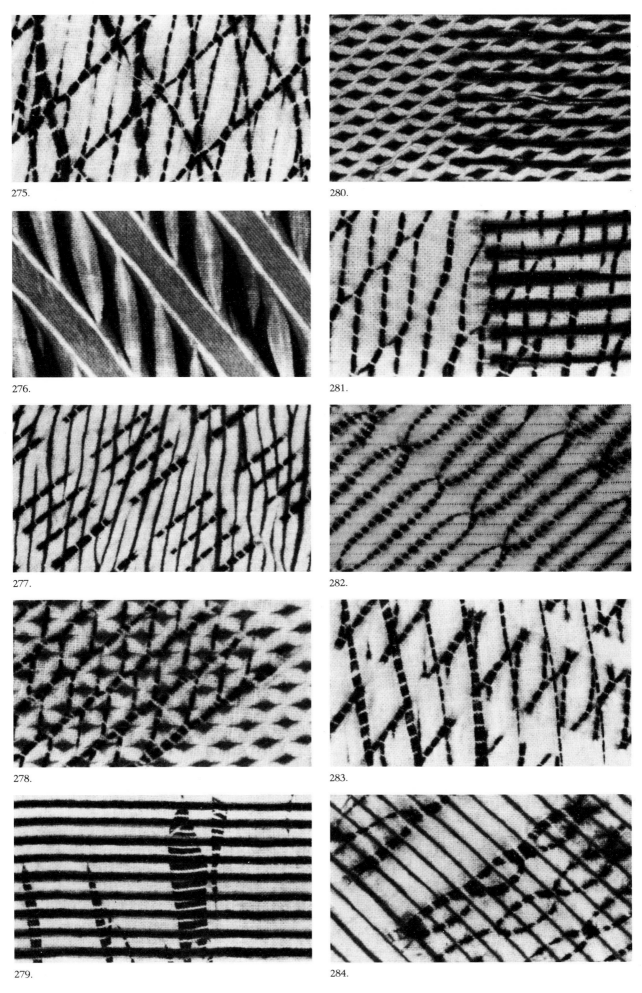

275.

280.

276.

281.

277.

282.

278.

283.

279.

284.

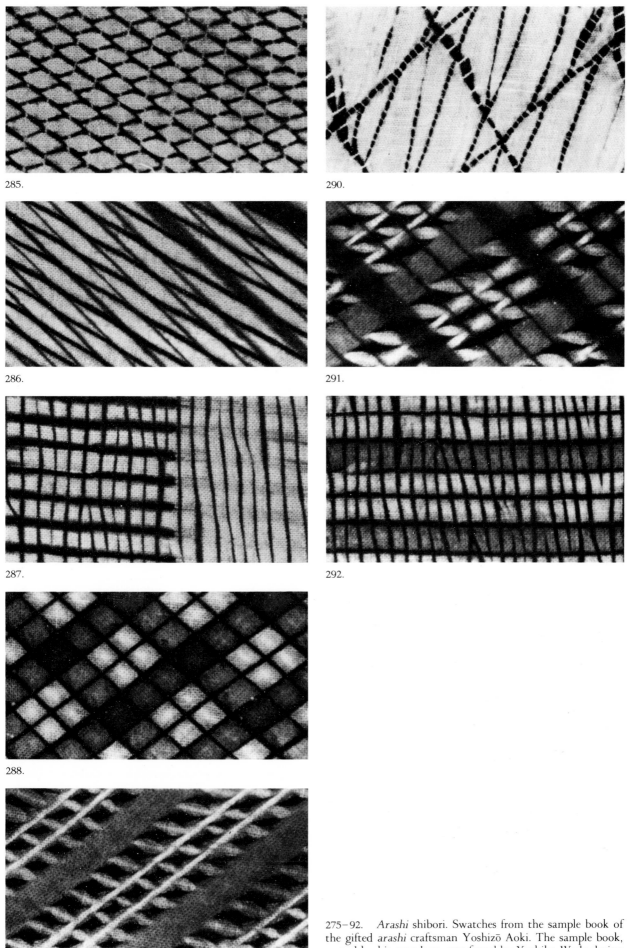

285.

286.

287.

288.

289.

290.

291.

292.

275–92. *Arashi* shibori. Swatches from the sample book of the gifted *arashi* craftsman Yoshizō Aoki. The sample book, owned by his grandson, was found by Yoshiko Wada during a visit to Arimatsu.

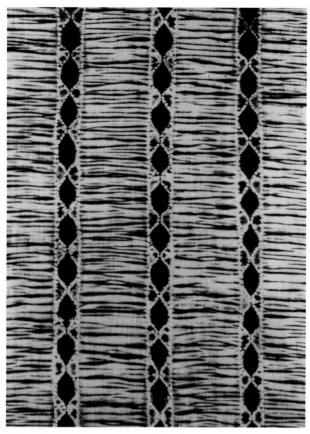

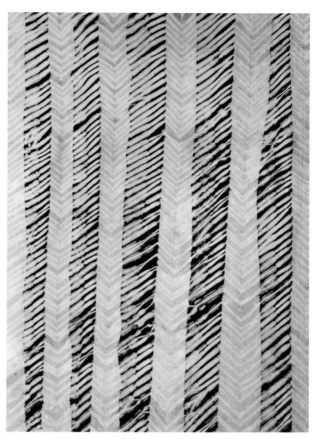

293. Mixed techniques: *arashi* horizontal wood grain (*yoko ōmokume*; p. 131) and *hishaku-nui* (p. 76) stitched stripes; cotton batiste and indigo

294. *Arashi* shibori, folding and medium diagonal stripes (*chūito ichido kairyō*; p. 128), silk broadcloth and indigo

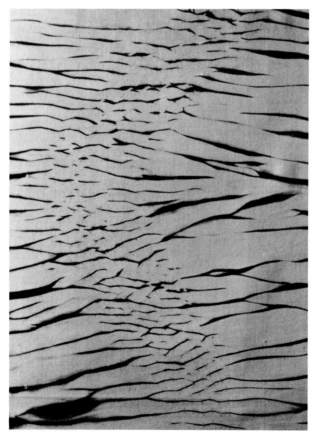

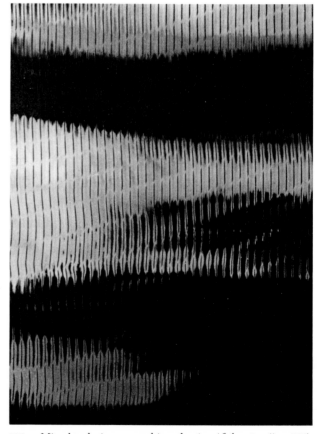

295. *Arashi* shibori, horizontal wood grain (*yoko ōmoku-me*; p. 131), meandering stream design; cotton sateen and indigo

296. Mixed techniques: machine pleating (*fukuzō suji*; p. 106) and *arashi*; silk crepe and discharge dyeing, purple, black, and beige

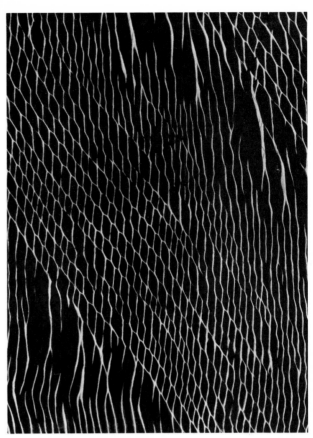

297. *Arashi* shibori, diagonal diamond net (*hasu ami*; p. 132); beige silk crepe, red-brown dye

298. *Arashi* shibori, same as Plate 297; black silk crepe, discharge dyed

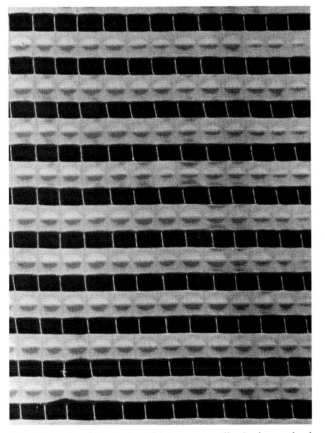

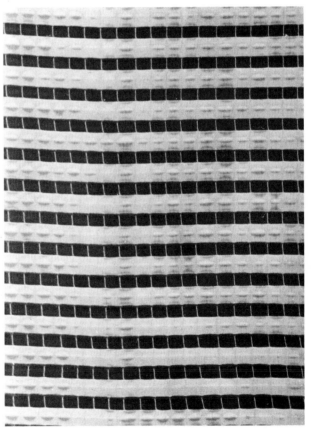

299, 300. *Arashi* variation, folding; gray silk, discharge dyed

300.

金五郎 中村芝翫

301.    Woodblock print by Toyokuni, portrait of the actor Nakamura Shikan. The kimono is *miura* shibori, and the small towel (*tenugui*) is *mame* shibori (compare Plate 9).

302.    Man's underkimono (*jiban*), hand pleating (*tesuji*; p. 105) and
resist wrapping (*kantera maki*; p. 108); nineteenth century

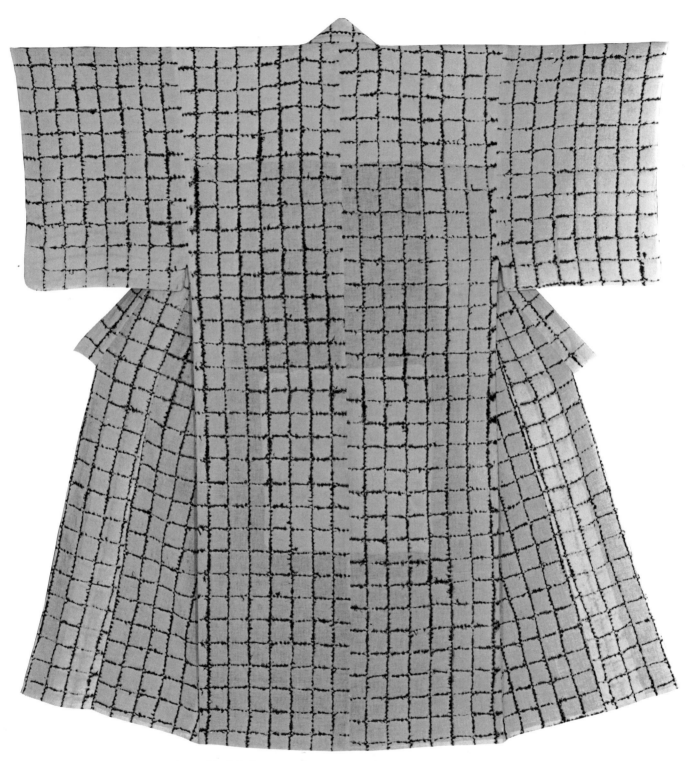

303.  Man's light cotton kimono (*yukata*), white shadow (*shiro-kage* shibori; p. 97), squares pattern

304.    Unfinished garment, white shadow (*shirokage* shibori; p. 97),
hemp leaf pattern (*asa-no-ha*; see Plate 191 for detail)

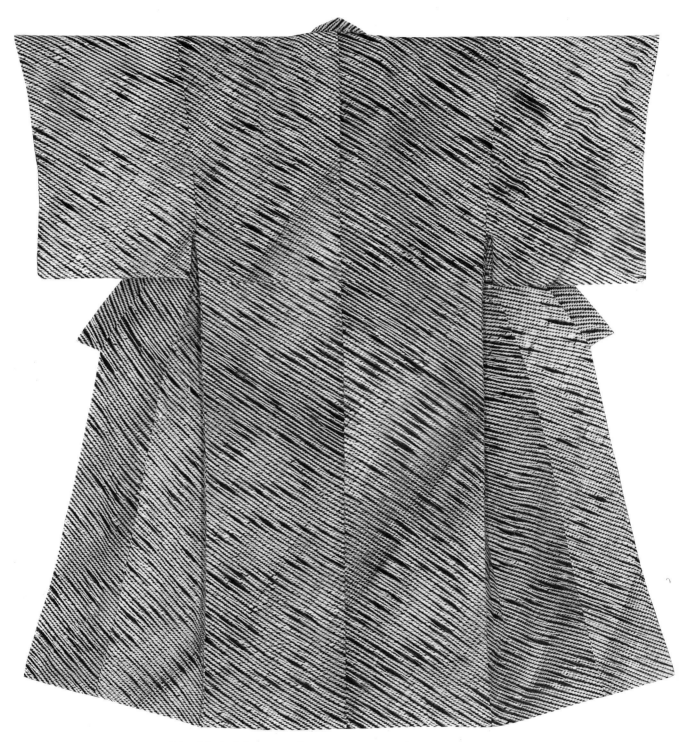

305.   Man's light cotton kimono (*yukata*), *arashi* shibori, pine wind diamond (*matsukaze ami sakura*; pp. 129, 134)

306.　Man's light cotton kimono (*yukata*), *arashi* shibori, variation
of crossed diamonds (*tate yoko chiri*; p. 134)

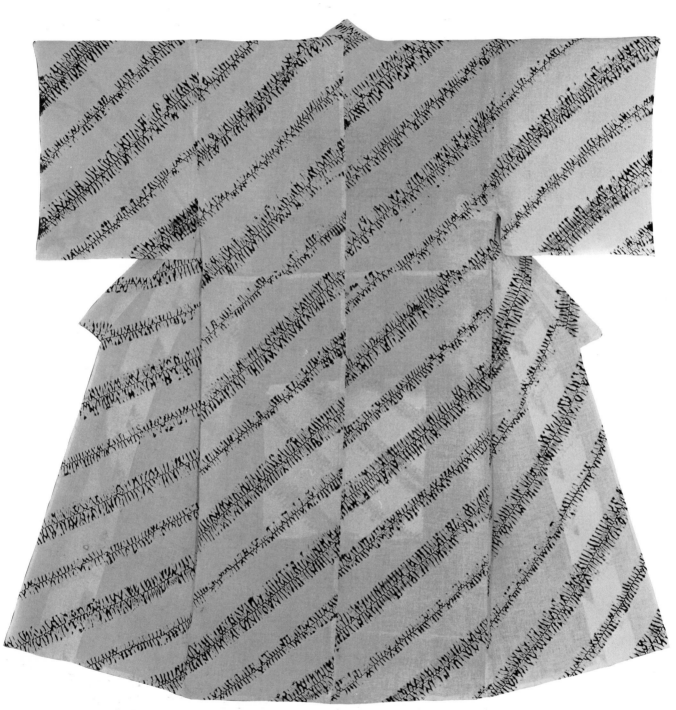

307.   Man's underkimono (*jiban*), *ori-nui* (p. 76) shibori bound
against a flexible core (*shin ire*; p. 100)

308.    Woman's light cotton kimono (*yukata*), *maki-nui* (p. 82)
variation; designed by Motohiko Katano

309.   Man's underkimono (*jiban*), *arashi* shibori, crossed diagonal lines (*koshi kairyō*; see *hosoito ichido kairyō*, p. 128)

310.   Unfinished garment, *arashi* shibori, angel wings (*hagoromo*; p. 135)

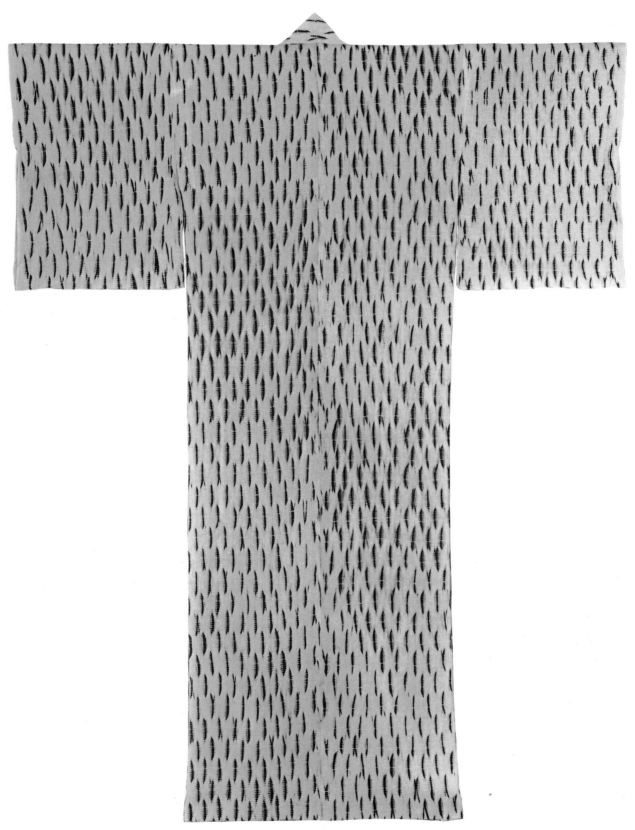

311.  Unfinished garment, reversed pleating (*midori* shibori; p. 110)

312, 313.   Woman's light cotton kimono (*yukata*), square ring dots (*yokobiki kanoko*; p. 63) and detail. The *kanoko* dots are rough and irregular, but the effect is charming and lively.

314.   Man's light cotton kimono (*yukata*), machine pleating; late nineteenth century

315.   Woman's light cotton kimono (*yukata*). Process unknown.

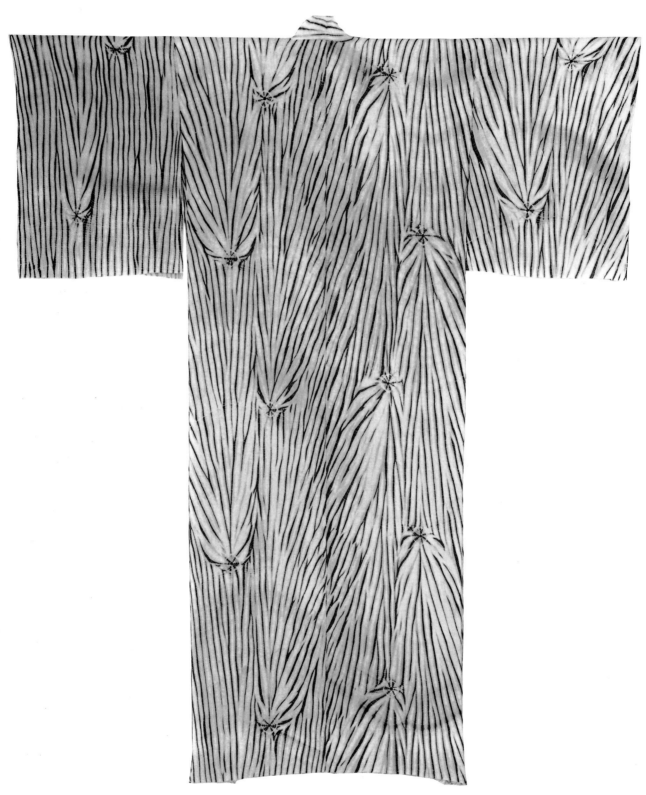

316.   Unfinished garment, willow (*yanagi* shibori; p. 111)

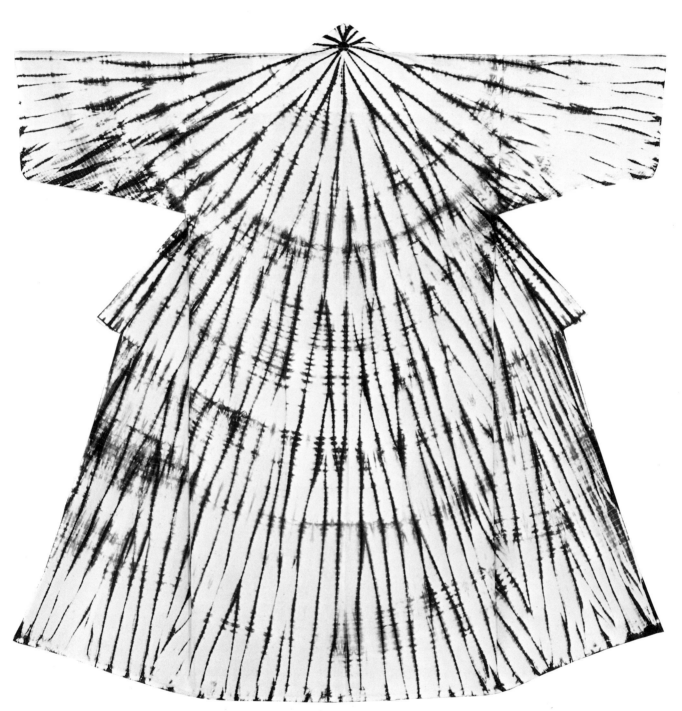

317.   Festival kimono, variegated pleating, straw raincape design.
Kōzō Takeda of Arimatsu believes the garment was made in Amagi,
Kyushu.

318.  Man's underkimono (*jiban*), double pleating (*nido suji*; p. 107) and resist wrapping (*kantera maki*; p. 108)

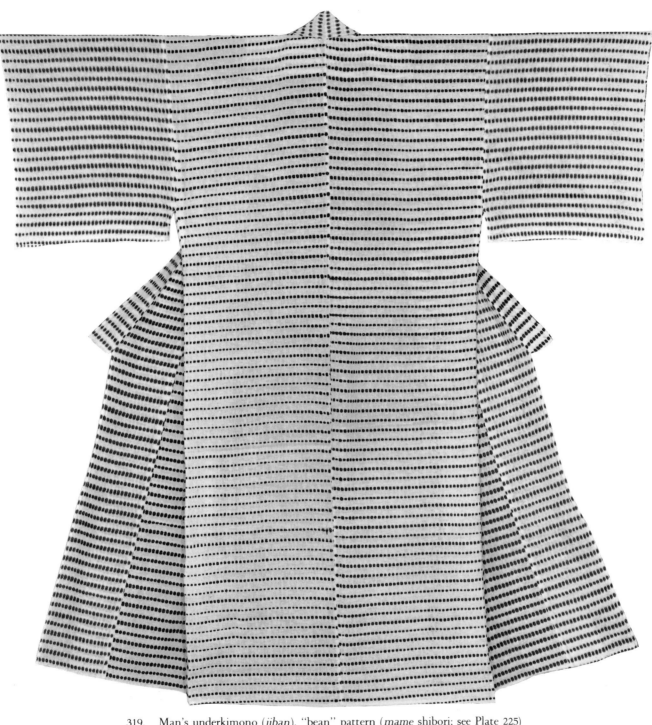

319.　Man's underkimono (*jiban*), "bean" pattern (*mame* shibori; see Plate 225)

320. Kimono, silk, tortoiseshell (*kikkō*) pattern, by Motohiko Katano. Exact process unknown (see also Plate 331).

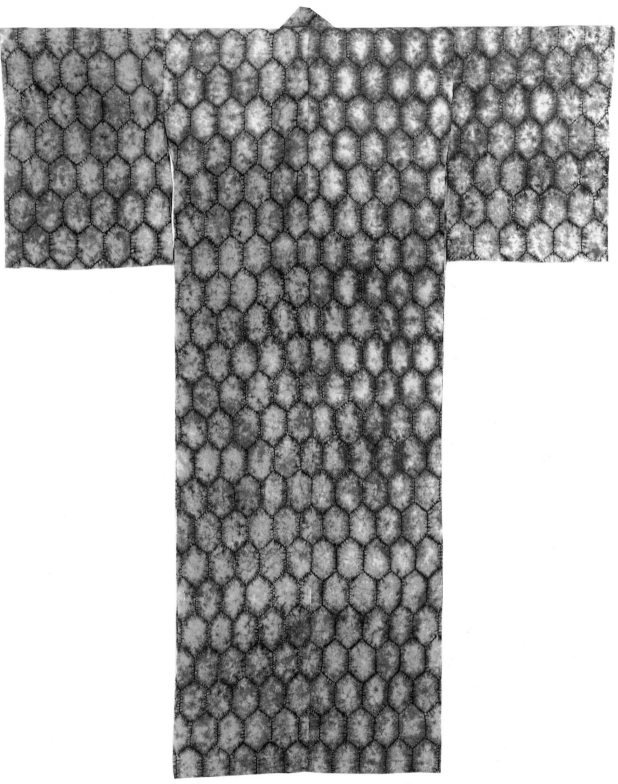

321. Unfinished garment, white shadow (*shirokage* shibori; p. 97), tortoiseshell (*kikkō*) pattern. The dye seepage has created a pleasingly soft yet strong effect.

322. Woman's light cotton kimono (*yukata*), *ori-nui* shibori, undulating line (*tatewaku*) pattern (p. 76). This and the next example are produced by the same *ori-nui* technique, clearly illustrating the design potential of even this basic shibori process.

323. Woman's light cotton kimono (*yukata*), *ori-nui* shibori, wavy line pattern

324.   Man's bath kimono (*yuagari*), *ori-nui* (p. 76) and *maki-age*
(p. 86) shibori and dip-dyeing (p. 88); butterfly design

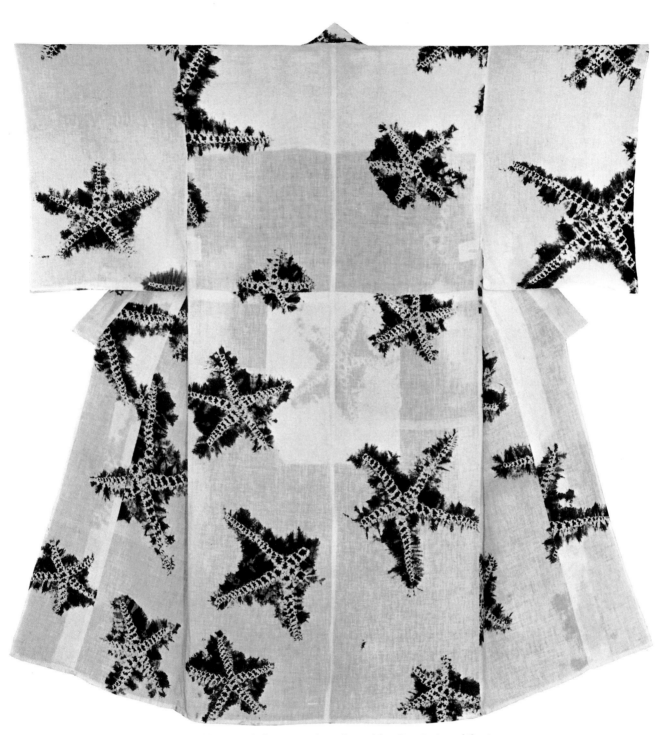

325.  Man's underkimono (*jiban*), looped binding (*miura* shibori;
p. 70) and dip-dyeing (p. 88); starfish design

326.    Festival kimono, *ori-nui* (p. 76) and *awase-nui* (p. 80) shibori,
capped ground. The bamboo medallions with the character *ka* in
center signify the Takeda family, Arimatsu shibori producers since
the early Edo period; nineteenth century.

327.   Festival kimono, looped binding (*miura* shibori; p. 70), *ori-nui* (p. 76) and *maki-age* (p. 86) shibori

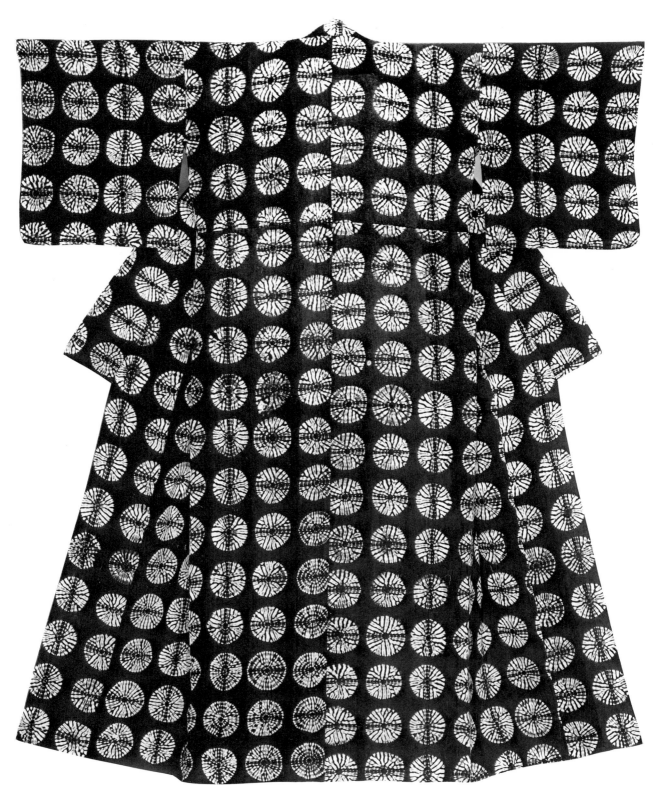

328. Woman's underkimono (*jiban*), Japanese larch (*karamatsu*
shibori; p. 78), by Motohiko Katano. Note how the direction of the
line along the center fold of each motif changes.

# Innovation

# Changing Dimensions

## CONTEXT: CRAFTS IN JAPAN

A harmonious relationship with nature, often cited as a key characteristic of Japanese culture, is at the heart of the Japanese craftsman's responsiveness to his or her materials. This attitude leads to an unforced approach to making objects, involving an openness to the process and an acknowledgment of the integrity of materials and techniques.

The concept of work in Japan is different from that of the West, in part because of a different sense of time. Traditionally, mastery of an art was achieved slowly in the apprentice system; technique was absorbed by the body over many years, not assigned to the head during an intense period of training. Today, however, the apprentice system is nearly dead and head training in art schools has supplanted it. Still, the Japanese attitudes towards work and time remain largely unchanged. The commitment of time, both in learning skills and in making objects, is a natural element of craftsmanship. The execution of the work, the *flow* of the process—this is the focus of the artisan rather than the passing or measuring of time; he is, so to speak, inside his labor rather than outside. The concept of man-hours has had no place in the traditional craftsman's world; "efficiency" is totally a function of the result desired. For example, if a certain background pattern involves seventeen steps but a compromise version could be achieved in six steps, the efficient means of obtaining the desired pattern—that is, the most effective way—would be the longer process. *Kanoko* shibori, as discussed previously, requires from ten years to a lifetime to perfect skill, and one to two years may be necessary to complete the tying of a single kimono.

Of course, this is an oversimplification of a traditional Japanesw work ethic, stated so as to provide a contrast with the familiar modern notion of efficiency and time-and-motion economics. The old attitude is still sufficiently alive in Japan to greatly influence the work of Japanese craftsmen, yet this labor-intensive craft heritage is too often incompatible with the reality of trying to feed a family in today's economy. The result is the rapid disappearance or overpricing of what were once common, everyday objects. These trends are evident in the world of shibori, and one of the purposes of this book is to document fast-vanishing techniques, with an eye to their creative potential.

Once a craft or medium has been chosen, it is rare for a Japanese to change to another, just as it is unusual in Japan for a student to switch colleges or an employee to leave a company. This dedication to one pursuit encourages the craftsman to acquire a deep knowledge of a craft and to survive the dry, difficult periods. When technique is mastered, the craftsman is freed to become an intermediary between concept and process. Only after technical competence has reached a level of naturalness can the craftsman make unconscious aesthetic decisions, simply because he or she knows the medium so well, and then it becomes possible to find solutions to problems at each step of the way.

The concept of craft in Japan embraces both craft and art, blurring (if not ignoring) the distinction between them that has been typical of their practice and appraisal in Europe and North America since the eighteenth century. Craft and art historically have been inseparable until relatively recent times. Before the Meiji era (1868–1912), the artisan's identity was primarily that of a member of a group performing a certain function within society. An artisan viewed an object he made in terms of the social group in which it would be used; that is, in terms of the object's destiny after it left the hands of the maker. Thus, an object's purpose included not only physical or practical use but also the function of providing visual pleasure and, often, conferring upon its owner prestige commensurate with social position. The rigid codes of behavior and appearance according to social class extended to the choice of objects used in daily life, as narrowly prescribed for aristocrats as for peasants. For example, it was not proper for one of the aristocracy to have a Karatsu dish or a Shigaraki vase (outside the tea room); the appropriate object was a Ninsei style bowl or Kakiemon vase.

The influx of western culture during the Meiji period brought with it emphasis upon the individual and a concept of art as an expression of individuality. Fine art became a new category distinguished from traditional crafts. Since the Muromachi period (1333–1573), however, there had been exceptions to the rule, craftsmen who enjoyed fame and patronage from a feudal lord or rich merchant. They were similar to present-day artists in that their works were done as individual statements with their signature, and they became well known through the popularity of their style. Still, they rarely worked alone; apprentices and other craftsmen assisted.

Textile art has occupied a central position within crafts throughout Japanese history. The majority of works have been in the form of clothing, and as in the case of other objects created for personal use, the style and fabric of a garment reflect not only the wearer's taste but his or her social life. Patterns and motifs seen on textiles also appeared on ceramics, lacquerware, and other items, the colors and designs setting the mood for the aesthetics of a period. This role of the garment as a framework for the craftsman's creation, as a canvas is used by a painter, reached a culmination in the dazzling Nō robes of the sixteenth century, which were and still are worn only for theatrical performances.

During the twelve centuries that the art of shibori has been cultivated in Japan, several distinct approaches reached outstanding levels of achievement in textile art. *Tsujigahana* textiles, Kanbun *kosode*, long-sleeved kimono (*furisode*) of the late Edo period, and folk textiles of Arimatsu–Narumi reveal different interpretations of the possibilities that shibori offers, each a manifestation of changing aesthetic criteria.

During the past fifty years the *mingei* movement has generated appreciation and support for Japanese folkcrafts. Sōetsu Yanagi formulated aesthetic criteria for folk objects: a natural, healthy beauty is the result of an object's utility, its participation in a distinct tradition, and the anonymity of its maker(s). Yanagi was also aware that the age of the anonymous artisan was over, and he proposed standards for the work of the artist-craftsman as well. It is not the place of this discussion to inquire whether shibori meets Yanagi's concept of *mingei*. Like all crafts in Japan, shibori is in transition. Its creative possibilities remain hidden even from many people closely associated with Japanese textiles, and there are surprisingly few people today who have dedicated themselves to shibori as compared to, say, stencil dyeing (*katazome*).

COMMERCIAL PRODUCTION—KIMONO

As seen in Part I, economic conditions have affected the evolution of shibori as a textile art. It is against the background of commercial production that most shibori craftsmen should be viewed, since the textile arts have always been geared toward supplying consumer goods, to make functional items of dress and accessories.

The freedom of movement and convenience of western clothes make them suitable for everyday wear, whereas kimono and other traditional garments have now become luxury items reserved for special occasions. Nonetheless, the kimono is still accepted and valued as traditional, native dress, and it is an integral aspect of arts such as the tea ceremony and Japanese dancing and singing.

There is a tendency to choose a kimono for its design rather than its practicality. The purchase may be likened to the acquisition of art objects such as paintings and luxury items such as diamonds or furs. Because kimono are so expensive they are an obvious symbol, and as the wearer's personal choice they serve as statements of cultural sophistication. A kimono is the acceptable formal wear for events such as weddings, funerals, receptions, parties, etc., and it can be worn for more years than a stylish western dress, which soon passes out of fashion.

A kimono employs designers, who are considered no different from the other craftsmen involved in making the kimono; their job is but one of many steps in the production process. A relatively recent trend is the patronage of artists who will design and create one-of-a-kind or a line of kimono. These artists have their own studios, and the kimono house acts as an agent or distributor, a link with the public. Most of the one-of-a-kind kimono created by these artists are considered works of art and are entered in exhibitions or displayed as creative statements in solo shows. Some artists are in great demand, and their works carry a high price.

**Kyoto and Arimatsu–Narumi:** Japan's two major shibori centers, Kyoto and Arimatsu–Narumi, are directly connected to the industry, and production is divided into small, specialized areas. Because the trade of fabric dyeing can require many complicated processes and must accommodate mass production, labor is delegated to many skilled workers. The *Kyō kanoko* tradition from the Edo period, which includes *hitta kanoko, te-hitome kanoko,* and *bōshi* shibori, is being continued in Kyoto and the surrounding area, where there are close to thirteen hundred small studios related to shibori. Recently there has been a sharing of expertise between Kyoto and Arimatsu–Narumi. For instance, shibori producers in Arimatsu–Narumi send cloth to be patterned in *hon hitta* and *te-hitome* (see pages 59 and 65) to Kyoto, where it is tied by women on the outskirts of town. Kyoto in turn benefits from the tradition of *miura* and *yokobiki* (see pages 70 and 63), tied by women in the Arimatsu–Narumi area and outlying rural regions.

Small craft shops are still economically viable in many instances and have not been replaced by mechanized industry. It is exciting to see the extensive networks of home businesses operating in modern Japan, which have no counterpart in the United States. This system coexists with production of *kanoko* using cheap labor in countries such as Korea, Taiwan, and the Philippines. Although a great increase in quantity and mechanical perfection is possible through the cottage-industry type of mass production, the spirit and high standards of refinement of earlier craftsmen have not been achieved. In the *Kyō kanoko* produced this way, some effort has been made to adapt their designs and colors to modern tastes, but the results are rather timid, since merchants and producers avoid speculative innovation and stick to tried, conservative designs that clearly display the expense of the garment. The majority of designs are copies of classic ones, but they have lost their original strength and justification. Most of the production in Arimatsu–Narumi has turned to silk kimono similar to *Kyō kanoko* because of its reputation as the expensive, prestigious shibori and popular ignorance of other shibori types. Traditionally the shibori-dyed light cotton summer kimono *(yukata)* made in Arimatsu–Narumi were very popular because of the lively and casual designs. A small quantity of such cotton kimono is still made, and there has been an effort to adapt the original designs (with some variations) to silk as well. Despite their beauty, they do not appeal to most buyers, who find them outdated. Examples of the survival of the Arimatsu–Narumi tradition may be seen in the bolts of cotton fabric (Plate 348) which, unfortunately, represent a small percentage of today's products.

**Morioka City**: The area around Morioka City in Iwate Prefecture has been famous for purple root *(shikon)* dyeing and Japanese madder dyeing for twelve hundred years. The old name for the region is Nanbu, and since the Edo period some shibori has been done in relatively simple forms dictated by the traditional dye process (Hanawa shibori, see page 84). The owner of a shop called Soshidō in Morioka City was inspired by this traditional craft and, after learning shibori in Kyoto, began producing much more complicated shibori textiles with innovative designs made possible by the use of chemical as well as natural dyes. Today his son continues to experiment with this Nanbu shibori, using mostly chemical dyes and depending on imports for his supply of natural dyes. The fabrics produced demonstrate an effective use of *maki-age* (stitched Plates 349–53 and bound shibori, page 86) to make an overall design (Plates 349–53). The choice of an overall pattern indicates that these are not intended for formal wear but are closer to folk tradition. Traditionally *kanoko*, capped (*bōshi*, page 89), and tub-resist (*oke*, page 94) shibori have been preferred for formal wear, in part because of the greater time and skill required to execute a kimono by these techniques. *Maki-age* is rarely used since it gives less control of patterning, as well as the fact that it is a less difficult process to master, resulting in a less expensive product. By restricting their colors to only shades derived from purple root or madder root dyes, the Nanbu shibori craftsmen have successfully concentrated upon designs that reveal the cloth's sensitivity to the shaping and dyeing process. The three-dimensional effect of shibori is enhanced by the use of purple root or madder root dyes, not only because monochrome makes tonal variation more apparent, but also because the mordanting process before dyeing coarsens the fabric, resulting in larger folds and creases.

THREE GROUPS OF CRAFTSMEN

For convenience in discussing Japanese textile artists, they can be grouped loosely according to three approaches. First there are those who devote their lives to one pursuit. They were trained in the traditional apprentice system, spending years in absorbing skill and afterwards continuing to work within the established craft. These are the "anonymous" craftsmen, often producing only one type of object (such as lanterns or wooden tubs) or pursuing only one specialized skill (such as indigo dyeing) without striving for recognition, much less fame. Though such craftsmen are fast disappearing, still a surprising number remain, and very recently there has been an increase in the number of young people drawn to such crafts.

The second group consists of those who learned traditional methods but emerged as individual artist-craftsmen. These artists use their own designs and values to create works that are new while still partaking of the tradition out of which they came. Such people are the mainstay of the textile field in Japan, and many groups and societies have been formed by artist-craftsmen. The giant associations or societies, that encompass all the crafts, such as Kokuga-kai, Nitten, and Dentō-kōgei, hold regular exhibitions open to the public; and each association has a different focus and style. One group expects all works to be utilitarian forms—in textiles this means mainly kimono and obi; another group emphasizes panels, screens, and wall hangings—stressing the fine art aspect. Although young artists just starting their careers may enter and show works in the exhibitions of a number of associations, it is not acceptable to continue such eclecticism. An artist is expected to decide to exhibit with one association and eventually acquire membership when his or her work has been recognized. The structure of these organizations follows the verticality characteristic of Japanese society; that is, there is a hierarchy within each association. Some sharing of ideas may occur within an association, especially in the smaller ones, but there is very little dialogue between them. Younger craftsmen of all fields are beginning to chafe under this system, and their discontent may prove to be a catalyst for change in the future.

The third group of craftsmen, which is relatively small, consists of artists working independently and pursuing personal expression. These artists are not usually products of tradition and sometimes speak out against it. They communicate and associate more freely with one another than do those within the other groups. Their work tends to be more conceptual, and the statement made is ultimately more important than the technique used. In common with many craftsmen of North America and Europe, their approach is individualistic, direct, and often experimental.

## CONTEMPORARY JAPANESE ARTISTS

Very few of the Japanese shibori artists discussed here belong in the third category of craftsmen outlined above. Although textile art developed an alternative role to the utilitarian and decorative, most textile artists in Japan still work—and think—within the framework of textiles as a traditional craft. Even when making exhibition pieces— and personal artistic expressions— most use the kimono form. Just as the canvas was the accepted form of painting in the West until recently, so costume has been the accepted form of textile art in Japan. Whereas contemporary painting and sculpture contain currents that flow away from traditional formats, a comparable development has not occurred in the textile arts. In recent years the folding screen and panel (fabric stretched on a frame) have been used in making artistic statements. These represent a departure from the past, but are little more than a simple borrowing of the canvas format, which has been questioned by painting for years. This approach, which basically makes textile art a kind of painting, perhaps is seen as the most immediate way to confer fine art status on this medium. But shibori illuminates other possibilities that originate in the materials and processes themselves. For example, fabric can be folded or pleated or hung in layers; the shape of the finished object can vary greatly, adding another dimension to textile art and extending the range of possibilities in creation.

Experimentation with the way shibori is presented occurs in Hiroyuki Shindō's large *Song of Indigo* (*Aidama no Uta*, Plate 343), in which an openwork weaving is placed in front of shibori images. This combination of shibori with a textile medium not consisting of surface design is unusual in Japan, as is the size of the work. It is quite rare to see dyed textiles used in forms much larger than kimono or folding screens. Another artist who has challenged the conventions of Japanese textile art is Shioko Fukumoto. She, too, makes large works in fiber, and she uses shibori in a way that explicitly reveals the process itself, keeping the three-dimensional shapes that result from pleating. Fukumoto's work has won recognition in Japan, where she is known for her fresh, surprising approach combined with restraint and regard for textile processes. Traditionally the transitional stages of shibori resist have not been intentionally retained as an element of the finished surface design, with the exception of *kanoko* (see Plates 101–04). An analogy with Fukumoto's treatment of pleats in the shibori hanging *Raging Surf* (*Shiosai*; Plate 347) would be, in stencil dyeing, to allow the resist paste to remain as part of the dyed surface. To our knowledge, Japanese artists have not yet explored this interesting idea.

Today, within the surface design tradition, the spirit of experimentation inspired by a revival of interest in *tsujigahana* has flowed into contemporary mixed-media works by artists of different backgrounds. Historically, *tsujigahana* was not the first time (in Japan) that pictorial design was created through dyeing, but it serves as an example

Plate 343

Plates 101–04
Plate 347

of utilizing shibori, silver- and gold-leaf stencil, embroidery, and brush painting. In a similar spirit, some of the contemporary artists discussed here have used shibori with other media. Furusawa uses shibori, painting, and stencil dyeing; Nakagawa uses shibori, paste resist, and painted dye application; and Kubota uses shibori, direct dye application, and paste-resist variations. In Furusawa's *White Herons* kimono (Plate 336) the soft-edged bird forms could not have been made by stencil dyeing, but the many tiny white petal shapes did require the precision and detail possible only by the stencil and paste-resist process. No two birds are identical, since each one reflects the direct touch of the artist's hands in stitching and gathering the fabric and capping it. The artist clearly understands the inherent qualities of both shibori and stencil dyeing and has chosen each process as a necessary means of obtaining a desired effect.

In contrast to Furusawa, Kubota uses mixed media in a flamboyant style, enriching the surface through the crinkles and creases that result from shibori. Shibori as a immersion dyeing process would not by itself yield the many colors in Kubota's work, but direct dye application and paste-resist variations enable him to achieve this wide range. Besides these surface embellishment techniques, Kubota utilizes various kinds of fabric with different textures or with gold thread. This mixture of rich effects gives an ornate, jewellike quality to the object.

While these artists step outside the boundaries of convention as they experiment with mixed media, there are other artists who choose to stay within the medium of shibori and its heritage, and their works are outstandingly creative without seeking to redefine the craft. Motohiko Katano is an excellent example of this quintessentially Japanese artistic spirit. The motif he chooses may not be new—in fact he often uses traditional patterns such as the wave *(seikaiha)* or tortoiseshell *(kikkō)* that have long been part of the vocabulary of Japanese craftsmen in all media. It does not matter that at first glance the motif looks familiar, for a transformation has taken place, and one realizes the artist's deep understanding of design, process, and material that enables him to unify them in an original way. In doing so, Katano participates in that tradition of Japanese art that recognizes creative interpretation as valid artistic work. He has devised new ways to make traditional patterns—and the resulting surface design is no longer quite the same pattern. For example, his tortoiseshell pattern kimono (Plate 331) has an affinity with "white shadow" *(shirokage)* tortoiseshell pattern (Plate 66) in the crisp dark linear design floating against a light background, but Katano has allowed the dye to penetrate the center of the enclosed areas. To obtain this particular effect in shibori is a unique accomplishment. The tortoiseshell kimono shows Katano's sensitivity and ingenuity in other ways as well. Whereas usually this and other traditional motifs are used as allover pattern, for example, the white shadow grid kimono (Plate 303) and the white shadow hemp-leaf kimono (Plate 304), Katano's use of large checkered blocks of pattern to create the overall garment design can be linked with the design of Nō robes. Like the work of the other artists presented in this book, Katano's kimono can be appreciated in themselves without specialized knowledge of Japanese textile art. Nonetheless, because Japanese artists refer to a tradition, even when departing from it to some degree, the history of shibori as well as its relation to other processes provide a rich source of appreciation.

Most of the Japanese artists presented in the following pages create their own designs and perform most of the complicated processes involved in the realization of them. Even when other craftsmen are employed, the artist maintains close control over all phases of work. The artist tries to be responsible for the entire process and takes seriously the development of a personal style within the tradition. A high level of technical competence is taken for granted. As the discussion of shibori outside of Japan will show, lack of tradition allows freedom; but it is only by utilizing the power of concentrated experience that is found in a long tradition that refinement occurs.

Plate 336

Plate 331
Plate 66

## SHIBORI IN THE WEST

Until very recently there has been little information in the United States on ways of patterning fabric other than weaving. Because there is not a strong tradition of dyeing in the U.S., shibori has been welcomed as a new method, in contrast to the prevalent attitude in Japan, where it is only one among many ways to embellish fabric. Beyond its novelty, shibori offers the artist an amazing variety of processes and effects, unified by a basic concept that inspires open-ended exploration.

## FIBER ART IN THE UNITED STATES

The very words "fiber art," compared to such terms as "weaving and dyeing" or "textile arts," reflect a redefinition of activity in relation to material and the processes it suggests. These processes need not be traditional ones, as the term "textile arts" implies, nor are they confined to the two primary methods (weaving and dyeing) that have been used to make objects mainly of utilitarian value. This redefinition reflects the artists' search for material and broadness of expression.

"Fiber" includes paper and pulp, plastic strips, metal coils, rubber tubing, wire, grasses, or any other materials that share the "tissue- or thread-like quality" that defines fiber. The techniques of "fiber art" include the traditional ones of manipulating fiber and just about anything else that the artist desires.

In the sixties and early seventies there was a surge of interest in fiber art as a rediscovered medium, coinciding with the new awareness of broadened means of artistic expression and the corollary attention paid to artistic identity. Within weaving, off-loom techniques continued to be explored and the two-dimensional woven surface challenged, which led to sculptural works. Dyeing also seemed to offer greater freedom, and this contributed later to an eager interest in shibori. Infatuation with Asian culture in general found popular expression in such fads as tie-and-dye. Although this is a kind of shibori, it was not fully appreciated as a craft; tie-dyed clothing was made and enjoyed for its bright colors and artless forms. It seemed freer and more exotic than other dyed fabrics such as those patterned by batik or silk screen. The fine Indian tie-dye products were not imported or sought after; only the less expensive, quickly executed type reached the market, exerting considerable appeal.

In 1972 the Museum of Contemporary Crafts organized an exhibition, "Fabric Vibrations," of tie-and-dye and fold-and-dye wall hangings and environments. This was the first major exhibition of shibori in the United States. The foreword to the catalogue of the show written by Paul Smith, Director of the Museum, gives a vivid picture of what was happening at that time.

> Tie-dye, fold-dye, stitch-dye—all of these are ancient methods for decorating fabrics with colorful and intricate patterns. There processes of decoration have been used by very early cultures in almost every part of the world. During the last few years there has been a revival of this art, particularly among young people. There is fascination with the spontaneity and mystery of the process; the end result, vibrations of color and pattern, relate directly to the youth culture today—their music, their interest in the mystical, and their life style. Fabric Vibrations is a collection of outstanding examples of the art of tie-dye in a contemporary idiom by eight artists.

## CONTEMPORARY WESTERN ARTISTS

Not all of the artists included in this discussion are still involved in the medium of shibori, but their earlier works reveal some of the creative territory that has been explored. Among the first, pieces by Chungi Choo and Marian Clayden in the sixties and early seventies reflect the mood of the time. The use of vibrant colors in seemingly free, bold forms of dyed silk was accepted by the public as fresh and inspiring. Often these works were suspended in space, responding to the light and air and offering alternative ways to view and relate to them. Choo and Clayden are among the artists who worked in shibori as an extension of their involvement with tie-and-dye and fold-and-dye without direct contact with Japanese shibori. For others, exposure to Japanese shibori caused a significant shift in their development as artists, and often their use of shibori is unconventional. As artists who were directly inspired by Japanese shibori, Nancy Marchant and Yoshiko Wada adapted traditional aspects of shibori and Japanese aesthetics to their own concepts, making literal images with multilayered meanings. Another response to Japanese shibori can be seen in the works of Erica Runstrom and Ana Lisa Hedstrom, who have concentrated upon a single process and its multitude of effects. Runstrom creates painterly images utilizing the linear elements of *arashi* (pages 123ff); Hedstrom uses a rich vocabulary of patterns and colors obtained through *arashi* in garments and other forms.

A few of the artists have explored techniques related to the principle of shibori without conscious analysis of the process or without awareness of the affinity between their work and Japanese shibori. Both Pam Scheinman and Lois Hadfield instinctively employ a medium similar to folded shibori (*suji* shibori), Scheinman using simple hand pleating or rolling of the cloth and Hadfield capitalizing on the folds created by permanent machine pleating.

Despite these differences in background and approach, a unifying factor among these artists is their use of shibori for personalized artistic expression, whether in the embellishment of clothing or in other forms. In the West, shibori is practiced outside of a traditional context and is open to many interpretations.

This book has suggested a definition of shibori that essentially removes it from its traditional context by understanding it as the manipulation of any two-dimensional surface into a three-dimensional shape, which is then dyed to record the process itself. Some of the contemporary western artists presented here are moving in this direction, for example Scheinman and also Mary Rice, who juxtaposes the resisted image and the folds created in shibori. Rice has also worked with paper, exploring the three-dimensionality of the process as an evocative aspect of the finished piece. Many Americans have become interested in using garments for artistic expression, whether or not the clothing is intended to be worn. Both Clayden and Hedstrom have created distinctive garments in shibori and they consider these works as important as their art in other forms. This development brings clothing closer to the kind of recognition given kimono in Japan, and it is perhaps ironic that the trend occurs at the same time younger Japanese artists are avoiding the kimono as an art form.

If this discussion of shibori encourages and facilitates interaction between artists of Japan and the West, one of the purposes of this book will be accomplished. Each side has much to offer, and the art of shibori will benefit from their mutual influence.

Preservation of crafts cannot occur in a vacuum, but must have a place within society. Conditions have changed so drastically in Japan that the age-old craft of shibori cannot continue just as it was before; and a tradition cannot be regarded as alive if it exists only in isolated examples or an individual museum piece. Reassessment of the function of kimono, the role of craftsmen, the appropriateness of traditional designs and techniques in today's world— all this and more is required. Perhaps the freshness of the American perspective can contribute to the Japanese rejuvenation of the craft and stimulate fresh approaches to aesthetics and the objects made. At the same time, Americans can gain immensely from the vast skills, talents, and sense of materials of the Japanese, obtaining not only technical information but something of the spirit that has fostered excellence in shibori and other arts for a millennium and more.

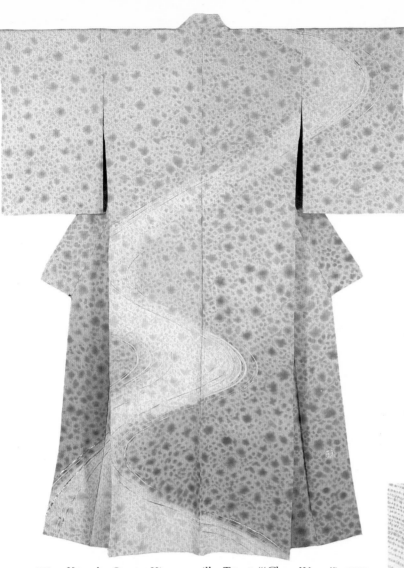

329.    Kensuke Ogura. Kimono, silk; *Tōryū* (*"Clear Water"*). 1962.

330.    Kensuke Ogura. Kimono, silk (detail);
*Shōrai* (*"Pine Wind"*). 1961.

331.   Motohiko Katano. Kimono, silk and natural indigo, *kikkō mon* (tortoiseshell pattern); untitled.

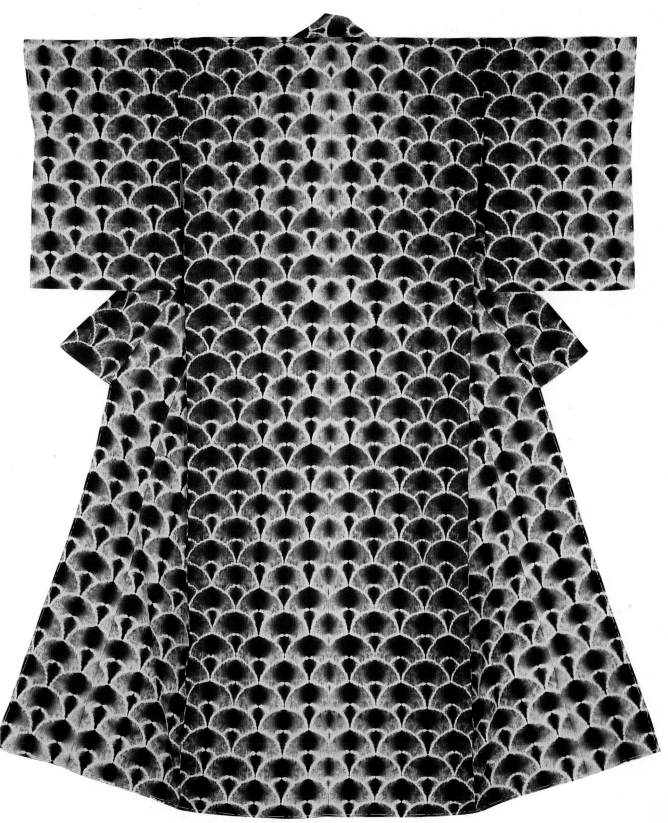

332.   Motohiko Katano. Kimono, silk and natural indigo, *seikaiha* (wave pattern); untitled.

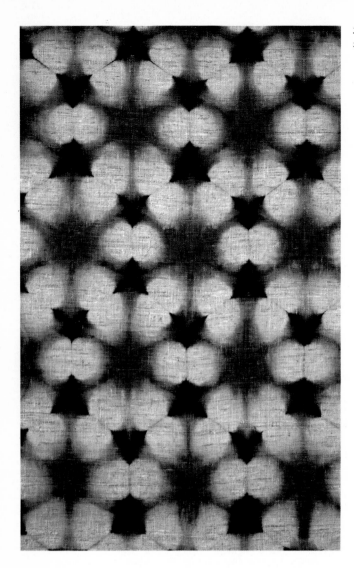

333.   Kaori Katano. Cotton broadcloth and natural indigo, *ren-zoku kikagaku monyō* (geometric floral pattern); untitled.

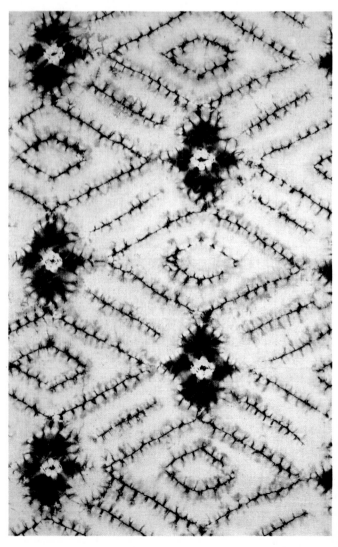

334.   Kaori Katano. Cotton broadcloth and natural indigo, *shiro-kage* ("white shadow") shibori; untitled.

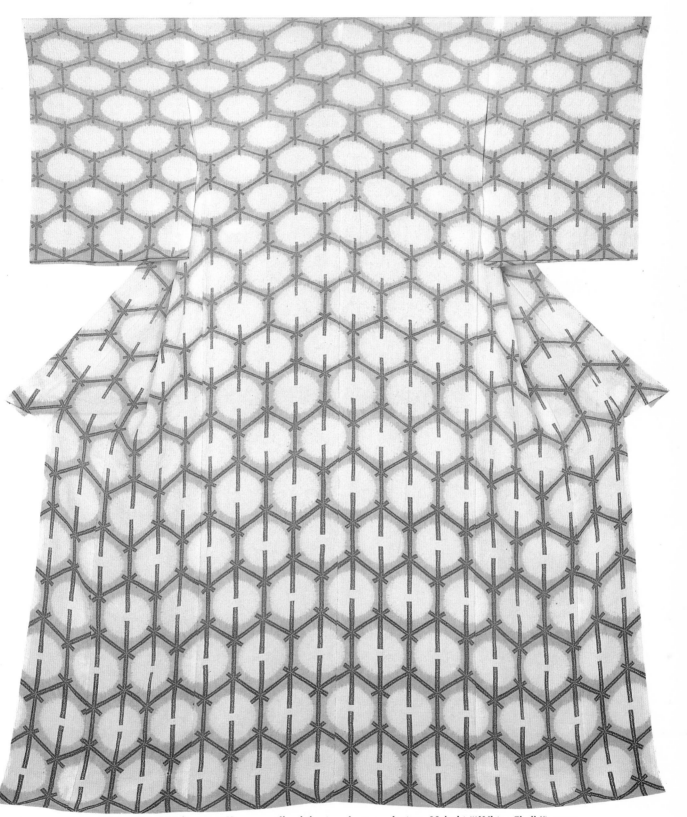

335. Shinji Nakagawa. Kimono, silk, shibori and *yūzen* dyeing; *Hakubi* ("*White Shells*"). 1977.

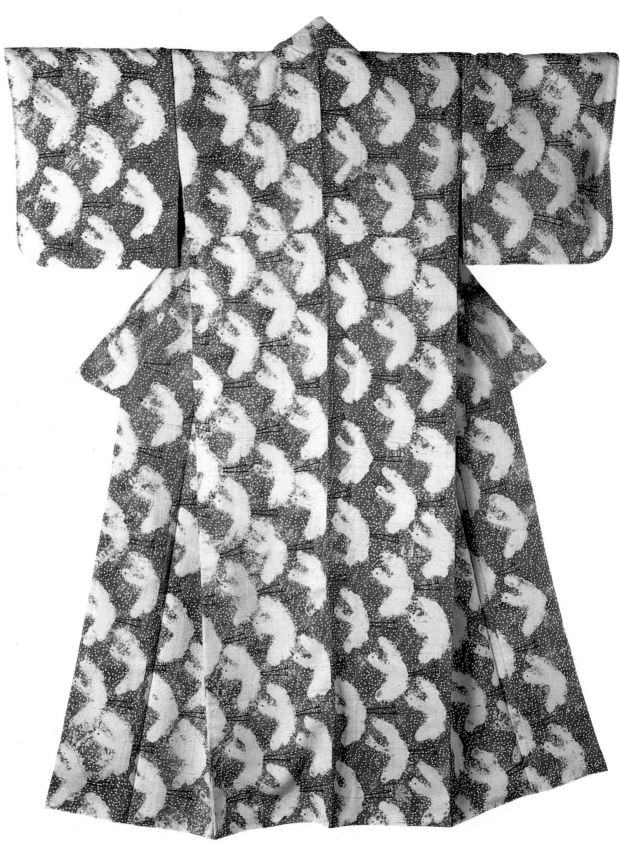

336.   Machiko Furusawa. Kimono, silk, shibori and stencil dyeing; *Shirosagi* ("*White Herons*").

337.   Machiko Furusawa. *Kosode*, silk; *Tsujigahana*.

338. Itchiku Kubota. *Kosode*, silk crepe; *Yōtō* ("*Wisteria*").

339.   Itchiku Kubota. Long-sleeved kimono (*furisode*), silk with gold thread (*kintōshi*); *Dō* ("*Movement*").

340. Shirō Ichinose. Kimono, silk (detail); *Ajisai* ("*Hydrangeas*"). 1978.

341. Shirō Ichinose. Kimono, silk; *Susuki* ("*Pampas Grass*"). 1977.

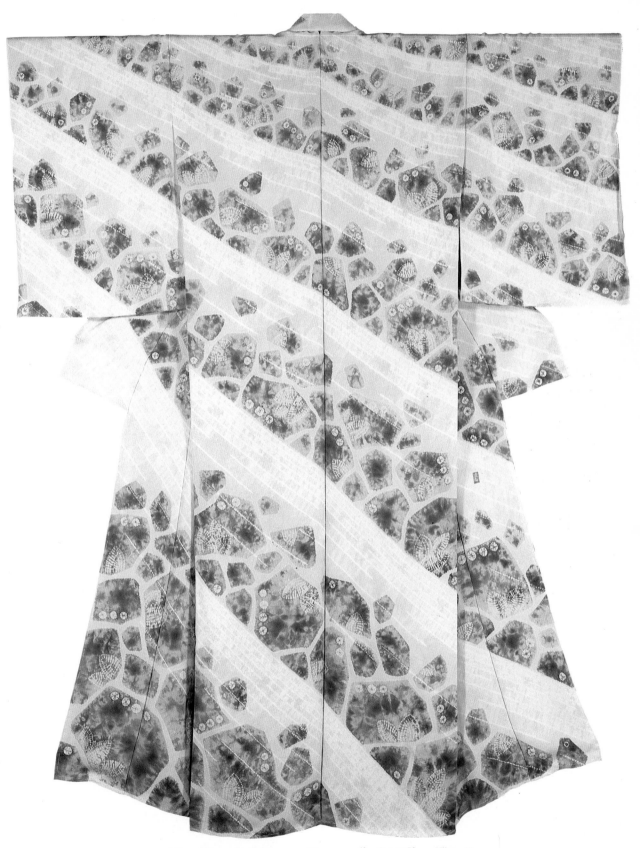

342.  Hirotoshi Fukumura. Kimono, silk; *Sei* ("*Clear Water*").

343. Hiroyuki Shindō. Tapestry, panel behind open weaving, natural indigo; *Aidama no Uta* ("*Song of Indigo*").

344. Hiroyuki Shindō. Hanging, hemp and natural indigo; untitled. 1982.

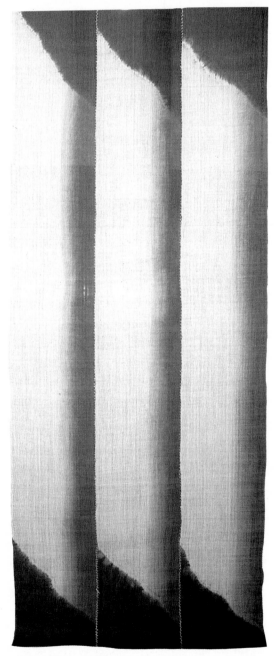

345. Hiroyuki Shindō. Hanging, hemp and natural indigo; untitled. 1982.

346. Shioko Fukumoto. Tapestry, cotton, natural indigo, logwood (detail); *Sazanami* ("*Ripples*"). 1978.

347. Shioko Fukumoto. Tapestry, cotton and natural indigo; *Shiosai* ("*Raging Surf*"). 1979.

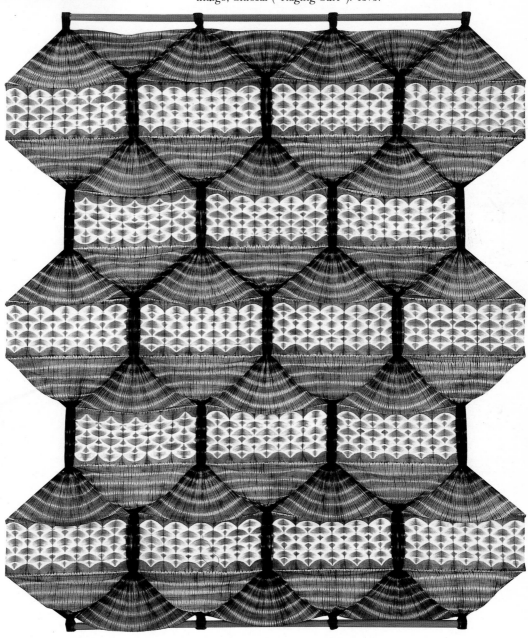

348.   Bolts of kimono material from Arimatsu, cotton and indigo.
Most of the types of shibori pictured are no longer made.

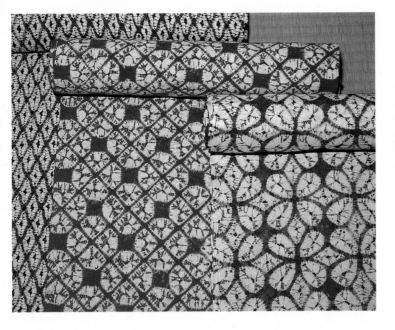

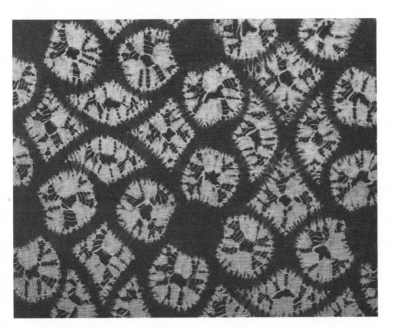

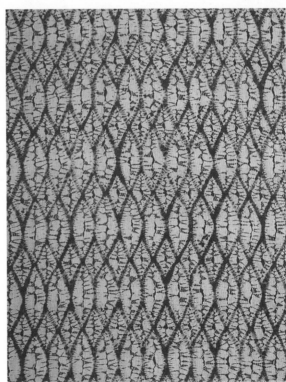

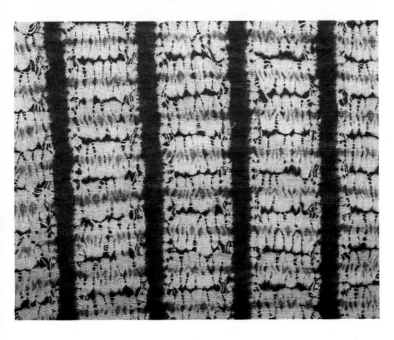

349–53. Kimono fabrics, Nanbu shibori, silk, purple-root and madder dyes.

239

354–57. Four underkimono (*jiban*), silk. These undergarments are often made of shibori fabrics and may display exuberant designs and startling color combinations. Plates 355 and 357 picture men's *jiban*, the latter showing a strange type of shibori.

240

358.   Marian Clayden. Dress. 1981.

359.   Marian Clayden. Jacket. 1981.

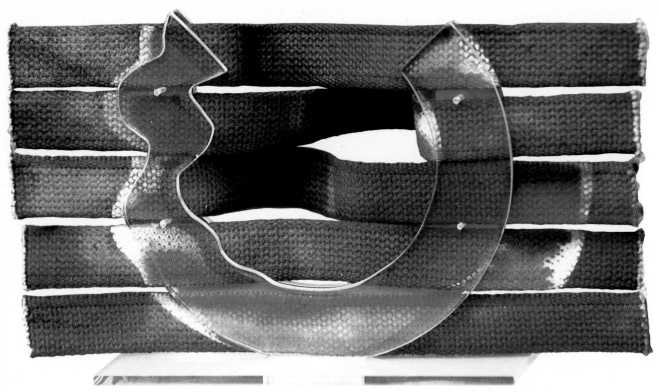

360. Marian Clayden. Plaited structure; *Dyer's Clamp*. 1980.

361. Marian Clayden. Hanging, silk; *Hand of Suttee*. 1980.

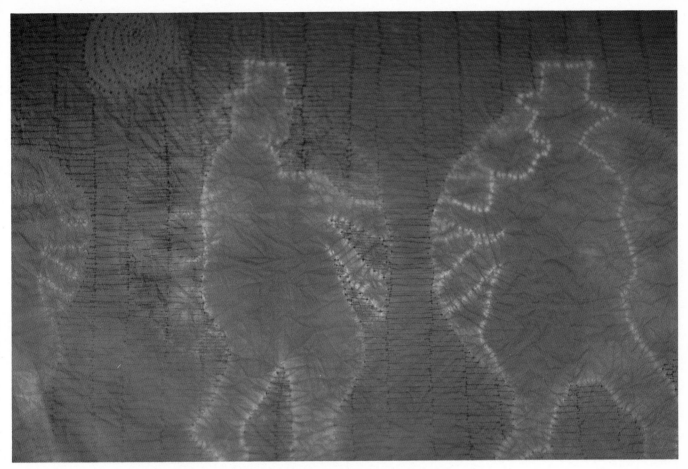

362.    Katherine Westphal. Hanging; *Hula Hoop Men*. 1975.

363.    Katherine Westphal. Garment, cotton and indigo with embroidery; *Santa Claus Hippari*. 1978.

243

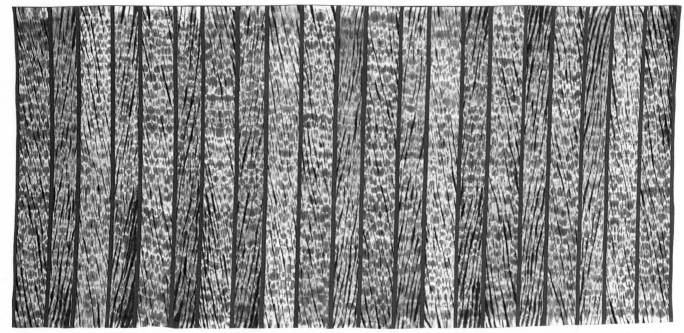

364. Katy Dolk. Hanging, pieced cotton; *Window*. 1979.

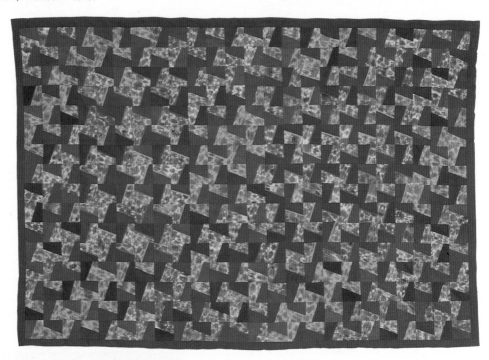

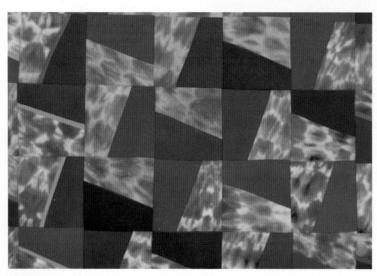

365, 366. Katy Dolk. Patchwork hanging and detail; *Serengetti II*. 1979.

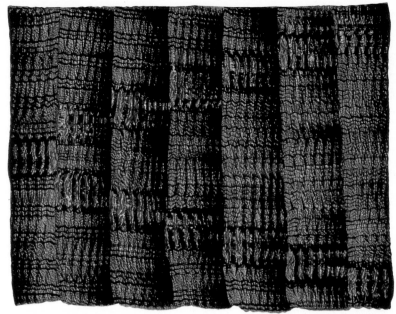

367. Pam Scheinman. Hanging; *Nightfall*. 1976.

368. Pam Scheinman. Work, rayon taffeta (detail); *Fandango*. 1977.

369, 370. Pam Scheinman. Work and detail, viscose rayon satin; *Lattice Fan*. 1981.

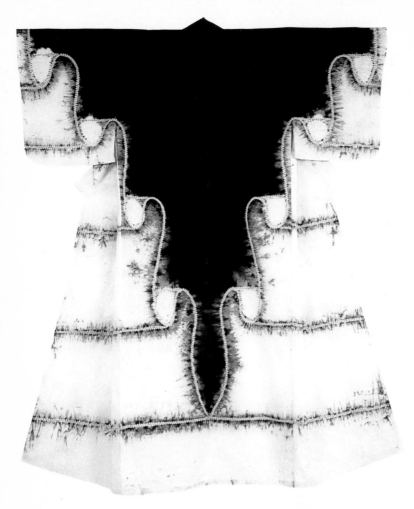

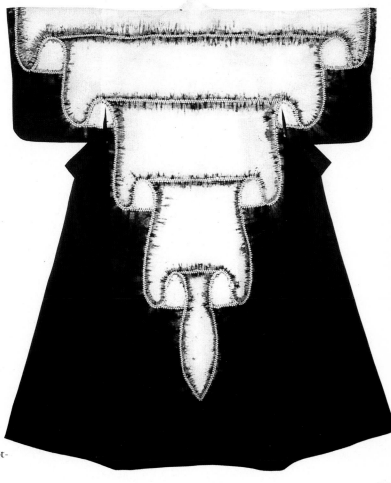

371–74.  Nancy Marchant. Series of four kimonos, cotton and indigo; untitled. 1977.

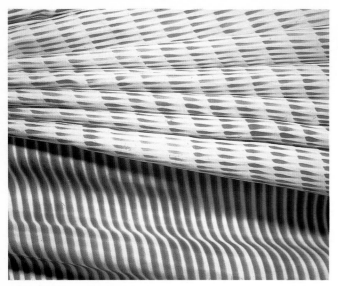

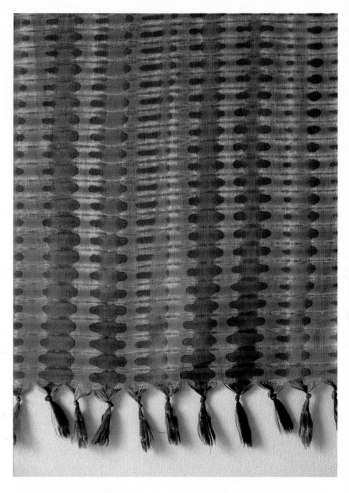

375–77. Lois Hadfield. Silk yardage (LOISILK).

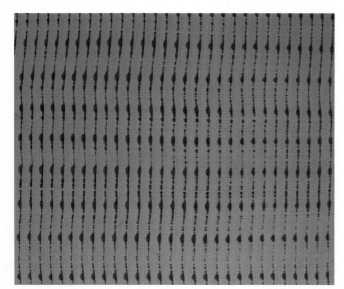

378. Lois Hadfield. Silk yardage (LOISILK); clothing by Ellen Hauptli.

248

379. Yoshiko Iwamoto Wada. Work, silk; *Valentine Jiban*. 1978.

380. Yoshiko Iwamoto Wada. Hanging, cotton, with painting; *Line Series #5.* 1982.

381. Susan Kristoferson. *Braided Ripples.* 1982.

382. Susan Kristoferson. Garment, pieced cotton; *Haori Vantage.* 1978.

383. Mary Kellogg Rice. Work, viscose rayon and indigo; untitled. 1980.

384. Mary Kellogg Rice. Work, silk and indigo; untitled. 1979.

385. Mary Kellogg Rice. Work, Japanese hand-laid paper (*washi*) and indigo; untitled. 1979.

386.   Ana Lisa Hedstrom. Small work, silk; *Miniature Piece*. 1978.

387.   Ana Lisa Hedstrom. Hanging, silk; *Arrow Hanging*. 1979.

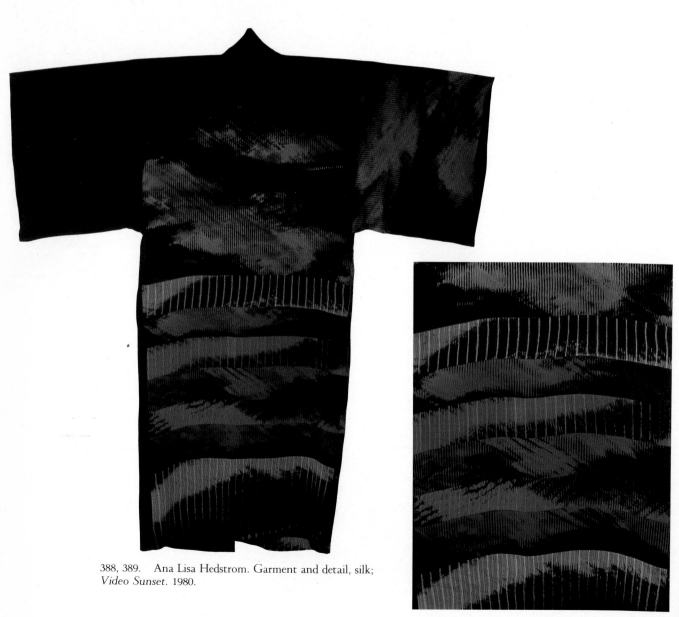

388, 389.   Ana Lisa Hedstrom. Garment and detail, silk; *Video Sunset*. 1980.

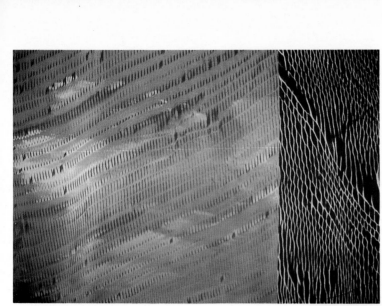

390. Ana Lisa Hedstrom. Silk fabric (detail).

391. Ana Lisa Hedstrom. Silk fabric (detail).

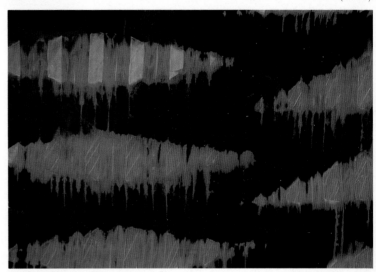

392. Ana Lisa Hedstrom. Garment, silk; *Neon Sunset*. 1981.

393, 394.   Erica Runstrom. *Orange Stripe* and detail. 1978.

395, 396.   Erica Runstrom. Hanging and detail, cotton; *Orange and Green Screen*. 1979.

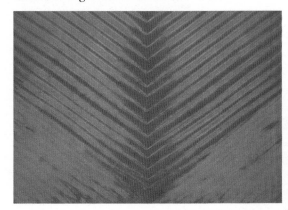

397. Erica Runstrom. *Cube Drawing* (detail). 1979.

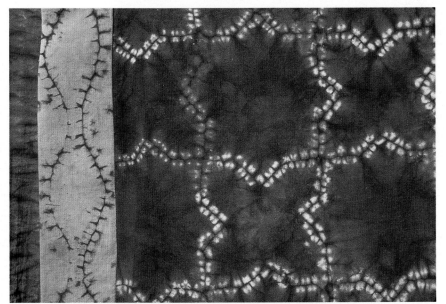

398. Virginia Davis. Garment (detail), cotton and indigo; *Orinui Jacket*. 1977.

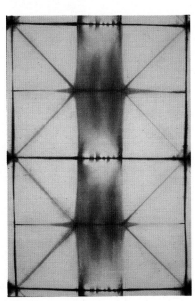

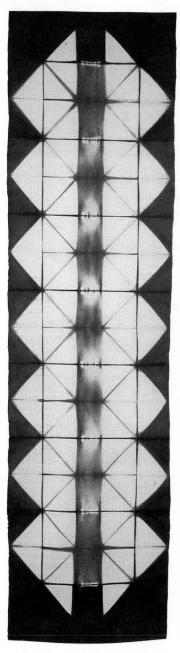

399, 400. Barbara Goldberg. Hanging and detail, cotton and indigo; untitled. 1982.

401.   Daniel Graffin. Work, cotton; *Tenet.* 1978.

402.   Daniel Graffin. Work, cotton and indigo; *Vingt-quatre Carré Approximatifs.* 1978.

# The Artists

KENSUKE OGURA (Plates 329, 330)

Kensuke Ogura has been working as a dyer for nearly seventy years, and his sustained fascination with the craft has kept him young and innovative. He began working as a merchant's helper when very young, but, because of his love for painting, later began to work in *yūzen* (see Glossary). His fluid brushwork attracted the attention of the Ogura family of *yūzen* dyers and he was adopted by them. While he worked developing his craft in the family business in Kyoto he came into contact with shibori, and his growing interest in the techniques led him to learn the craft directly from shibori artisans.

By then he was in his forties. His career benefited from the help of two important people: Toshijirō Inagaki, a stencil dyer who was at that time head of the design department for Matsuzakaya Department Store, and Someto Akashi, the noted textile scholar. They both encouraged Ogura to continue his work in shibori and suggested that he study the old surviving *tsujigahana* textiles. Inagaki gave Ogura the opportunity to see actual examples from the Matsuzakaya collection, and for ten years he copied these elegant textiles. During this time, Matsuzakaya asked him to make special kimono adapted from the original *tsujigahana* garments.

Ogura's attempt to capture the essence of *tsujigahana* was not limited to technique and style alone. He went beyond copying designs and a superficial grasp of technique and boldly enhanced his approach to shibori with the experimental quality evident in old *tsujigahana* textiles. He works with a wide repertory of shibori techniques, and his use of them is always innovative, reflecting sensitivity toward the process and respect for the hand of the artisan.

In the work pictured in Plate 329, Ogura uses *miura* shibori (see page 70) exclusively with a classic motif of a curving stream. The entire kimono is dappled; this extensive use of *yatara miura* (page 149) on silk kimono is very unusual since it is a technique generally chosen for casual wear such as cotton kimono or for silk underkimono. The misty atmosphere of Ogura's kimono is created by the mixture of large and small *yatara miura* units, varying in shades and tones of gray—warm, cool, dark, light. Added touches of gold embroidery further highlight the stream, as if the flowing water is catching the rays of the afternoon sun. After contemplating the overall effect a few moments, one may sense a shift in impression, from a close-up view of water rippling over pebbles to a distant view of a river wrapped in mist, floating in light. Ogura's restraint in choice of hue and form seems strikingly contemporary.

Ogura again uses a bold motif in *Pine Wind* (*Shōrai*; Plate 330). The pine trees are executed in stitched-shibori (page 73), while the white areas of the background are capped and reserved by *bōshi* shibori (pages 88ff). Thickened dye was applied by brush to the stitched and gathered folds of fabric (*ori-nui*; page 76), resulting in thin lines on the white background. These lines, which move across the kimono, give the feeling of wind blowing through trees, and the fluidity of these soft lines contrasting with the stark trees creates a pleasing tension. In their resemblance to dry brushstrokes, they add to the vigorous calligraphic image.

MOTOHIKO KATANO (Plates 331, 332)

The achievement of Motohiko Katano in the medium of shibori is remarkable because only in his late fifties was he persuaded by Sōetsu Yanagi to change his medium from that of wax resist *(roketsu)* to shibori. Yanagi was concerned with the disappearance of this traditional craft from the Arimatsu–Narumi area, near which Katano lived. He introduced Katano to Kanjirō Kawai the potter and Keisuke Serizawa the stencil dyer, two craftsmen of the *mingei* persuasion who impressed and greatly influenced him. Katano was inspired especially by the philosophy of Kawai and his almost religious approach to creative work. Kawai had told Katano to burn the old shibori and use the ashes to enrich the field where the seeds of the new shibori would germinate.

Aware of his teachers' expectations and accepting his mission, Katano devoted all of his efforts to creating his own style. During this long and difficult process, he ingeniously transformed many of the traditional techniques of shibori and developed a personal vocabulary to articulate his ideas and feelings through cloth and dye.

Through a new combination of two shibori techniques, pleating and stitching, Katano created his own distinctive, highly individual style (see pages 113–15). The narrow fabric is pleated lengthwise, and geometric designs are stitched through the layers of cloth. After the cloth is dyed and opened up, continuous symmetrical patterns appear; this is repetition produced by the folding of the cloth. The stitching plays a determining role by exerting pressure, which results in white lines or areas and gradations of color. In referring to this distinctive technique here, it is called Katano shibori in recognition of its inventor.

The disappearance of natural indigo dyeworks from Katano's area, the Nagoya region, eventually forced him to set up his own indigo dye bath. He worked very hard to understand the secrets of natural indigo. This natural dye requires a full commitment from the craftsman. There are many variables involved, and traditionally the quantities of ingredients, methods of handling them, assessing development of the dye, temperature to be maintained, and even the season chosen for setting up the dye vat have been highly personal matters. But the results of this challenge were rewarding for Katano. By working with his hands in his own dye bath, he had the freedom to control the seepage of the dye and the depth of its color.

Katano's success in obtaining sensitive gradations of indigo tones is the result of his creative combining of shibori and indigo dyeing techniques. For example, in the wave pattern *(seikaiha)* kimono (Plate 332), the rich tonal variation is produced by careful control of dye penetration and oxidation.

The tortoiseshell *(kikkō-mon)* kimono (Plate 331) reveals Katano's further exploration of the possibilities of pleating and stitching, resulting in a complex pattern that utilizes both crisp delineation and soft-edged forms. Probably the fabric was folded into triangular shapes as in *sekka* shibori (page 116) and stitched along one edge through all the layers, thereby creating the sharp, dark lines of the hexagons. The logic of the progression from the basic compressed triangular unit that yields the hexagonal shapes to the larger design units that combine with the white blocks in the overall pattern flows from Katano's deep understanding and his mastery of the entire process.

KAORI KATANO (Plates 333, 334)

Kaori Katano worked with her father, Motohiko Katano, shibori artist and indigo dyer, assisting him with sewing, binding, and dyeing. Since his death, she has carried out his mission to foster the growth of a revitalized craft.

She works by herself at every stage of the shibori process, creating the design, sewing, binding, and dyeing, as well as caring for the natural indigo bath. Her strength lies in the technique of Katano shibori and in her control of the dye, as is apparent in the series of works on broadcloth of allover geometric patterns. Kaori Katano's superb mastery of her craft—her unerring knowledge of the amount of pressure applied to the cloth by the stitches, and of the seepage and degree of oxidation of the dye—is the result of long experience and lessons learned from a craftsman who demanded much from himself and from his daughter. Her patient dedication and sensitive touch can create the softest edges and the most marvelous range of blues, from the pale tone of winter ice to the dark sky of a summer night.

The floral pattern in Plate 333 is part of the geometric pattern series. Katano's magic works perfectly with the heavy, soft, handwoven cotton broadcloth, whose supple texture allows the dyer to manipulate it easily. The indigo forms evolve in their own space, seemingly three-dimensional images emerging from the dark background.

In the white shadow shibori (shirokage; Plate 334), not only does Katano demonstrate artful mastery of one of the most difficult processes in shibori, but she also displays a sense of charming yet austere elegance. The combination of blue motifs with floral centers and concentric, blue-on-white linear diamonds creates a harmonic study in contrasts and expands the design possibilities of this shibori type.

While there is a naiveté in Kaori Katano's approach to design, this contrasts markedly with her technical mastery, and perhaps it is her very naiveté that allows such a pure understanding of, and involvement with, the processes of shibori. Like her father, she possesses a special quality of the supreme Japanese craftsman, giving herself to the creative work with infinite respect for materials and techniques. Without intellectualizing or emphasizing their identity as artists, father and daughter have set a standard of excellence in the traditional practice of shibori.

## SHINJI NAKAGAWA (Plate 335)

Shinji Nakagawa is a *yūzen* dyer (see Glossary) whose family has been working in the craft of dyeing fabric for three generations. He and his brother are unusually versatile; their skills include designing, stencil cutting, application of paste through stencils, *yūzen*, wax resist, and dyeing. These are often specialized professions in which a craftsman devotes a lifetime to one skill. Besides his professional work in *yūzen*, in 1975 Nakagawa started to incorporate shibori in his work for one of the annual national exhibitions. Living in Nagoya close to the folk shibori centers of Arimatsu and Narumi, Nakagawa had long been interested in these techniques, and a revival of interest in *tsujigahana* brought to his attention the challenge of these masterpieces that utilized shibori in harmony with other media.

In the *White Shell* (*Hakubi*; Plate 335) kimono, allover geometric patterns are executed through the combination of *yūzen* and shibori. The white capped circles float through fine, meticulously rendered *yūzen* patterns. The softness of these white shibori forms relieves the tension of the linear elements done in *yūzen*.

## MACHIKO FURUSAWA (Plates 336, 337)

Machiko Furusawa was originally interested in becoming a painter. After studying painting for about five years she realized that she felt a stronger affinity with dyeing and changed her medium to paste-resist stencil dyeing *(katazome)* and hand-painting. Later she learned shibori as well.

Most artist-dyers in Japan work within the established system of traditional crafts where many specialized craftsmen perform such tasks as making paste, dyeing ground color, cutting stencils, and sewing and binding. However, unlike many such artists, Furusawa prefers to cut her own stencils, prepare paste from flour, and carry out all the processes of shibori by herself. She values direct contact with materials at every step of the way. In each piece there is always an element of surprise, whether it is an uncommon combination of techniques, unusual motifs, or lines and shapes that carry a naive, childlike strength. The bleeding of dyes and the blurring of shapes are elements in Furusawa's work, and its simple beauty is inspiring and refreshing. Whereas in Japan perfection of a single skill is conventional, Furusawa seeks to expand her art by embracing new ideas.

When Furusawa was studying stencil dyeing she became especially fond of *bingata*, the colorful paste-resist stencil dyeing of Okinawa, and mastered various methods unique to the craft, including layering of colors and images with several stencils. Her interest in multiple techniques and images is always evident in her work; she usually chooses to apply other techniques over a stenciled pattern—sometimes shibori is used, individual color areas are hand-dyed by brush, and linear patterns are hand-painted. One of many such wonderful mixed-media pieces is *White Herons* (*Shirosagi*; Plate 336). Numerous white petal shapes were stencil dyed, then almost abstract shapes of birds were sewn and capped (*bōshi* shibori; page 88) and touches of painting were added to convey the features. The simple shapes of the herons with soft edges characteristic of stitched forms give movement and volume to each bird and make a vivid contrast with the fine, sharp stencil pattern of the ground.

Some shibori work is done without a cartoon to be transferred to the cloth to guide the stitching of the design, as in *Tsujigahana* (Plate 337). Basically Furusawa treats the fabric as white canvas. The openness of her approach allows images to be redefined and reborn as a frolic of colors and patterns. In her reproduction of historical *tsujigahana*, Furusawa tried to create not an imitation or duplication of *tsujigahana* style but rather the spirit of the elusive beauty of dyed textiles of this era. She succeeded in conveying the quality so vital to *tsujigahana*—spontaneity supported by laborious and careful craftsmanship. One of the typical techniques seen in *tsujigahana* textiles, hand painting in sumi ink, was also applied here, but the style is Furusawa's own.

### ITCHIKU KUBOTA (Plates 338, 339)

Itchiku Kubota started working for a *yūzen* dyer as an apprentice when he was fourteen years old. He was granted early independence from his master at the exceptionally young age of nineteen. Besides working as a *yūzen* dyer, he found time to begin studying painting, went to exhibitions and museums, and worked on his own. When he encountered *tsujigahana* fragments in a museum he was mesmerized by their beauty.

The war interrupted Kubota's career, and he was unable to return to *yūzen* dyeing until 1951, after six years as a prisoner of war in Russia. In 1959 he began to research and experiment with ways to re-create the beauty of *tsujigahana*. Inspired by classic examples, he first tried to use shibori techniques, which seemed to him the way the patterns in these textiles had been made. Using these seemingly obvious techniques led to failure, and only after long trial and error did Kubota reach the unique technical solutions that could help him achieve the goal he pursued.

In 1977 he had his first solo show of his own style of *tsujigahana* textiles, which he calls "Itchiku Tsujigahana." Since then he has continued to explore his new-found art, wishing to establish his own style rather than reproduce the classic objects he reveres. His major pieces are kimono, which are filled with floral and other traditional motifs delineated by the puckers created by stitching. The soft puckered shapes are filled with and float against richly muted colors. Some of the details have been done in fine sumi ink painting.

What Kubota has achieved with dyes is remarkable. In some cases he applies the dye by brush to each shape before stitching is done; in other cases the dye is applied by brush after shapes and lines have been stitched and drawn up tightly. The combination of shibori and direct application of dye create halos around shapes, and the images seem to glow and move gently through space, as in the *Wisteria kosode* (*Yōtō*; Plate 338). For some pieces Kubota uses heavy silk crepe *(chirimen)*, while for others he chooses silk with gold threads woven in *(kintōshi)*. Both are enhanced by the crinkles that remain from stitching. The division of the *Wisteria kosode* into three large design areas follows Japanese costume tradition. Here the boundaries are delineated by the hard edges of a classic design motif often found in *tsujigahana*, the "pine-bark lozenge" *(matsukawa-*

bishi). Kubota made this *kosode* to be worn by a Japanese dancer, along with a narrow obi and under-*kosode*, which he also dyed. The garment is similar to sixteenth century kimono, with long shallow sleeves. The design of the *kosode* is planned to accommodate a narrow obi rather than the wide sash worn with modern kimono.

One of Kubota's most ambitious works is the *Sunset (Rakuyō)* series of five kimono in which he conveys changing atmosphere and dramatic shifts in color. The central piece in this series, suggesting the splendor of sunset with splashes of red and gold, is the long-sleeved kimono called *Movement (Dō;* Plate 339). The *kintōshi* shows a full range of response to light—areas free from binding positively shine, whereas puckered areas shimmer softly, and the gold almost totally disappears in the expanse of white-resisted shapes across the shoulders. Viewed together, the five kimono form a sequence of color and light that records a phenomenon in time, from evening prelude through sunset to twilight. Kubota goes beyond the realm of costume embellishment in his use of traditional garments in a series similar to a group of paintings or poems.

## SHIRŌ ICHINOSE and HIROTOSHI FUKUMURA (Plates 340–42)

These two young dyers, who work mainly in shibori, have in common the experience of serving apprenticeships in the studio of Kensuke Ogura. Hirotoshi Fukumura served as an apprentice for ten years. During the first three years he learned *yūzen* and thereafter began working in shibori as well. Since 1973 he has been an independent dyer in Kyoto and has shown shibori pieces in various exhibitions.

The imagery of *Clear Stream (Seiryū;* Plate 342) seems to refer to stones at the bottom of a clear-running river. Judging from the effects Fukumura has achieved, his procedure was probably something like first stitching the diagonal parallel lines (*hira-nui;* page 74), then stitching the outlines of the stones, and adding *maki-age* (page 86) circles and *miru/karamatsu* (pages 78–79) leaf shapes within the stones. The single lines were drawn up, and the entire garment was dyed in pale gray; then the outlines of stones were drawn up, and blue was applied by brush to each puckered area. The mottled blue gives texture to the stones and suggests the shimmering water through which they are seen. Using a restricted number of design elements, Fukumura successfully integrates them with shibori methods.

Shirō Ichinose begins with the particular effects of shibori in mind, and his sensitivity toward technique flows into the image he plans. In the *Hydrangeas* kimono (*Ajisai;* Plate 340), the individual petals have been stitched before dyeing, so their outlines remain white, separating the petals within each cluster and setting off the flowers from the leaves. In the lower area of the kimono the combination of white outlines and rich blue color gives these blossoms, thrusting forward, volume and texture. *Bōshi* shibori (pages 88ff) was used to reserve the ground area, giving the impression that the shrub is seen against bright light, yet the network of foliage with its subtle tonal changes is not a flat silhouette. Ichinose's use of the soft edges of stitched forms, variegated gray and blue both within individual shapes and in the overall design, white open spaces, and apparent shifts in point-of-view contribute to the illusion of space and volume.

Ichinose again chose not to use any hand painting in the *Pampas Grass* kimono (*Susuki;* Plate 341), in which the fluffy curving stalks of pampas grass are superbly depicted by *ori-nui* (page 76). *Susuki* is one of the seven autumn grasses of Japan, well known in popular culture as well as in classic literature and art; thus this kimono has immediate seasonal associations, evoking an autumn field where pampas grass sways and bends in the wind. It is one of Ichinose's gifts to be able to match extremely well an object or phenomenon in nature with a specific shibori method. For example, *ori-nui* shibori is especially well suited to portray pampas grass. In another kimono (*Rose of Sharon; Mukuge*), the soft edges and traces of crinkling remind one of the exact texture of flower petals. Ichinose's keen response to nature and his unforced interpretation of shibori are unified in works that never seem labored and never lose their vital connection with life.

### HIROYUKI SHINDŌ (Plates 343–45)

Hiroyuki Shindō is an artist with the strong conviction that life itself is an integral part of the creative process. This belief is evident not only in the works he has produced but also in his approach to the process of dyeing with natural indigo, a skill that demands enormous care and expertise. Shindō is one of the few dyers carrying on the classic natural indigo tradition, which is now almost lost in Japan.

Although he was educated in the fine arts and went on to teach at a college, Shindō chose to leave his position in favor of pursuing his creative work. In his early twenties Shindō became fascinated by the beauty of indigo blues and the mysteries of the natural dye, which seemed to have a life of its own. After repeated attempts to understand the secrets of the dye, his persistence was rewarded when he met Motohiko Katano, the indigo dyer and shibori artist, who shared his knowledge and opened Shindō's eyes to the significance of nature in understanding and establishing rapport with indigo.

Shindō's expertise and his dedication to producing works using natural dyes have been realized in a series of contemporary tapestries and shibori hangings in which only natural materials—silk, cotton, linen, and vegetable dyes—have been used. But however traditional the source of his materials, his resultant works are stunningly modern.

Shindō's tapestry *Song of Indigo* (*Aidama no Uta*; Plate 343) is a large panel of stitched and capped cloudlike shapes mounted behind an open weaving. There is an effective harmony between the two planes, achieved by the use of floating warp threads that give the weaving the transparency to reveal the soft edges of the cloud shapes on the panel behind it. The juxtaposition of these elements with the woven indigo circles, shaded for volume, adds further depth to the overall effect.

The more recent work pictured in Plate 344 is a large stitched shibori hanging dyed on old hemp cloth. The gradations of blue on three lengths of kimono cloth required successive dipping. The tonal continuum reveals Shindō's outstanding control of indigo dyeing. He has made use of simple shapes, reversed and staggered. Dark and light meet along the curving line where the fabric was stitched and capped. The edges of the fabric strips provide hard edges running vertically through the piece, and the staggered arrangement of the three strips makes adjacent areas affect each other with varying impact. The gradations seem to suggest space and shadow, next to the flat, dark areas, which seem solid.

Another piece done in a similar manner is seen in Plate 345. The bold white areas are created by stitching and capping. Each of the three strips of cloth was dipped repeatedly along one selvage to create a shadowlike stripe becoming lighter toward the top. This simple element adds volume to each unit, giving the impression of a white surface that curves away, like a roll of paper. Shindō's pieces are most effective when suspended in open space, where they can be viewed interacting with light and air.

In Japan an artist with Shindō's fidelity to natural materials is expected to work with traditional design motifs and forms. Rarely does a craftsman of Shindō's technical ability choose to work in nontraditional ways. Perhaps his images seem recognizably modern in western terms rather than "very Japanese," but in fact Shindō expresses a sensibility that is true to contemporary Japan, with its blend of old and new.

### SHIOKO FUKUMOTO (Plates 346, 347)

The work of Shioko Fukumoto has recently appeared in the major crafts competitions and exhibitions in Japan. She has received recognition for offering a fresh view of traditional crafts techniques and using them in a totally contemporary, innovative manner. She was originally a painter and sculptor who worked on textural wall pieces. She belonged to an avant-garde art group, which was less interested in products than in the interaction between material and process, and this interest has been consistently displayed in Fukumoto's work in shibori. The need to use shibori for her own work stemmed from her recognition of the pliable quality of fabric and the beauty of the three-dimensional forms given to the fabric during the shibori process. Fukumoto also realized that indigo is the most effective dye to use for resist-dyeing, since it produces the widest range and most subtle shades of blue. These qualities create a striking three-dimensional effect on the surface of the fabric. Using these essential characteristics of material and process, Fukumoto creates works that are at once subtle and bold.

In her earlier work (Plate 346) she used units of narrow fabric, exploring the thin vertical stripes and light horizontal lines inherent in the *nui yōrō* process (see page 106). Sections of the cloth are left in dark folds from the stitch-pleating and dyeing. Other sections are opened to reveal patterns of light and dark indigo that reflect the tension exerted on the fabric while it was being dyed. The combination of compressed and open units governs the distortion of horizontal lines, giving movement and volume to the multifaceted whole.

In a more recent work (Plate 347), Fukumoto again expressively uses kimono cloth of the standard (36 cm/14 in) width. The units of fabric have been folded vertically in accordion pleats using the horizontal stitches of *nui yōrō*, and deeper vertical folds have also been made, stitched to create the rhythmical geometric and linear designs characteristic of Katano shibori. Because of the three-dimensional form of the fabric in the earlier stages of the process, it naturally maintains its pleated shape. Fukumoto adds structural support to the material to connect several vertical units of fabric, and this support at the same time shapes the plane of the fabric. Thus the basic forms of the fabric as it has been manipulated are retained in the closed, partially open, and fully open units that fit together in the finished piece. She preserves the excitement of going through the process of shibori, from the bundled forms concealing a design to the secrets revealed when the cloth is unfolded. She successfully harmonizes the vertical elements—the original pleats, the dyed stripes on the surface, and the shadows cast by the pleats—with the horizontal elements of the bold surface pattern, or, in her earlier work, with the subtle traces of the parallel stitches characteristic of *nui yōrō*. Fukumoto's pieces provide an interesting synchronization of process and result.

## MARIAN CLAYDEN (Plates 358–61)

Originally a painter, Marian Clayden was led by her need for more textural surface to create collages using fabric and paper. She was attracted by the enormous tactile satisfaction to be experienced in the fiber medium. This pleasure combined with the process of dyeing inspired Clayden to continue her pursuit of new possibilities. Her determination to find what she called "new visual electricity" drew her to the techniques of resist dyeing—binding, clamping, and using discharge to create designs. Intrigued by the way in which the familiar two-dimensional surface could be broken up, she began to work in three dimensions, using various nonloom techniques to create new forms and textures but keeping the process of manipulation and the structure of each piece very simple. Her works include three-dimensional braided and plaited structures such as *Dyer's Clamp* (Plate 360) as well as two-dimensional fabric hangings.

In her early work on fabric Clayden used a stitch-binding technique. By tying and dyeing carefully selected areas of material, she created irregular patterns, which reflect the folding of fabric, dyeing, and discharging. Linear and aerial images neither float nor define but vibrantly penetrate the surface of silk in colors that are audacious and extravagant. The variations in tone and hue resulting from the stitching, binding, and dip-dyeing create an illusion—the planes seem to oscillate with resonance, echoes of colors underlying colors. Clayden's powerful phrase "visual electricity" is a perfect description of the neonlike appearance of the brilliant edges of dyed and discharged colors that pulse across the surface of the work. When spontaneity and love of the unexpected grip her, there is danger of losing a certain degree of control. But Clayden is "prepared to destroy beauty in order to take the final statement further," and it is this paradox that characterizes her involvement with process and becomes her strength.

In Clayden's later work such as *Hand of Suttee* (Plate 361) and *Dyer's Clamp* (Plate 360), clamping is the preferred technique; and an attempt to blend control and spontaneity in her dyeing has become increasingly apparent. In the designs produced by clamping, the bolder images are defined by the shapes of the boards that hold the cloth between them in either single or multiple layers. Areas on which pressure is exerted are reserved, and thus the clamped shapes are revealed and the colors beneath are defined. Compared to her earlier work, the use of color is relatively subdued in the overall tone of *Hand of Suttee*, but the brilliantly illuminated focal points contrast sharply with the background, giving an illusion of space filled with ethereal color. The red captured by clamp resist within the hand imparts a feeling of fire and a desperate grasping at life.

In the past few years Clayden has also used shibori to create a line of clothing. She devotes part of the year to developing these garments and part of the year to working on her "nonfunctional" art. Like a number of other artists, she finds challenge in making wearable art. In the coat of Plate 359, she has created a dramatic composition in monotone. The sleeves were clamped and dyed in grays to match the collar and the bodice. The images and mottled ground on the sleeves add fluidity to the garment and at the same time make a strong visual statement. Although Clayden has become more interested in designing garments and accessories, she acknowledges that what she loves is the process of dyeing and the colors made possible by it.

KATHERINE WESTPHAL (Plates 362, 363)

Looking at Katherine Westphal's work is like reading the diary of someone who is constantly involved with creative work and loves it. She uses or combines materials, media, and images with an enthusiasm and spontaneity that have inspired other artists.

Counting her childhood as the beginning of her creative career, she has devoted more than sixty years to the exploration of the visual arts. At university Westphal majored in fine arts and later became an industrial textile designer. Her designs for commercial fabrics were eclectic—variously inspired by magazines, advertisements, patterns from nature, and from classical and modern textiles. This work naturally led to an interest in and involvement with specific processes of fabric printing and dyeing. The more she studied techniques, the more convinced she became that direct interaction with processes and materials were much more important than the end product.

Among the techniques Westphal has explored are embroidery, wax resist, shibori, appliqué, hand-painting, collage, and drawing, as well as such unconventional processes as heat transfer, Xerox copy, blueprint, Kwik print, and rubber stamps. She uses without prejudice not only such traditional materials as fabric, yarn, dye, paint, and paper, but also photographs, postcards, magazines, plastic, and metal. Any object may be adopted as her material, and any process may be employed to transform it. Every experience is potential inspiration for Katherine Westphal, and though her creative framework is not limited to a single discipline as is that of the traditional Japanese craftsman, they share the achievement of becoming one with process and material.

Westphal has done a number of pieces incorporating shibori techniques to produce unusual graphic effects. In the small tableau *Hula Hoop Men* (1975) (Plate 362), images are outlined by plain stitching (*hira-nui*; page 74) and it seems as if these bulky figures are seen through dense fog. The white spots that result from *hira-nui* make the shapes glow, delineated by points of light. The men are in formal attire—top hat and tuxedo—suggested by minimal means. The simplified shapes in themselves are almost comical, besides the unexpectedness of men in dress clothes playing with hula hoops. Westphal has allowed the crinkles from the shibori process to remain in the fabric as an enrichment of the surface along with the fine black lines filling the background.

In the *Santa Claus Hippari* (Plate 363), Westphal uses stitched shibori (see pages 73–74) extensively to create a pictorial image in a fairly realistic style, while the overall tone and white resisted elements give the impression of a blueprint. The touch of embroidery in red and white sparks the surface with accents of color and texture. The ingenuity of expressing such familiar (in modern Japan as well as the West) images as Santa Claus and McDonald's hamburgers in traditional indigo shibori, in the form of a Japanese garment, expands the boundaries of the craft. The humor evident in this piece—with its edge of social comment—is often found in Westphal's work. Her work is full of such surprises, which arise from an insightful combination of new and old. Even more surprising in view of the risks she takes is Westphal's consistent creative success, which always challenges the viewer's preconceptions about fiber art.

### KATY DOLK (Plates 364–66)

Katy Dolk has been working in the field of textile arts since college. In both her weaving and fabric construction she shows consistent interest in the intrinsic geometry of textile structure. Her method of fabric construction is mainly piecing, based on traditional patchwork methods, including Seminole Indian work. Each geometric unit contains small pieces of fabric; many such units are assembled into larger shapes—squares, long rectangular strips, or parallelograms—which again are assembled into a large rectangle and finished in the style of a quilt.

Besides the solid-color fabrics that she dyes, Dolk has been making patterned fabrics by dyeing them in the manner of shibori. Strips of fabric are braided tightly, and thickened dyes are applied over the braided surface. When the two types of fabric are combined, a refreshing contrast between solid color and mottled areas, as well as between hard and soft edges, adds movement and depth to the whole surface, as in *Serengetti II* (Plate 365). The braid-and-dye method used is found mainly in Africa.

After Dolk learned about Japanese shibori, she combined the braid-and-dye method with pole-wrap resist (*arashi*; pages 123–37) in her fabric construction *Window* (Plate 364). Strips of fabric were dyed while braided to give soft, small, allover patterns, and each multicolored strip was wrapped diagonally around a tube (or pole), pushed into compact folds, and dyed. The surface of the little folds received the indigo dye, creating dark, sharp linear patterning, which runs diagonally across the fabric. Piecing of narrow strips of dark blue with shibori-patterned strips gives a structure to the overall design and also intensifies the direction of the dark diagonal lines. When fabric is dyed on a tube, the folds on either end cannot be packed as tightly as in the middle. This causes the dye to penetrate more at both top and bottom, creating heavier lines. Dolk has carefully arranged these characteristic elements of *arashi* to create subtle changes of the visual planes; some vertical units appear to recede while others come forward, partly because of the overall tonal gradation of the ground pattern. This piece is enriched by the layering of two kinds of shibori.

### PAM SCHEINMAN (Plates 367–70)

Pam Scheinman was introduced to textile arts through weaving, but she felt drawn to dyeing and printing and finished her graduate work in the field of printed and dyed textiles. Her earlier fascination with shadows led her to use screens in the discharge printing of black taffeta.

Scheinman's sensitivity is well expressed in *Nightfall* (Plate 367). Her interest in patterning and surface brought her attention to means of manipulation such as pleating, smocking, and quilting. Here she uses a shibori method to create patterns by rolling the fabric, binding it to maintain the three-dimensional shape, and then dyeing it. Besides the surface patterns, Scheinman was intrigued by the three-dimensional quality achieved by the process. The crinkled folds remain in the fabric after dyeing, and Scheinman decided to capitalize on this aspect and set the folds permanently by steaming and heating. The irregular creases follow the surface pattern and cast shadows over it. By discharging the black color, the resisted areas of taffeta that are free of bleach remain black, and other areas become enriched by the gradation of rusty oranges. The black patterns are the shadows of the folds and binding threads, and produce an intriguing interaction with the actual shadows. The light-to-dark tonal gradation across each column is caused by the rolled form of the fabric, since the inside portion was less affected by the bleach than the outside, leaving more of the original shiny black. This gradation creates an illusion of three-dimensionality, giving a feeling of volume, which is enhanced by the richly textured surface.

Scheinman continues to explore surface texture and accompanying pattern in another piece, *Fandango* (Plate 368). This dynamic piece consists of forty-two units, which are formed by an accordion-pleated fabric being folded in half and opened into a fan shape. The dark areas are the impressions of the binding across the width of the pleats, and the orange areas result from color being discharged. When the units are assembled into a large square by alternating the direction of each fan-shaped unit, their linear patterns create a bold gyrating movement. Each indentation of the binding stands out on the surface of the folds, contributing to the rich overall texture.

In a more recent piece, *Lattice Fan* (Plates 369, 370), Scheinman again uses accordion-pleated fabric in a similar structure, but here each rectangular piece of cloth was first painted in four colors. Then the pleated satin fabric was bound and again painted, creating an effect like that of *tesuji* shibori (pages 104–06). As in *Fandango*, Scheinman retains the folds of the fabric as part of the finished piece. Over the bold colored areas, a very fine linear element is added where only the exposed edges of the pleats received paint. This piece is an example of Scheinman's application of dye pigment, showing an understanding of the shibori process that allows her to extend its interpretation.

### NANCY MARCHANT (Plates 371–74)

When Nancy Marchant received her M.F.A. in textile art, her thesis show consisted of kimono-shaped pieces all executed in the shibori techniques of stitching, capping, folding, and dipping. The exhibition displayed impressive control of the medium, which she achieved in a relatively short period of time. The major theme in this body of work is the illusion of planes in space that is achieved so effectively by the three-dimensional quality of shibori. The soft edges and tonal variations in shades of indigo create enormous visual satisfaction.

Marchant's compositions are simple and boldly define the planes. Her choice of shibori techniques and her sensitivity to the shape of the kimono as a framework for her creative statement combine to display her concern for the total synthesis of technical and visual elements. Marchant's exploration of shibori led her to study Japanese aesthetics of costume, where details such as linings are carefully considered. Her highly disciplined approach is epitomized by her series of four kimono (Plates 371–74). Here the illusion of undulating cloth is executed in four positive and negative compositions.

Before dyeing, the stitches on the edges of the design were drawn up, and the areas of the pattern to remain white were capped. The exposed fabric accepted the dye, and the natural seepage of indigo into the stitched areas produced strong radiating lines along the edges of the shapes, contributing to the illusion of depth. Thus the stitching technique results in white lines that define the apparent planes of the overall design, and the bleeding and blurred edges typical of stitched shibori add volume to the shapes.

In these works in shibori, Marchant plays with the image of cloth in a totally contemporary manner. Using illusory folds, she graphically depicts the supple qualities of fabric. To achieve these illusory folds she has manipulated and contorted the fabric itself into a form that accepts or resists the dye. Finally she has created the complete garment—and the whole is greater than the sum of its parts. The image of cloth moving across the surface of a garment, which will naturally undulate when worn, reinforces the idea of movement and depth. The interplay between all these elements utilizes the distinctive characteristics of shibori, resulting in a strong, coherent series.

## LOIS HADFIELD (Plates 375–378)

Lois Hadfield has been exploring surface design since her undergraduate education and did her graduate work primarily in silk-screen printing. Her principal interest at first was the building of patterns by placing elements into a selected framework, superimposing units of design to create moiré patterns.

Hadfield's love of structure and repeated patterning is apparent in the work she has produced recently. She has developed a dye technique similar to mechanical pleating (*fukuzō suji*; page 106), in which machine-pleated folds provide a structural basis for a variety of dyeing processes. The dyes cast highlights and shadows along the ridges of the folds. Ridges are further enhanced by the transparent treatment of air brushing, causing delicate shifts of color and linear patterns, which float across the surface like soft wind. One inspiration for this technique was the costume design of Ellen Hauptli, which displays an inventive use of pleating. The harmony and balance of pieces that Hadfield and Hauptli have created together show a successful synthesis of the elements contributed by each.

In a group of designs called Companion Pieces (Plates 357–77), Hadfield superimposes monochrome and polychrome patterns over a variety of kinds and sizes of pleats. There is an overriding sense of rhythmic order in the way the lines of color dance across the ridges of pleating—like echoes or shadows of pleats and ridges on a flat surface. Her sensitivity to the qualities of the dye and the enduring simplicity of her design combine to create fabrics with a delicate resonance of movement and color, which are complemented by Hauptli's costume design (Plate 378).

## YOSHIKO IWAMOTO WADA (Plates 379, 380)

After majoring in textile arts in Japan, Yoshiko Wada came to the United States, where she resumed her early interest in painting and drawing. This period of working in the fine arts in the late sixties significantly influenced her growth as an artist. Wada learned not to confine herself to a single conventional medium or material. Wada again became involved in the textile arts through teaching and gradually started to produce work in the field using various types of Japanese resist dyeing.

Wada's work in fiber generally falls into two categories. One is an extension of her installation work and expresses her fascination with planes that are either illusionistic (created within the fabric surface) or realistic (an arrangement of a series of panels). In order to create illusionistic planes, Wada has employed a variety of processes: dyeing, weaving, stitching, painting, creasing. The images used in this category of work are minimal and austere. The second category of her work is parody based on her cultural heritage. Whether her interpretation of an aspect of contemporary culture is a pun, a parody, or a satire, the transposition of images, materials, processes, and social context is personal and original and the statement is entertaining. A shibori piece, *Valentine Jiban* (Plate 379), is an example of this latter category in the form of a traditional garment. Japanese women, after they marry and grow older, wear outer garments of restrained colors and designs, avoiding long, swinging sleeves *(furisode)*, large, bold patterns, and red and other bright colors. But bright, often fiery red is discreetly reserved for the undergarment *(jiban)*, often in bold positive and negative patterns. This paradoxical custom of forbidding vivid color outwardly yet retaining it inside inspired Wada to create *Valentine Jiban*, a parody on the tradition. To complete the parody the garment form remains unfinished, implying that it is a garment not meant to be worn. A white curvilinear pattern of capped shibori (see pages 88ff) is repeated on both sides of narrow kimono fabric. When the strips of fabric are sewn together to complete the garment, the white shapes become hearts cut in half, and the two halves do not match precisely. One heart shape is executed in *mokume* shibori (pages 75–76), and the effect evokes the three-dimensionality of an actual heart.

A recent piece, *Line Series, Cotton* #5 (Plate 380), shows another direction Wada has taken in exploring shibori. She is interested in qualities of line—for example, in relation to the degree it becomes a part of the fabric or remains on the surface. In this work the lines achieved through dyeing permeate the fabric. The white diagonal lines were created by board clamping (pages 115ff) on nine strips of narrow hand-woven African cotton. Each strip was folded into a small rectangular unit, sandwiched diagonally between two boards, clamped, and dyed. When the fabric was opened, the diagonal elements formed a zigzag pattern. In the completed piece these units are slightly offset to give the appearance of interwoven lines, which seem to shift and retreat from the flat surface. The strips were sewn together by feather-stitching in threads dyed in the six colors used for shibori. Here and there accents of colored lines were painted by hand, defining different planes as if some of the strips were behind others. The soft ambiguity of edges produced by shibori is essential to the effect of the work, allowing the gentle definition of line. The repetition of three hues invites the eye to perceive certain strips as lying on the same plane and to make connections across the different colors.

SUSAN KRISTOFERSON (Plates 381, 382)

Susan Kristoferson's work shows her versatility as a textile artist. During graduate study and since completing a degree in textile arts she has utilized different media, including felting, painting with dyes on canvas, and shibori. Among her large paintings on canvas the consistent use of small, quasigeometric shapes in a maplike, deliberate randomness reveals her major interest in images that are broken down and reassembled.

Analogous to her painting is the shibori in *Haori Vantage* (Plate 382), where Kristoferson has taken fabrics dyed in various types of shibori and cut them into smaller, "alphabetlike" components, although the intention is not to have them "spell" anything as they are sewn back together. During the process of making this garment, Kristoferson's attention was focused not on the dynamics of the overall design but on each shape and each area, gradually building up the whole. The inspiration for this type of image came originally from her interest in aerial view maps. She was fascinated by the designs apparent on the surface of the earth—the endless feast of odd shapes and colors, some areas that suggest rhythmic order and others that seem chaotic. In *Haori Vantage* she shows her great care and sensitivity in the use and creation of each shape. The intensity of the pattern within each shape, the amount of light and dark, and the direction and movement of linear elements are the unique impressions of various shibori methods. The complexity of pattern entertains the viewer with its subtlety.

*Braided Ripples* (Plate 381) reveals Kristoferson's continued interest in working with modules, building from a number of small units. Using three or four basic types of dyed squares, she arranges them in a larger visual system. The squares were rolled around a piece of string in a variety of ways—diagonally from one corner, diagonally from two opposite corners to the center, or horizontally. Then three or four of these rolled units were braided together; sometimes a length of string was substituted for one of the rolled pieces of cloth. These braids were dyed by immersion in indigo, about twenty-one dips to achieve a rich blue. By itself, braiding tightly would produce a mottled, chevronlike effect (see *Serengetti II* and *Window* by Katy Dolk, Plates 364–66), but use of string inside the rolled fabric before braiding yields this sharper, netlike pattern. The squares are combined in such a way as to efface the individual units and draw attention to the larger movement of the overall pattern. Because of the distribution of blue on each square and the interrelationships among these areas of color, the system of initial units is broken down. Each square is stitched to the backing only along the top, left free on three edges to move in the breeze. One of the pleasures of contemplating Braided Ripples is the variety of patterns within it that gradually emerge. Plates 364–66

In addition to exploring traditional techniques such as Katano shibori, Kristoferson has come up with other exciting ways to create patterns by masking, machine stitching, and resist dyeing. Sewing is sometimes done on the fold to form a pocket where the dye does not penetrate. Another process involves cutting various shapes with masking materials, which are applied to the fabric, and then wrapping the fabric around a pole or tube, binding it with threads to secure it. However, it is important to note that the fabric surface is not shaped; the pole or tube is used merely for a backing or support during the application of dye. The masking material creates flat, sharp images, and the binding threads leave fine white lines. Again this is a departure from traditional shibori, a take-off differing in principle from rigid-core methods such as *arashi* and *shirokage* (see pages 97–100, 123ff), where a pole is used to secure the fabric and pressure is exerted upon the contorted fabric to maintain its three-dimensional shape through the dyeing process. Some of Kristoferson's innovations are possible by using dye paste (which opens up a more painterly approach) rather than dye liquid, but recently she has worked more with indigo.

## MARY KELLOGG RICE (Plates 383–85)

After studying art in college, Mary Rice worked in weaving, mainly tapestry and later sculptural pieces. She has always enjoyed painting, especially watercolor, but her major emphasis has been on the textile arts. While she lived in several Asian countries she had an opportunity to work closely with local weaving cottage industries, as well as numerous occasions to visit and study provincial crafts of countries where long traditions of handcrafts exist. Through these experiences she gained insight and understanding into the nature of crafts in a cultural context.

When she was exposed to Japanese shibori in 1975 Rice was immediately attracted to the responsiveness of materials and process to the artist's hand. The directness of the relationship between her hand and the resulting images created through shibori gave her the kind of control she feels is very important to create a work with integrity.

Initially Rice concentrated on basic, simple elements, sometimes executing designs entirely in *mokume* shibori (page 74). Varying the stitch size as well as the space between rows of stitching creates variation in the size and distribution of dark and light elements, which in turn creates the appearance of three-dimensionality.

When she was working with stitched shibori (pages 73ff), Rice was amused by the heavily crinkled surface that retained the original shaping of the cloth and the elasticity that remained after the dyeing process was completed and the threads had been removed from the tightly gathered cloth. By playing with the cloth at this stage, Rice was inspired to explore the property of three-dimensionality in a slightly different manner. The piece in Plate 384 was executed simply by *ori-nui* shibori (page 76), where each parallel line was sewn on the fold with double rows of stitching, drawn up tightly, and then dyed, creating many parallel white lines. In this piece she utilized the crinkled surface as well as the soft white resist shapes that appear and disappear against the gentle blue ground, with crisp linear elements defined by the folds in the cloth and the shadows cast by them

In order to emphasize the textured surface and its elasticity Rice partially restitched the lines of the original folds and let the cloth stretch where no stitching was restored, and a featherlike image appeared. The vertical folds change the light which is cast on the surface, and the dark dotted lines made by restitching and the textured surface contribute to tactile as well as visual satisfaction.

These elements Rice worked with in the piece in Plate 384 were extended into the work in Plate 383, where they are dealt with more spontaneously. The gentle swaying lines move with an ease reminiscent of brushstrokes or pencil lines, but they bear distinct traces of *ori-nui* shibori and stitching. Rice's discriminating attention to the subtlety of each effect contributed by the processes and materials plays a key role in making a statement so rich in detail, yet so simple and pure.

Rice's approach to shibori expanded into another dimension when she began working with Japanese handmade papers (Plate 385). Paper retains the shape into which it has been manipulated, and this can be viewed both as an added surface element and as a new form. Folded paper was placed over a tube and was bound and dyed. After drying, the paper was removed from the tube and gently opened.

### ANA LISA HEDSTROM (Plates 386–92)

Ana Lisa Hedstrom originally studied art and ceramics, but after three years of travel through Southeast Asia and India she began weaving, experimenting with natural dyes, and spinning yarn. In 1975, when she first learned about shibori, she was strongly attracted to the process and the directness of contact it offered. Hedstrom felt that among the many techniques of shibori, *arashi* shibori epitomized the effects that interested her.

As she began to explore the possibilities of *arashi* shibori, she was delighted by the elements with which she was working—the folds in the fabric, the tension exerted upon the shaped fabric, and the transformations of colors that occurred during dyeing and discharging. The result contained infinite variations of color, pattern, andtexture.

The development of *arashi* shibori demanded exceptional creativity and ingenuity in the craftsman who invented it, Kanezō Suzuki. The rigor apparent in classic *arashi* shibori work is also evident in Hedstrom's approach. She has discovered the essential balance between spontaneity and control in the creative process. She thoroughly explores a pattern and its variations, working until she realizes all the possibilities and limitations. Sometimes the fabric is wrapped on the pole as many as four times, dyed or discharged at each step. The layered patterns on the surface of *Arrow Hanging* (Plate 387), its rich field of colors and shapes, and the large directional patterns create an overall design that reflects the movement of smaller components within the piece. The ripples on the silk and the tiny floating shadows were recorded by the dye in a rich array of muted into deep, subtle colors—colors that Hedstrom calls "atavistic."

In *Miniature Piece* (Plate 386), the resilience of the silk allows the three-dimensional quality of shibori to survive, retaining the sculptural, tubular shape into which the fabric was molded during the dyeing process. The ripples and folds are tactile and intriguing and have led Hedstrom to employ them as part of the finished product. Hedstrom has become increasingly involved with colors and patterns, and has started to use fabrics and patterns freely to make collages within a garment form. In doing so, she has gained freedom to combine surprising elements of shapes, colors, and patterns. In *Video Sky* (Plate 388), the distinctive *arashi* shibori patterns appear in various striking, electrified colors that, accentuated by the dark forms which repeatedly appear between them, generate the effect of a flickering electronic image. *Neon Sunset* (Plate 392) shows Hedstrom's sophistication as a colorist. Piecing together rectangle after rectangle of various fabrics, she creates a dramatic pattern that complements the overall rectangular form of a straight-cut garment. Recently, Hedstrom has begun applying bleach by brush to create a cloudlike effect that transforms her garments into an image of the sky.

ERICA RUNSTROM (Plates 393–97)

As a painter Erica Runstrom responded to many materials and processes and articulated her personal engagement with them. Drawing from a wide range of materials, she became particularly interested in fiber.

After studying shibori techniques, Runstrom focused on *arashi* shibori (pages 123ff) because she particularly enjoyed the physical pleasure involved in the large-scale manipulation of the cloth. She chose to concentrate on the basic pattern intrinsic to *arashi—ichido kairyō* (page 128)—where the diagonal lines are created by the way the cloth is wrapped and pushed on the pole. Runstrom says that her focus on *arashi* came after doing embroideries and studying Hiroshige's *Shinotsuku* ("Lines of Rain"). She comments, "The field or pattern inherent in the *arashi* is just an observation or my own interpretation of a macrocosmic and microcosmic view of our physical existence."

In her hanging Orange Stripe (Plates 393, 394), Runstrom repeatedly dyed and discharged to create a strong statement whose color and linear detail are immensely rich yet understated. Soft directional lines define the penetrating colors, which become muted and blurred after being dyed and discharged many times. The linear design becomes a textural field filled with colors so fluid it becomes impossible to distinguish between positive and negative space. The method of folding the cloth before wrapping it on the pole creates the staggered effect and reflects the peak and valley folds and the way they receive the dye.

Each of the panels of *Orange and Green Screen* (Plates 395, 396) was folded in half vertically, dyed in *arashi* shibori, and discharged. The orange color appears translucent and seems almost to vibrate, as a result of the way the dye reacted to discharge. Along the edges of the orange lines there often appears a thin, faint halo typical of discharging. The three lengths of cloth serve as a container for this image of a folding screen.

In her indigo and white piece entitled *Cube Drawing* (Plate 397), Runstrom again uses *arashi* shibori, with more emphasis on line alone yet employed to suggest volume. Here the patterns superimposed on one another are more distinct. The cloth was flattened as it was pressed against the pole, and the thread wrapping the cloth was recorded as a series of broken white lines over the dark lattice of a classic type of *arashi* shibori. The light geometric shape reveals an area of the cloth that was masked with tape to resist dye. The tonal variations create the illusion of a three-dimensional form that floats on a space defined by lines, which are the inevitable mark of *arashi* shibori. Runstrom works with the simplest elements in a straightforward manner, achieving both strength and subtlety in the visual impact of her art.

VIRGINIA DAVIS (Plate 398)

Virginia Davis has been working in ikat weaving and shibori dyeing since about 1965. It is in ikat that her major interests have been explored most fully, and her themes have centered on tonal values and on the illusion of dimension. Her effort to minimize forms and to explore the greatest possible permutations in the most subtle tonal values leads her to move gracefully in indigo blue from light to dark, with various tones between. Then, by combining tie techniques with the structure of the weave, Davis presents the viewer with shifting tonal images, progressing from light on dark to dark on light.

Many of the themes Davis develops in ikat find their way into her work in shibori. In her shibori jacket (detail, Plate 398), the light linear pattern on a dark blue background is taken from Islamic tile design and executed in *ori-nui* shibori. Caught within this pattern are a series of undulating positive and negative shapes, each separated from the other by pale blue soft-edged lines of varying degrees of intensity, all of which contribute to the subtle distortion of planes and the creation of a repetitive pattern that is alive and moving, rather than static. The edging on the jacket is executed in *shirokage* shibori, which gives a refreshing contrast to the dark fabric. In this garment, Davis integrates her contemporary aesthetic concerns with age-old techniques.

### BARBARA GOLDBERG (Plates 399, 400)

Barbara Goldberg was exposed to tie-and-dye in the early 1970s, when there was a great interest in eastern culture, but at that time felt that the control and sophistication she could achieve were limited. She moved on to silk screen, but later encountered shibori and began to see the potential for expression and control she could achieve through various traditional techniques. Working with indigo also forced her to focus on the subtlety of images: hard edges versus soft edges, sharp images versus fuzzy images, and the wide range of the color blue. Simple mechanism and direct process are important factors in her work because they enable her to feel physically involved every step of the way. Even some of the long and laborious methods of stitching and binding can be viewed as being active periods for creative and meditative thought. The untitled work in Plate 399 combines the soft, blurred quality of the center with the geometrically precise lines of the designs on either side. The fold-and-dye technique as used by Goldberg is unconventional and sophisticated.

### DANIEL GRAFFIN (Plates 401, 402)

French artist Daniel Graffin's works in his 1979 solo show at the Allrich Gallery, San Francisco, included a number of pieces done in shibori. They were part of a series called "traces." Graffin's choice of the word "traces" indicates his concern with the cloth's sensitivity to process, its memory of the experience. Graffin has worked in unconventional ways with fiber materials, mainly cloth, often constructing pieces by sewing, and has made large sculptural works.

In the series "traces," the bleeding or soft edges characteristic of shibori, the crinkles left on the blue ground, the creeping of the dye into white areas, and the variation in blue are all reminders of the process, preserved purely and with no unnecessary elements. Graffin is able to see the essential aspects of making an image by a particular technique. In the catalogue for the solo show, Graffin explains his approach:

> One could call the dyeing operation the structure of work. It is the framework and the tool by which the colorant is deposited in the fiber support. In the preparation of the textile before dyeing, I have deliberately separated all direct action of the hand, putting between it and the support the intervention of a mechanical tool.

Graffin's attitude provides an interesting contrast to that of other artists who appreciate shibori for the possibility of direct physical involvement with materials. In a way his work shows a very pure grasp of the concept of shibori, using minimum steps, limiting variables, and eliminating irregularities. Graffin is interested in the basic process rather than effects that can be achieved through variations. His focus is clear in the images he chooses—the most basic shapes of intersecting lines, squares, and rectangles, all of which are created by straight line machine stitches on folds of cloth. His effort to stay with essential elements is rewarded by the results, which are stark, forthright, and visually convincing.

# Appendices

# Cloth and Dyes

Until the late nineteenth century, fibers from plants and animals and coloring substances from trees and other plants, sea creatures, insects, and minerals provided the world's weavers and dyers with all their materials.

In Japan, silk and hemp *(asa)* together with numerous other bast fibers were the textile fibers used until the introduction of cotton in the fourteenth century. The first appearance of silk in Japan is obscure, but it appears to have come from the Asian mainland in the second or third century. An indigenous sericulture was encouraged in the third and fourth centuries, and weavers of silk gained special status among Japanese artisans. Cloth woven of silk was worn by a privileged few; hemp and ramie *(asa)* were worn by all classes.

For centuries before the Christian era, India was producing superb cotton cloth, but cotton came late to China—where it was not cultivated until the twelfth century—and later still to Korea and Japan. The cotton plant *(Malvaceas gossypium)* was first cultivated in China's northwestern provinces, but due to opposition from producers of hemp and silk, it was slow to spread. It did not come into general use until the latter part of the Yuan dynasty (1276–1365). From China cotton cultivation spread to Korea. Cotton fiber and yarn found their way to Japan from Korea in the fourteenth century. In the sixteenth century, Japanese pirates brought back cotton seeds from raids on the Korean coast. Once introduced into Japan, the growing of cotton spread. The plant flourished in many areas and provided the common people with an alternative to hemp and other bast fibers for clothing. However, not until the Meiji period (1868–1912) was it in general use for all manner of articles—bedding, including filling for quilts, undergarments, sturdy work clothes, and light summer kimono *(yukata)*. Cotton was grown quite early in an area near Arimatsu, and the availability of cotton there may account in part for the popularity of Arimatsu shibori during the Edo period. Shibori processes were readily and quickly adapted to cotton cloth, and new designs and ways of shaping the cloth were devised.

All traditional garments in Japan are made of narrow cloth. The width derives from the one that is most convenient to weave by hand, particularly on the backstrap loom widely used in Japan. The width of the cloth (35.5 cm/14 in) was standardized during the Kamakura period (1185–1333), most likely as an aid to computing quantities of the silk that was exacted as tax. Although most cloth is now machine woven, the narrow width has until recently prevailed because the construction of traditional Japanese garments is based on it. Four widths of cloth are used to construct a garment, whether it is a formal silk kimono for an elegant lady or a short cotton jacket for fisherman or farmer. This cloth width affects all the decoration processes used for textiles as well as the scale of the designs that result.

The shibori techniques that evolved in Japan were devised for this narrow cloth; wider cloth, naturally, eliminates some of the design limitations inherent in the narrow width. While the shibori processes are affected by all the cloth's characteristics—its weave, width, weight, and softness, etc.—it is the type of fiber that determines what dyes can be used successfully. Natural dyes tend to have a preference for certain fibers; the behavior of synthetic dyes is similar.

The development and use of color in Japan, according to Seiroku Noma in his book *Japanese Costume and Textile Arts*, can be traced to the Asuka period (552–645), when Chinese color terms were introduced. In earlier terminology only very simple color distinctions were made.

During the Nara period (645–794), dye techniques were perfected, the number of dyed colors increased, and terms for shades of color appeared. Subsequently, the range of colors increased greatly, and the dyer's art evolved to become one of great subtlety and complexity.

The most important of the ancient dyes used in Japan are indigo *(ai)*, madder *(akane)*, gromwell or purple root *(shikon)*, sappanwood *(suo)*, a tall miscanthus *(kariyasu)*, and *Phellodendron (kihada)*.

In Japan after World War II a revival of interest in plant dyes occurred as a result of the folkcraft *(mingei)* movement, which focused attention on indigenous techniques and ancient processes. In America, at about the same time, attention to natural dyes developed through an interest in plants and a curiosity about their special properties on the part of knitters and hand weavers. Natural dyes today have become a source of interest and inspiration for both fabric artists and hobbyists.

Before the discovery of synthetic dyes in the mid-nineteenth century, the use of a particular dyestuff was governed by tradition—favorable conditions for the growth of dye-yielding plants, the availability of the proper mineral deposits, and the availability of the dyestuff through trade. Unlike the dyers of other centuries, the contemporary dyer has an immense range of dyes and colors to choose from—synthetic as well as natural.

The natural dyes touched on here are those of greatest historical importance in Japan. This discussion is not intended as an introduction to Japanese natural dyeing methods; a full coverage of this large and important subject is beyond the scope of this book and the expertise of its authors. Because information on chemical dyes is easily available, space demands that their discussion be kept to a minimum.

The historic dyes of Japan fall into two classes—vat dyes and mordant dyes.

Vat dyes, of which indigo is the original and most important example, are dyes that must first be converted by reduction (a process that removes oxygen from the liquid in which the dyestuff has been mixed) into a soluble form. When the cloth that has been immersed in the dye solution is removed and exposed to the air, the dye is oxidized and fixed on the cloth's fibers. The process of reduction is carried out through the addition of certain chemicals to an alkaline solution containing the dyestuff. The large vessel and the dye bath that it contains are both referred to as the vat, and the process of preparing the dye bath is called vatting. Vats are differentiated by the method or chemical used in the reduction process, for example, fermentation vat, zinc-lime vat, hydrosulphite vat.

Vat dyes will successfully dye cellulosic fibers—cotton, linen, hemp, and viscose rayon—as well as the protein fibers of silk and wool.

Mordant dyes, unlike vat dyes, require the presence of an additional substance—a mordant—which, by combining with the dyestuff, forms an insoluble compound (or "lake") to produce a fixed color in the fiber. The principal mordants are alum, iron, chrome, copper, and tin. Although mordants were used in antiquity—there is evidence to suggest their use in India five thousand years ago—the chemical reason for using them was not understood. The name mordant, from the French word *mordre*, to bite, was given to these substances because at one time it was thought that they were corrosive, pitting the surface of the fibers and thus opening the way for the dye to get inside.

The first-century Roman naturalist Pliny the Elder (ca. 23–79) in his *Natural History (Historia Naturalis)*, writing of the ancient Egyptians, describes the process of painting with different mordants on undyed cloth and then dyeing it in a single dye bath.

> Garments are painted in Egypt in a wonderful manner, the white cloth being first coated not with colors but with drugs [mordants] which absorb the colors. Although the dyeing is of one color, the garment is dyed several different colors according to the different properties of the drugs which have been applied to the different parts; nor can the dye be washed out.

Pliny's description is of a polymorphic dyestuff, one which is capable of producing different colors with different mordants. Madder and sappanwood were the two polymorphic dyes available to the Japanese dyers of old.

Mordants are applied in several ways: the cloth is treated with the mordant before or after it is steeped in the color substance; or the mordant can be combined with the dyestuff in the dye bath. Japanese dyers combined mordants as well as the dyestuffs to obtain many colors and shades of great subtlety.

# TRADITIONAL JAPANESE DYES

INDIGO *(ai)*: Indigo is the most ancient dyestuff known. The leaves and stalks of any one of a large group of leguminous plants of wide distribution yield the color substance indican from which this superb blue dye is obtained. A garment dyed with indigo, which has been dated 3,000 B.C., was found in Thebes. Indigo and madder remained the most important dyestuffs from ancient times until the late nineteenth century and the advent of synthetic dyes. Indigo was synthesized in the last years of the nineteenth century and produced at a price with which natural indigo could not compete, bringing to an end the large-scale production of natural indigo, which had been the basis for a lucrative world trade.

The indigo plant grown in Japan *(Polygonum tinctorium;* Japanese; *tade ai)*, was introduced from South China in the eighth century. It was grown widely in Japan and became the most readily available dyestuff. Most villages had an indigo dyer, and many country people grew enough plants to produce dye for their own use.

The process they used in the preparation of the dye-yielding plants and the dye vat is best told in the words of the late Ayano Chiba (from Barbara Adachi, *The Living Treasures of Japan)*, who all of her long life grew her own indigo plants, made the dye, prepared the vat, and dyed the hemp, which she also grew, spun, and wove into cloth.

"We're getting the seeds ready now for planting next year's crop of *ai* (indigo) in June, and all those bags up on shelves over the dye tubs are full of dried *ai* leaves. We pick the *ai* in late July, the second crop in September. It has nice pink blossoms, you know. We strip off the leaves and then I crumple them up and put them on rice-straw matting out in the sun to dry. In good weather, three days is enough. Then we store it in those net bags. I filled sixteen bags this year. Once the leaves are dry, we store them until January. We make the dye when it's very cold, and oh, it really does get cold here in January. But it's nice here in the winter, nice and quiet. Right after New Year's, I made a sort of bed out of lots of rice straw right down on the floor in front of the dyeing tub. Then I stuff some big bags made out of rice-straw matting with the *ai* leaves that have been washed in water but left wet. You have to stuff the bags full but not too much. Too little is no good either, just the right amount. We wrap the bags in more rice straw, put weights on top, and let the bags sit here on the dirt-floored section of the workroom. In a week, the leaves start to ferment, but I leave the bags without peeking in them for twenty days. Then I open up the bags and stir those fermenting leaves around very well—you have to be sure to give them a really good stir, then, wrap them up again and put the stones or weights back on. The leaves have to sit like that for one hundred days altogether. The next job is to pound the leaves just the way you pound rice to make rice cakes at New Year's. We pound them with a wooden mallet in a stone mortar, in several batches, until it gets all into a ball. I break up these cakes of indigo paste into bits, about the size of a plum, and set the lumps out to dry for three to seven days, depending on the weather. And there you are—those are the *ai-dama* ("indigo balls") that make the dye, just the way they did it in the old days!"

Mrs. Chiba explained that the stacks of charcoal by the house were oak wood. The charcoal would be burned in the *irori* (open hearth) and *hibachi* (brazier) in the main house all winter, as the ashes would supply the lye for the dye. "Not those white ashes, but those black bits at the bottom. I measure out the *ai-dama* and lye by weight, five parts to four. Then I pour in warm water—not too hot, not too cold, just right—just enough to cover the *ai* and lye. Then every day for a week I pour in a little more water—it can be hotter—until I get just the right amount. Too much is no good. Then I stir it very carefully and cover it. It has to sit for thirty days."

In order to dye a roll of the buff-colored hemp material, Mrs. Chiba inserts twelve flexible bamboo ribs [*shinshi*] along the selvage of the bolt, dips it into water, and then dips it into the vat of dye. "I put it in once for just the right amount of time—a few minutes—then take it out and let it drip back into the tub. Then in again, and once more. Once the dripping stops, I hang it up to dry. Once it dries, I give it three more dips. I do this dipping and drying six times, sometimes nine times, for each bolt of material. When I lift the cloth out of the vat, it's sort of green, but in the breeze it turns blue—right in front of my eyes it changes color."

The process of vatting described by Mrs. Chiba is a completely natural one in which reduction in the vat takes place as a result of fermentation. Hers was a slow process that fit the rhythms of her life. Professional dyers using pure natural indigo and the fermentation vat who want quick results add various substances such as honey and bran to induce fermentation.

There are many recipes for fermentation vats in books on natural dyes as well as for the hydrosulphite vat. In the authors' experience the less common zinc-lime vat is a practical one for home or studio use. Directions for preparing and maintaining it are given below. The zinc-lime vat was developed in Europe in the mid-nineteenth century. It has a number of advantages: it can be made with natural indigo or synthetic indigo powder; it is not caustic; dyeing can be done in a cold vat; and the vat can be maintained ready for use for many months.

Indigo and shibori are natural partners. The indigo dye process itself may result in fortuitous and accidental effects that enhance those created by the planned shaping of the cloth.

Indigo has a special natural affinity for cotton, but it will successfully dye all plant fibers derived as well as silk and wool. It yields many shades of blue, from the palest tint to a rich blue-black. The depth of shade depends upon the strength of the vat and number of times the cloth is immersed in the dye. Indigo can be dyed over shades of yellow to yield a wide range of greens and dyed over red to produce purple.

Indigo, being a vat dye, does not require a mordant to fix the color, but mordanting substances may be used to alter the quality of the blue. For instance, iron, which is naturally present in the water of some areas used for rinsing indigo-dyed cloth, changes the blue to black. The tannin found in peach bark *(shibuki)* is widely used in Japan in the final rinsing of the cloth to brighten the blue and remove the somewhat purple cast of the indigo.

Indigo is fast to light and washing but, unlike most dyes, it does not penetrate the fiber; rather, it is fixed to the fiber's surface, rendering it weak to abrasion.

MADDER *(akane)*: Madder is the archetypal mordant dye. This crimson dye is found in the roots of the Eurasian herb *Rubia tinctorium*. A species of madder—*Rubia cardifolia L.* var. *Mungista Mig.*—is native to Japan and since early times has been used to dye cloth a vibrant red. In the Nara period the color was restricted to the garments of third-rank members of the imperial court. Later, as the color of happiness, it came to be used widely on festive occasions. Newborn babies were wrapped in scarlet cloth, and brides still wear red.

In addition to the red shade obtained with alum mordant, madder yields maroon to red-brown with iron, yellow-brown with copper, red-orange with tin, and crimson with chrome.

The ancient process used in Japan is similar to the one used in dyeing with purple root. A contemporary recipe and method is given on page 283.

PURPLE ROOT *(shikon or murasaki)*: During Nara times the roots of the plant *Lithospermum erythroryzon*, which grows wild in Japan, flourishing in open fields of mixed vegetation, were the source of a purple dye reserved for the garments of the royal princes and court ministers of the highest rank.

Poems in the eighth century anthology the *Man'yōshū* praise the color and speak of its beauty and elegance. This purple *(murasaki)* is still admired by the Japanese, and cloth dyed this subtle color is highly prized.

The purple root plant, also known as gromwell, was cultivated for its medicinal properties in closely guarded fields owned by the imperial court. The dyed cloth and the roots of the wild plant were collected as a tax. Today the dried roots can be purchased in Chinese medicinal herb shops, the plant's medicinal use having survived its use as a dyestuff.

A unique remnant of a once flourishing craft of dyeing with both purple root and madder remains in Japan in the town of Hanawa, in the far north on the island of Honshu. One man and his wife, the Kuriyamas, produce ten to twenty bolts of shibori-resisted cloth each year in purple and the vibrant red of madder, following the slow, traditional way of dyeing.

Purple root, like madder, is a mordant dye. The mordanting process carried on by the Kuriyamas is lengthy and laborious. A description of the process as well as the preparation of the dyestuff and the dyeing may provide an understanding of the effort expended by dyers of old to produce the prized purple and red cloth.

The mordant is obtained by burning branches of certain trees or woody shrubs that contain alum. The shrub *Camelia japonica*, the most common source, does not grow in the cold climate of the north, therefore in the Hanawa area the branches of a small tree called *nishi kohori* are used. The fresh branches gathered in early spring before the leaves appear are burned in a copper pot, water is added to the ashes, and the mixture is boiled for thirty minutes. The liquid is poured into a wooden barrel, where the ash particles settle to the bottom, and the clear liquid, the ash lye, is drawn off (see leached ash solution, page 285).

During the summer months, the cloth is dipped repeatedly into the ash lye solution and dried in the sun. Purple root dyeing requires thirty dips, madder takes fifty immersions. The slow build-up of the mordant stiffens the cloth, and the mordanted cloth is allowed to cure during the winter months. If it is to be resist dyed, the stitching and binding of the cloth is done by Mrs. Kuriyama while the cloth is curing. Distinctive designs result from the limitation imposed by the stiffened cloth.

In the autumn following this long preparation, dye is extracted from the roots of plants, and the cloth is dyed. Early in the morning of the dyeing day, which is selected for the right weather conditions, the dried plant roots are crushed in a stone mortar. The pounding continues for an hour or so. The crushed roots are transferred to a bamboo sieve, and hot water (not in excess of 60°C/140°F) is poured over them. This solution is used for the first immersion of the cloth. A fresh batch of dye liquid is used for each dip. Ten to thirteen dips are usually required to obtain the desired depth of color. For each batch of dye the roots are crushed further, and fresh hot water is poured over them. When the roots are thoroughly pulverized, the mass is placed in a hemp bag, which is laid on a wooden board and pressed with a heavy piece of wood to extract as much of the remaining liquid as possible.

When, in the dyer's judgment, the most beautiful depth of color has been achieved, the dyeing is halted and the cloth is rinsed. The rinsing removes all traces of the mordant, and the cloth's original softness is restored. When the cloth is dry, the binding and stitching threads are removed. The cloth is then carefully rolled and placed in a chest of paulownia wood or in a tin-lined wooden tea chest and stored away from light and air for three to four years. It is claimed that during this resting period the color becomes richer, clearer, and brighter and is permanently fixed in the cloth's fibers.

SAPPANWOOD (suo): Sappanwood is a red wood of the East Indian tree *Caesalpinia sappan*, which yields a soluble dyestuff. A similar tree *(Caesalpinia brasiliensis)* is native to Brazil and accounts for the common name Brazilwood often used for these red woods.

Sappanwood found its way through trade to Japan in the eighth century. Like madder, it is a polymorphic dye substance and was therefore very useful to the early dyers. It is capable of yielding shades of pink to red with alum; lavendar to purple with iron; and greenish bronze to rich red-brown with chrome. Combining mordants and overdyeing with indigo further extends this color range.

The color substance is easily extracted from the wood chips by boiling them in water (recipe, page 283). The unmordanted cloth may be immersed in the color extract, after which it is dried and then painted with different mordants to produce several colors, or it may be painted in different areas with various mordants, dried, and then immersed in the color solution (the method described by Pliny the Elder). If the entire cloth is dyed in one color, it is either mordanted first with a single mordant and dyed, or colored first and then immersed in the liquid containing the mordant.

Sappanwood is a natural dyestuff offering the contemporary fabric artist interesting possibilities. It would reward experimentation with any of the shibori processes.

PHELLODENDRON (kihada): Phellodendron is a small genus of aromatic deciduous trees of the family *Rutaceae* found in eastern Asia. The trees have compound leaves, which turn yellow in autumn. The inner bark of *Phellodendron amurense Rupr.* is used in Japan to produce a greenish yellow dye. *Phellodendron* and *Miscanthus tinctorius Hackel (kariyasu)*, a tall reed, were the early sources of yellow. These two somewhat different yellows overdyed with indigo provided many shades of green. *Phellodendron* bark is available in the United States. A recipe for its use is given on page 284. *Kariyasu* is not available outside Japan.

SAFFLOWER (benibana): The flowers of the safflower plant *(Carthemus tinctorius[compositae])* yield a dye that produces yellows, oranges, reds, and pinks on cotton, linen, hemp *(asa)*, and silk. Used extensively in India and Indonesia to produce all of these colors, in Japan it is used primarily to dye cloth in reds and pinks, which have an especially lovely, soft quality. In early times the red from safflower was used for rouge. It is the traditional color for women's underkimono. The lovely shades drawn from these flower petals are not very fast. However, since the Japanese admire evanescence, the dye's impermanence is accepted.

In Japan the flower petals are fermented and formed into small flat cakes. The fermentation process reduces the yellow dye substance. In America, the loose dried petals may be purchased from Chinese herb shops and dealers in natural dyestuffs, or the plants can be easily grown.

## PREPARING CLOTH FOR DYEING

Before dyeing, all cloth must be treated in some manner, even if it is only gently washed. Naturally such preparation of cloth for dyeing should be done before any shibori processes are undertaken. (Fabrics prepared for dyeing are available direct from Testfabrics Inc., a company that supplies ready-to-dye fabrics to commercial dyers. Address, page 294.)

Silk contains a protein called sericin that binds together the twin filaments secreted by the silkworm. Commercial silk usually has the sericin removed by a process known as degumming. If the silk is soft and has a sheen, the sericin has been removed and all that is required is a long soak in warm water to remove oil and starch used in spinning and in finishing the cloth.

*Washing silk*: Fill a large kettle with enough warm water (39° to 50°C/100° to 120°F) to cover the fabric, and put the kettle over heat. The silk may be folded in half lengthwise if it is too wide to fit in the kettle. Ease the cloth over the edge of the kettle and down into the water to prevent the formation of air pockets, which make it difficult to keep the cloth completely submerged. The water temperature should be kept constant for three hours. When the cloth is removed, it should be allowed to cool, after which it is rinsed in clear water. The silk must be handled carefully to avoid wrinkling or crumpling, because it is difficult and sometimes impossible to remove wrinkles made in wet silk. It should never be wrung, but hung flat to dry.

*Scouring cotton*: Cotton fibers contain a natural waxy substance that acts as a resist and must be removed before the cloth can be successfully dyed. Cotton is scoured in a boiling solution containing caustic soda and soap. Besides removing the waxy substance and any impurities, scouring increases the absorbency of the fibers, improving the quality of the dyeing. Mercerized cotton has been scoured and need only be washed. The following scouring recipe is for 500 grams (a little more than 1 lb) dry weight of cotton.

> 10 liters (quarts) water
> $13\frac{1}{2}$ grams ($\frac{1}{2}$ oz) sodium hydroxide (caustic soda)
> $4\frac{1}{2}$ grams ($\frac{1}{7}$ oz) neutral soap (Ivory Snow)
> wooden stick for stirring
> Large kettle—large enough to allow plenty of room for the solution to boil up vigorously without splashing over

*Caution: caustic soda burns.* Wear rubber gloves, work in well-ventilated place, stand to one side of the kettle, and avoid breathing the fumes. *Never* add water to caustic soda; the dry soda should be added to a large volume of water. Be careful not to let the liquid splash up into the face or eyes.

*Procedure*: Measure the water into a large kettle and put the kettle over heat. Weigh the caustic soda on a piece of paper, then drop it, paper and all, into the water. The water will bubble and roil vigorously the moment the caustic soda enters it, so stand well away from the kettle. When the bubbling stops, add the soap. Bring the water to a boil. Ease the cotton into the liquid and keep it submerged for thirty to forty minutes. The liquid will turn the color of tea.

Wearing rubber gloves, remove the cloth from the liquid to a clean container. Two sturdy sticks are convenient to do this. Take care: the cloth is boiling hot and the solution is caustic. Allow the cloth to cool, then rinse it thoroughly in cold water until no odor of caustic soda remains.

## PREPARING AN INDIGO VAT

There are two basic ways to bring about the necessary reduction of indigo in order to make and keep the dye soluble—natural fermentation and chemical solution. Natural fermentation (see page 277 above) is too involved and time consuming for most dyers. Of the two major types of chemical vat, the hydrosulphite vat is used commercially, and some dyers like it because it is quickly prepared. It has several disadvantages—it is caustic, does not readily yield a rich dark blue, and the vat cannot be maintained for any length of time. The zinc-lime vat is not caustic, has no unpleasant odor or caustic fumes, it yields rich, deep shades of blue, and can be maintained in one's studio ready to use for many months. Directions for setting up a hydrosulphite vat are readily available; only the zinc-lime vat is described here.

The zinc-lime vat is prepared in two parts—basic bath and stock solution. The basic bath is a large volume of water containing lime (calcium hydroxide) and zinc metal dust. The stock solution is indigo powder dissolved in methyl alcohol added to a small amount of hot water solution of calcium hydroxide and zinc metal dust. Later the stock solution is added to the basic bath. The newly prepared indigo vat must stand for six or seven hours before it can be used.

The indigo in the following recipe is sufficient to dye approximately twenty pounds of medium-weight cotton. A smaller vat may be prepared by cutting the recipe in half and using a proportionately smaller container.

When the indigo in the vat is exhausted, a new stock solution of the dye may be prepared and added to the original basic bath (see page 282).

*Equipment*

120-liter (30-gal) plastic trash container with cover, preferably one without ridges on the bottom

1½-meter (4-ft) wooden stick for stirring the vat. A mop or broom handle works well. It should be smooth and clean.

small saucepan or bowl—enamel, stainless steel, or plastic—for skimming the vat

8-liter (2-gal) enameled or stainless steel pot with lid

½-liter (1-pt) pyrex measure

stainless steel or sturdy plastic spoon

scale—a 500-gram scale is an essential piece of equipment. One with ounces as well as grams is useful.

thermometer—a metal thermometer with a dial on the top is easy to read, but a conventional glass candy thermometer will do as well. If a candy thermometer is used, keep it for dyeing only. **Never** use dye pots, measures, spoons, or any other equipment used to work with dyes and chemicals for food.

*Basic Bath*

100 liters (26½ gal) water

100 grams (3½ oz) calcium hydroxide (slaked lime; $Ca(OH)_2$)

30 grams (1 oz) zinc metal dust

*Procedure*: Fill the plastic container—the vat—with the water for the basic bath, then add the calcium hydroxide and zinc metal dust. Stir to dissolve the lime, then cover the container.

*Stock Solution*

6 liters (quarts) warm water

100 grams (3½ oz) indigo powder (either natural or chemical indigo may be used)

½ liter (1 pt) methyl alcohol

200 grams (7 oz) calcium hydroxide (slaked lime; $Ca(OH)_2$)

60 grams (2 oz) zinc metal dust

*Procedure*: Fill the enameled or stainless steel pot with 6 liters (quarts) of warm water. Place the pot on very low heat—just enough to keep the water warm.

Weigh the indigo and put it in the pyrex measure. Add the methyl alcohol a small amount at a time and mix carefully to a smooth paste. This takes time. Be sure the paste is smooth and thoroughly mixed. Lower the measure into the pot of warm water and gently stir indigo paste into the water. Work slowly and carefully. Do not wash out the dregs of indigo remaining in the measure; rather, use the "dirty" measure for the next step.

Mix the calcium hydroxide and zinc in the pyrex measure with enough of the indigo and water solution to make a smooth paste. Add this paste to the indigo solution by again lowering the measure into the liquid and blending in the paste.

Stir the indigo solution very gently with a clean stick. Turn up the heat just a bit. The temperature of the stock solution *must not* exceed 60°C (140°F) at any time. Use the thermometer and adjust the heat. Continue to stir the solution for about five minutes. The stock solution will change to a greenish color, a metallic looking film will form on the surface, and shiny dark purple bubbles will appear on the surface.

Remove the pot from the heat. Cover and allow the stock solution to rest for three to five hours. To test the solution to be sure the indigo is properly reduced, dip a small strip of white cotton cloth into it. The cloth should be a yellowish color when it is removed and should turn blue when exposed to the air.

*Combining the stock solution and basic bath*: Remove one liter (quart) of liquid from the basic bath and set aside to use in rinsing out the pot containing the stock solution. Add the stock solution to the basic bath and rinse out all of the sediment with the reserved liquid. Stir the bath, cover the vat, and let it stand at least six hours before dyeing.

## DYEING WITH INDIGO

The zinc-lime vat is not caustic; however, always wear rubber gloves to protect the hands from the chemicals. Indigo is easy to remove from porcelain sinks or vinyl flooring; simply scrub with detergent and, if necessary, with a cleanser containing mild bleach.

Generally, cloth should be wet before it is dyed. However, certain effects may be obtained with shibori by immersing dry cloth in the indigo—the dye tends to penetrate more deeply into dry cloth. This practice has the disadvantage of introducing oxygen into the indigo solution, which hastens the need for sharpening the vat (see below).

Soak cloth of cellulosic fibers (cotton, linen, viscose rayon) in water for five to ten minutes. Silk and wool should be soaked in soft warm water for at least twenty minutes. Cloth shaped by one of the shibori processes should be moved around in the water to be sure it is wet thoroughly.

An indigo vat in good condition always has an accumulation of bubbles on the surface. This is called the "indigo flower" and is composed of a dark bronzy blue foam in the center, surrounded by bubbles of a lighter blue. It usually floats in the center of the vat. Before dyeing, the small saucepan or bowl is used to skim off this indigo flower, together with any additional bubbles. This is set aside and is returned to the vat when the dyeing is completed for the day. The vat should not be used for more than two hours at a time.

Slowly immerse the cloth in the dye bath. Shibori shaped cloth will have air trapped in it. Try to ease the cloth into the vat in such a way as to minimize the amount of oxygen that enters the liquid. Hold the cloth a few inches under the surface and move it around slowly and gently. Take care not to let the cloth reach the zinc and calcium sediment on the bottom of the vat. After three to ten minutes remove the cloth, and, holding it over the vat, squeeze out the indigo.

Lay the wet dyed cloth on newspaper and, to ensure complete oxidation of the indigo, carefully open out the folds and gathers to expose the cloth to the air. If possible, do this outside in sunshine and air and enjoy watching the change in color that takes place. To obtain the maximum color fastness, the cloth should dry after each dip.

Each immersion of the cloth in the dye bath results in a darker shade of indigo. When the cloth has dried after the desired shade has been achieved, remove the stitching and binding threads and rinse thoroughly in cold water. Rinse until the water is clear of all blue.

Add vinegar to the final rinse water when dyeing silk or wool to counteract the strong alkalinity of the dye bath, which is harmful to animal fibers.

Though a mordant is not necessary with indigo, some dyers use one to obtain certain color nuances. See page 286 for peach bark (shibuki) tannin rinse.

### Care of the Indigo Vat

The zinc-lime indigo vat can be maintained for many months—for as long as any dye substance remains—with a little care. One must stir the vat once a day and maintain the chemical balance by adding calcium hydroxide and zinc as needed.

*Stirring the vat*: The vat is stirred with the long wooden stick, keeping one end on the bottom of the vat and stirring in a clockwise direction. Stir vigorously for a few minutes until the liquid forms a whirlpool. Keeping one end of the stirring stick on the bottom of the vat, stop stirring and hold the stick still. This stops the whirling motion of the liquid and brings all the bubbles formed on the surface—the indigo flower—together in the center of the vat. Remove the stick and cover the vat. The vat should be allowed to rest at least six hours (preferably overnight) after stirring before dyeing is done. For this reason, it is convenient to stir the vat the last thing each night.

*Sharpening the vat*: The condition of the vat can be judged by the appearance of the indigo flower and the color of the bath liquid. The flower of a healthy vat is made up of a dark, bronzy blue foam thickest at the center, surrounded by bubbles of a lighter blue. All the bubbles should look shiny and lively when the vat has been stirred. The size of the flower varies, but it should be about 15 to 20 centimeters (6 to 8 in) in diameter.

The color of the bath itself when it is stirred will be a greenish yellow-brown. If it is a bright greenish yellow—the color of Coleman's mustard—it probably contains too much zinc. The color of a good French mustard is about right. When the vat is stirred and it is in good condition, blue streaks appear in the brownish mustard-colored liquid. If there is an excess of zinc in the vat, it will adjust itself in a few days, but be sure to add more calcium hydroxide to keep the chemicals in balance. Add the chemical one teaspoonful at a time. Do not sprinkle the powder, but plop a full teaspoonful onto the liquid; the calcium hydroxide will stay together and float on the surface. If it is absorbed quickly, add more. When it floats without being dissolved into the liquid, the vat contains enough calcium.

The alkalinity of the dye bath can be checked with hydrion pH papers, which are available from chemical suppliers. It should be between 11.5 and 12.5.

A darkening and change in the color of the dye bath (it will turn green) when it is stirred and a decrease in the size of the flower are indications that the indigo in the vat is reverting to its insoluble state and zinc is needed to bring it back to its reduced or soluble state. This hs called sharpening the vat. Double check the need to add zinc by inserting a white plastic cup below the surface of the vat. If the liquid is light blue or colorless instead of being a greenish yellow when seen against the white cup, add 30 grams (1 oz) of zinc and some calcium hydroxide. The amount of calcium depends on the conditions of the vat. Add 10 grams (x oz), one teaspoon at a time. The vat may require as much as 100 grams ($3\frac{1}{2}$ oz). Stir the bath thoroughly and let it stand for six hours. Check the vat, and if reduction has not taken place, repeat the sharpening process.

When the indigo in the vat is exhausted, the liquid is clear, no indigo particles float in it, and sharpening has no effect. To replenish the vat, remove six liters (quarts) of the basic bath and prepare a new stock solution using this liquid; add this new solution to the old basic bath and stir.

## DYE RECIPES

### SAPPANWOOD (suo), Caesalpinia sappan

Sappanwood yields a polymorphic dyestuff. From it different reds are produced with tin and alum mordants, purples and browns with chrome, and purple with iron. (Iron should not be used as a mordant for silk since it causes the silk to deteriorate.) Sappanwood comes in the form of thin wood chips, and the dye is extracted in a series of boilings. The amount extracted in the following recipe is sufficient to dye one kilogram (2.2 lbs) of silk.

Alum is the least toxic of the mordants. If other mordants are used, pay particular attention to precautions given for their use, storage, and handling (see page 286).

*Extracting dye*:
- 125 grams ($\frac{1}{4}$ lb) sappanwood chips
- 2.5 liters (quarts) water

Place the chips in an enameled or stainless steel pot, add the water, and boil twenty minutes. Strain off the liquid and set aside. The process is repeated seven times, using the same chips and the same amount of water each time. The liquid from the first four extractions is reserved in one container, that from the last four, in another.

*Dyeing*:
- dye liquid from the first four extractions
- 10 grams ($\frac{1}{3}$ oz) alum (potassium aluminum sulphate; $KAl(SO_4)_2 \cdot 12H_2O$)

Heat the liquid from the first four boilings of the chips, add the cloth, and allow it to cool and remain in the liquid for at least two hours. Remove the cloth and squeeze out the liquid.

Dissolve the alum in lukewarm water. Add the cloth to the water containing the mordant. Let it stand for twenty minutes. Squeeze out the mordant.

Heat the liquid from the last four boilings, add the cloth, and allow it to cool in the liquid.

*Rinsing dyed cloth*:
- 7.5 grams ($\frac{1}{4}$ oz) cream of tartar (potassium bitartrate; $KHC_4H_4O_6$)

Dissolve the cream of tartar in lukewarm water. Add the cloth and soak for thirty minutes. Rinse three times in water and dry in the sun. The cream of tartar produces an acid rinse; it neutralizes the alkalinity of the alum mordant.

### MADDER (akane), Rubia tinctorium

The roots of the madder plant are used to produce a wide range of reds with different mordants. The Japanese use a native variety of madder—*Rubia cardifolia L. var. Mungista Mig.* The procedure of extracting the dye substance is similar to that used for purple root *(shikon)*. The following recipe using alum as the mordant produces a pure vermilion.

*Extracting dye*:
Chop up the roots, cover with water in an enameled or stainless steel pot, and boil for twenty minutes. Strain off and reserve the liquid. Repeat this procedure three times.

After boiling the roots for the third time, pound them in a mortar and repeat the above procedure of adding water, boiling for twenty minutes, straining off and reserving the liquid. Repeat seven more times, pounding the roots each time. Reserve the liquid from the first five extractions in one container, that from the last five in another.

*Mordanting cloth*:

    alum (potassium aluminum sulphate; $KAl(SO_4)_2 \cdot 12H_2O$)

Soak the cloth for twenty minutes in lukewarm water; squeeze out the water.

Dissolve the alum (3 percent of the dry weight of the cloth) in enough lukewarm water to cover the cloth, add the cloth, and soak it for twenty minutes. Squeeze out as much liquid as possible and open the cloth and allow it to air.

*Dyeing*:

*Dyebath One*: the dye liquid extracted when the madder roots were boiled the first five times.

Heat to 80°C (160°F), add mordanted cloth, and maintain temperature for twenty minutes. Remove from heat and allow the cloth to cool and remain in the dye liquid for at least two hours or overnight.

Remove the cloth, rinse two or three times, and dry in the sun.

*Dyebath Two*: the dye liquid extracted when the madder roots were boiled the last five times.

Heat dyebath to 80°C (160°F), add cloth, and maintain temperature for twenty minutes. Remove from the heat, allow the cloth to cool and remain in the dye liquid for at least two hours or overnight. Remove the cloth and squeeze out the excess dye liquid.

Soak the dyed cloth in wood ash lye (page 285) or a solution of potassium carbonate ($K_2CO_3$) for one-half hour. Squeeze out the liquid, open out the cloth, and let it stand for one hour before rinsing it.

Rinse the cloth two or three times and dry in the sun.

To produce a deep shade of red, repeat the entire process of mordanting and dyeing, allowing the cloth to cure for one week after each dyeing.

PURPLE ROOT *(shikon), Lithospermum erythroryzon Sieb et Zucc.* (soft purple root) or *Lithospermum euchroma Royle Arnebia euchroma* (hard purple root).

*Preparing cloth*:

Soak the cloth for fifteen to twenty minutes in freshly made ash lye leached from the ash of *Camelia japonica* (page 285). Squeeze out the liquid and thoroughly dry the cloth. Repeat several times a day for three or four days. Store the dried fabric in a dark place for at least two weeks. The longer the storage period—months are better than weeks—the better the results of the dyeing will be.

*Extracting dye*:

Pound the roots in a large mortar, add the crushed roots to a pot of very hot water, let them soak for a little while, and work out the dye. Strain the dye liquid through a fine cloth.

*Dyeing*:

Soak the cloth in the dye liquid until the dye is absorbed.

Repeat the process of extracting the dye from the roots as long as they yield color, and soak the cloth in each batch of liquid. When the root particles become fine, they may be placed in a cloth bag and the dye liquid extracted by pressing the bag with a heavy piece of wood. When either the dye substance in the roots is exhausted or the desired depth of color is reached, dry the cloth thoroughly.

Rinse the cloth in cold water until the rinse water runs clear.

PHELLODENDRON *(kihada), Phellodendron amurense Rupr.*

*Phellodendron* comes in the form of small chips, made from the inner bark of this East Asian aromatic tree. With alum mordant it produces a clear greenish yellow on silk.

*Extracting dye*:

    250 grams ($\frac{1}{2}$ lb) *kihada* chips (this dyes 500 gm/1 lb of cloth)

    2.5 liters (quarts) water for each boiling

Place the chips in an enameled or stainless steel pot, add the water, and boil for twenty minutes. Drain off the liquid into a container. Repeat the process seven times, using the same chips and the same amount of water each time.

*Dyeing silk*:

    half the extracted dye liquid

    10 grams ($\frac{1}{3}$ oz) alum (potassium aluminum sulphate; $KAl(SO_4)_2 \cdot 12H_2O$)

Pour the dye liquid into an enameled or stainless steel pot, add the cloth, and simmer for ten minutes. Allow the silk to cool and remain in the dye liquid for two hours or longer.

Dissolve the alum in lukewarm water. Add the cloth, soak for twenty minutes.

Return the cloth to the dye liquid, simmer for fifteen minutes, then allow it to cool and remain in the liquid for two hours or longer. Rinse it three times and let it dry in the sun.

Repeat the entire procedure using the remaining half of the extracted dye liquid. Rinse the cloth and dry it in the sun.

SAFFLOWER *(benibana)*, *Carthemus tinctorius (Compositae)*

Two dye substances are present in the blossoms of the safflower plant. Used together they produce a rich orange-yellow that can be rendered more permanent by the addition of acid to the dye process. Used separately, they yield yellow and red. The following recipe for red will dye 100 grams ($3\frac{1}{2}$ oz) of cloth.

Any trace of oil that is transferred to the dried petals from utensils, work surfaces, and the hands will adversely affect the dyeing. Wear rubber gloves at all times when handling the petals. The exact pH of the dye liquid and final acid rinse is very important. It can be determined with pH indicator papers available from chemical suppliers.

*Extracting dye*:

    100 grams ($3\frac{1}{2}$ oz) dried safflower petals

    8 grams ($\frac{1}{4}$ oz) potassium carbonate ($K_2CO_3$)

    6 liters (quarts) warm water

Place the dried petals in a cloth bag, cover with plenty of warm water, and allow to soak overnight. Squeeze out the yellow liquid. This is the yellow dye substance. It may be set aside and used later, but it has no use when dyeing red. Soak the petals a second time for several hours, squeeze out the liquid, and rinse the bag of petals in running water.

Dissolve the potassium carbonate in a small amount of lukewarm water. Add it to 6 liters (quarts) of warm water. Soak the petals for three hours. The liquid will have a brownish color. This is the red dye liquid.

*Dyeing*:

    the extracted dye liquid

    10 grams ($\frac{1}{3}$ oz) citric acid. The dye liquid should have a pH of 3.

Pour the dye liquid into an enameled or stainless steel pot and add the citric acid a little at a time. The liquid will turn from a murky brownish color to a clear red.

Soak the cloth in warm water, then place it in the dye liquid. When the cloth is saturated with dye, remove it, squeezing the cloth and letting the liquid drain back into the pot. Open out the cloth, air it for a few minutes, and return it to the pot. Repeat this entire procedure twice and then leave the cloth to soak in the dye bath for thirty minutes. Squeeze the dye liquid, air the cloth, and set aside.

Heat dye bath to 60°C (120°F) and add cloth. When it is thoroughly saturated, squeeze out the cloth, letting the liquid drain back into the pot. Open out the cloth and air it and return it to the pot. Repeat this sequence of soaking, squeezing, and airing the cloth twice, and then return the cloth to the dye bath and allow it to soak for thirty minutes.

*Rinsing dyed cloth*:

Add 2 grams ($\frac{1}{15}$ oz) acetic acid ($CH_3COOH$) to the rinse water. White vinegar may be substituted for the stronger acetic acid. In either case, the rinse water should have a pH of 10 to 11. Soak the cloth for thirty minutes, rinse well in clear water, and dry in the sun.

LEACHED ASH SOLUTION (lye)

A strong alkaline solution (lye) containing potassium carbonate is obtained by leaching the ashes of various kinds of wood. Certain kinds of wood have a high alum content as well. The most common source is the shrub *Camelia japonica*. It is widely grown in the more temperate areas of North America and Japan. Alum obtained from the ash of a small tree (*nishi kohori*; botanical name elusive) is still used by some dyers in Japan as the mordant in dyeing with purple root and madder. *Camelia japonica* ash may be substituted.

*To prepare ash solution*: Ash from freshly burned small branches, twigs, and leaves (all must be thoroughly dry) are placed in a large container, and an ample amount of boiling water is added. When the ash has settled, the solution should be clear and golden yellow in color; the liquid should make a squeaky sound when rubbed between the fingers. If it feels slippery and does produce a sound, it is too strong and more water should be added.

*To treat cloth before dyeing*: To treat 500 grams (about 1 lb) of cloth use 5.5 liters (quarts) of ash solution. Heat the solution and pass the fabric through it. If it is a heavy silk, pass it through the hands, gently squeezing the cloth. Stretch silk with *shinshi* and *harite* (page 61) and dry.

## Peach Bark Tannin *(shibuki)* Solution

Some Japanese indigo dyers use a final rinse prepared from the bark of the mountain peach. If it comes in the form of hard lumps, these must be crushed with a hammer.

Place the crushed bark in a glass jar with a tight-fitting cover. Fill the jar with water and let the bark stand overnight or until the bark particles soften. It will keep for a very long time. If mold forms on the surface, simply remove it. Place the cloth to be rinsed in a container and barely cover with bark tannin liquid diluted with water to the color of strong tea. Soak the cloth for a few minutes, squeeze out the liquid, and dry. Because this tannin will dye white cloth a light brown, shibori-resisted cloth that has been indigo dyed should be rinsed in the tannin before the stitching or binding threads are removed if one wants to preserve the original color of the cloth. Tannin from other sources may be substituted with somewhat similar results.

## Soybean Solution *(gojiru)*

A solution made by adding water to crushed soybeans is used in Japan to prepare cloth for dyeing. It acts to allow an even application of dye, especially with silk.

Soak one cup of dried soybeans overnight (or until soft) in enough water to cover, then liquefy the beans in a blender or food processor or finely pound them in a mortar. Add water until the liquid looks like watery milk, then strain through a cloth. Soak fabric in this liquid and dry it completely before dyeing.

Soybean milk, if it has no additives, may also be used.

## Metal Salts Used as Mordants

Mordants are water-soluble salts of metals that help bond fiber and dye color. Many of them are extremely toxic. Know what you are dealing with and handle, store, and use carefully. *A Handbook of Dyes from Natural Materials* by Anne Bliss has an excellent section on mordants and chemicals used as dye assistants.

General precautions are: store all chemicals in a safe place, tightly capped in glass or plastic containers and clearly labeled. Buy these chemicals in lump or crystal form in preference to powders, which are easily airborne and might be inhaled. Wear rubber gloves when handling dry mordants, mordant baths, or unrinsed wet-mordanted fabrics. Work in a well-ventilated place. Fumes from chrome, copper, and tin are particularly toxic. Clean up the work place.

*Alum (potassium aluminum sulphate; $KAl(SO_4)_2 \cdot 12H_2O$)*
  Alum is the least toxic of the mordants.

*Chrome (potassium dichromate or potassium bichromate; $K_2Cr_2O_7$)*
  Chrome is extremely poisonous. Fumes are irritating.

*Copper (blue vitriol or copper sulphate; $CuSO_4$)*
  Copper sulphate is deadly poisonous. An unlined copper pot or boiler can be used instead of copper sulphate.

*Iron (copperas or ferrous sulphate; $FeSO_4$)*
  The mordanting liquid made with iron crystals is toxic. An iron pot can be substituted.

*Tin (stannous chloride; $SnCl_2$)*
  Stannous chloride is an extremely poisonous white crystal. Always be sure to add this chemical to water, never put it in a container and pour on water. Very toxic fumes are released.

## Chemicals Used as Dye Assistants or to Alter pH Levels

*Sodium hydrosulphite; $Na_2S_2O_4$*
  Toxic, must be kept dry.

*Cream of tartar (potassium bitartrate; $KHC_4H_4O_6$)*

*Caustic soda (sodium hydroxide; $NaOH$)*
  Deadly poisonous, extremely caustic, can cause severe burns. Never add water to caustic soda, it boils up furiously; always add caustic soda to a large amount of water.

*Tannic acid ($C_{14}H_{10})_9$*
  A mildly poisonous acid, present in sumac, black tea, black walnut hulls, Japanese mountain peach, etc.

*Vinegar or acetic acid* (CH$_3$COOH)

Vinegar contains from 4 to 6 percent acetic acid. Glacial acetic acid may be used but is more dangerous to handle.

*Washing soda (sodium carbonate:* Na$_2$CO$_3$)

CLASSES OF CHEMICAL DYES SUITABLE FOR SHIBORI

*Direct dyes* for cotton, linen, viscose rayon, hemp (cellulose fibers)
    Brand names:   Miyako, Ciba Chorantine.
    Properties:   Moderate to good light fastness, poor to moderate wash fastness.

*Acid dyes* for silk, wool (protein fibers)
    Brand names:   Miyako, Kiton.
    Properties:   Very good light fastness, moderate to good wash fastness.

*Fiber reactive dyes* for cotton, linen, viscose rayon, hemp (cellulose fibers)
    Brand names:   Procion, Cibacron, Dylon.
    Properties:   Good to excellent light and wash fastness.

*Vat dyes* for cotton, linen, viscose rayon, hemp, silk
    Brand names:   Cibanone, Soledon, Durindone, Caledon, Inkodye (already reduced).
    Properties:   Have the greatest light and wash fastness of any dyes known.

*Note:*   The reduction process used for chemical vat dyes differs from the one that is used with chemical or natural indigo. Follow the manufacturer's directions.

# ARASHI NOTES—Suggestions for Beginners

1.  Start with a cylinder no larger than 10 centimeters (4 in) in diameter. The greater the diameter of the cylinder, the more difficult it is to push the cloth along it. The cylinder must be perfectly smooth. Polish it with the finest grade steel wool (000 or 0000) or apply paste floor wax (Johnson's is good) with steel wool and polish the wax with finest grade steel wool. If the wax is polished with steel wool, it should not come off onto the cloth. A cylinder length of 1 meter (3 ft) is sufficient for most purposes and easy to manipulate.

2.  The cloth is secured on the cylinder with short (2.5 cm/1 in) pieces of masking tape or by stitching. If the cloth is wider than the circumference of the cylinder, the edges or selvages will overlap. This overlap may be cut off, ignored, or used for decorative effect, as you choose. Masking tape is easy to use if the selvages or cloth edges meet or if any overlap lies flat on the cylinder. Stitching is convenient to make cloth cylinders to fit on the plastic cylinder core, whether or not there is any overlap of cloth.

    The masking tape pieces are removed just before the thread winds over them. If they are left in place, the cloth may be somewhat more difficult to push, but the reason they are removed is to avoid the undyed patches they leave. Such patches might not matter, depending on what you are doing with the cloth.

3.  At first it may be easier to control the rotation of the pole and the tension on the thread from a sitting position on a chair or stool. Place the cylinder at an angle, with the end on the floor also braced against a wall or some object so it turns more or less in place. Rest the cylinder against the inside of the left knee with the right leg over the cylinder. Keep both feet flat on the floor. Turn the cylinder with the left hand. The thread is held with the right hand about 15 to 20 centimeters (6 to 8 in) from the cylinder.

4.  The right amount of tension on the thread is a bit tricky at first, and success must come through practice. First be sure that the thread winds easily off its spool or core, whether you hold the spool with your right hand or just use the hand to control tension. If the thread tension on the cylinder is too tight, the cloth will not move; if too loose, you will have a mess. The only way to master this is to do it. There is no right way. Do what you find to be best for you.

5.  Wind the thread for no more than 7 to 8 centimeters (about 3 in) before compressing the cloth into folds. If too much thread is wound, the cloth is difficult, if not impossible, to push along the cylinder. The main drawback of the plastic cylinder is that, unlike the tapered wooden poles once used in Japan, it is uniform in diameter, resulting in greater difficulty in compressing the cloth. Winding the thread for short distances is a necessary adjustment that must be made. With experience one learns just how much of any given cloth can be wound with thread before it is pushed.

    When compressing cloth into folds, exert pressure on the cloth rather than on the thread.

*Hint*: A gradual and easy way of gaining experience in the *arashi* technique is first to stitch the cloth into a tube that fits snugly on the cylinder, then condense the cloth without winding it with thread. Without thread, one can more easily get the feel of moving the cloth along the cylinder. Of course, without the thread to guide the folds, the resulting pattern will be irregular lines.

When one has the feel of compressing the cloth without thread, one can try using thread with the same kind of stitched cloth tube, then graduate to winding the cloth in a spiral around the cylinder

# GLOSSARY

*akane.* Madder *(Rubia cardifolia)*; roots are used in dyeing to produce shades of red-orange.

*aobana.* Dayflower *(Commelina communis)*; juice extracted from the petals of this blue flower is used as a fugitive ink for marking fabric to be dyed; disappears upon contact with water (see fugitive color). Synthetic fugitive ink is available, but it requires steaming for removal. Marker pens with fugitive color are also available.

*asa.* A general term for a variety of bast fibers, used specifically to denote hemp *(Cannabis sativa)* but also for ramie *(Boehmeria nivea)*, jute, flax, and other fibers.

bast fibers. Woody plant fibers used to make rope, basketry and matting, textiles, and paper. The major Japanese bast fibers used for textiles until cotton became generally used in the late nineteenth century are:
*asa* (q.v.), like the English word "hemp," is a general term for many bast fibers, but usually refers to the most common such fiber used in Japan, *Cannabis sativa*.
*choma* or *karamushi*, China grass *(Urticaceae Boehmeria nivea)*
*ira kusa*, nettle *(Urticaceae, Urtica urena)*
*fuji*, wistaria *(Wistaria floribunda)*
*kuzu* (q.v.) (also romanized *kudzu*), erroneously called arrowroot *(Pueraria lobata)*

*bu.* Traditional Japanese unit of length measurement, one-tenth of one *sun*; 0.119 inch.

*chirimen.* Silk crepe. The warp thread is untwisted reeled silk; the weft thread is highly twisted reeled silk. Ordinary crepe is woven alternating two Z-twist and two S-twist threads. When this plain-weave cloth is boiled and scoured, the highly twisted weft creates the rippled texture characteristic of *chirimen*.

discharge dyeing. Removing dyed color from fabric in order to create design. A bleaching agent such as hydrosulphite may be used. See Plate 298.

*dōfuku.* A medium-length outer cloak worn by the warrior class during the Muromachi period (1333–1573).

*e-moyō.* "Pictorial design," as opposed to geometric or abstract patterns.

fugitive color. An impermanent color that disappears upon contact with water or exposure to sunlight, such as *aobana* blue (q.v.) and safflower red. Used to mark textiles for dyeing.

*furisode.* Kimono with long swinging sleeves that nearly touch the ground, worn by young unmarried women from mid-Edo period to the present day.

gromwell. See *shikon*

*hakama.* Full-cut trousers or culottes worn by both women and men during the Heian period. Heian court ladies wore long, red pleated *hakama* under *jūni-hitoe* (q.v.). Later, as *kosode* became the accepted formal wear, *hakama* were no longer worn by women but continued to be part of men's dress. Today they are men's wear for formal occasions.

*harite.* Wooden bars used to stretch bolt of kimono cloth (see page 61).

*haori.* A short, kimono-style jacket worn over the kimono. The front is left open rather than overlapped and is tied with silk cords.

*heko obi.* Men's soft silk kimono sash for casual wear.

*hitatare.* A three-quarter length outer garment evolved from the *suikan*, worn by men of the warrior class during the Kamakura period (1185–1333). It is distinguished from the *suikan* by its overlapping neck band; it was worn tucked into pants usually made of matching fabric.

*irosashi.* Application .of color or dyes in the *yūzen* (q.v.) process and certain stencil dyeing processes.

*itajime*. Resist process in which cloth is folded and clamped between wooden boards or sticks then vat-dyed. This method of patterning was popular especially for red and white fabrics for lining and undergarments. See also *kyōkechi*.

*jiban* (or *juban*). Undergarment worn beneath the kimono; its construction is similar to that of the kimono. Traditionally the patterns and colors are bold. *Naga-jiban (naga-juban)* are ankle length, and *han-jiban (han-juban)* are hip length.

*jūni-hitoe*. Attire of Heian period court ladies. Literally, "twelve unlined robes"; each robe is dyed a different shade or color and all are worn together in a way calculated to show in subtle combination at neck, sleeves, and hem.

*kaki-e*. Hand-painting on fabric, usually with *sumi* ink. The best-known example is the use of *kaki-e* in *tsujigahana* textiles (see Plate 13).

Kanbun *kosode*. Style of *kosode* first popular during the Kanbun era (1661–72), easily recognizable by the full-length design sweeping from shoulder to hem, with a large area of open ground.

*kariginu*. Literally, "hunting robe"; attire of men of the Heian period nobility consisting of a casual top worn over trousers. Originally for traveling, hunting, and other sports, but later for everyday wear.

*kasuri* (the Japanese term for ikat). The process of patterning cloth by binding yarns before weaving to reserve areas from dye; involves calculation of where the reserved areas of yarn will appear in the final woven piece.

*katabira*. Originally unlined summer *kosode*. Later the term specifically referred to an unlined summer garment of *asa* (q.v.) or summer silk (silk that still retains gum so the texture is crisp), while similar articles of cotton and silk were called *hitoe*.

*katazome*. Paste-resist stencil dyeing. Rice paste is applied through a special paper stencil to resist selected areas from dye. Often dip-dyed, but sometimes dye is applied by brush or thickened and applied by tube. *Bingata* is the bright, polychrome *katazome* developed in Okinawa.

Keichō *kosode*. A style of *kosode*, first popular during the Keichō era (1596–1614). Typically, interlocking or overlapping areas of contrasting colors and complex, disparate designs fill the entire ground. *Somewake*, shibori, and *nuihaku* were most often used.

*kesa*. Shawllike vestment worn by Buddhist priests, draped over other garments; often made of patchwork to suggest the patched clothing of the poor.

*kikkō*. "Tortoiseshell"; hexagonal motif used as an allover pattern or as a single unit. Has felicitous connotations because the tortoise symbolizes longevity.

*kimono*. The traditional garment of Japan, developed from the *kosode* during the early Edo period (1615–1868). A straight-cut, wrap-around robe worn with sash (obi).

*kintōshi*. Silk fabric woven with gold threads.

*kōkechi*. Ancient term for tied or bound resist. Examples from seventh and eighth centuries are in the Shōsō-in repository.

*kosode*. Originally an undergarment during the Heian period, with smaller sleeves and sleeve openings than the outer robes (such as *jūni-hitoe*). Later it developed into the outer garment and then evolved into the modern kimono.

*kuzu*. Bast fiber from stems of the *kuzu* plant *(Pueraria lobata)*, used for weft with cotton (q.v.), or silk warp to make *kuzu-fu* or *kappu* (*kuzu* cloth). This cloth is slightly stiff and has an attractive sheen. The root of the *kuzu* plant yields a starch commonly used in Japanese cooking and also has medicinal uses.

*kyōkechi*. Ancient Japanese resist process in which cloth is folded and then clamped between carved wooden blocks. Several colors are applied through holes in the blocks, which form reservoirs to contain dye. Examples from the seventh and eighth centuries are in the Shōsō-in collection

madder. See *akane*.

*matsukawabishi.* "Pine bark lozenge," a geometric motif composed of three superimposed diamond forms (see page 26) used as an allover repeating pattern as well as a single unit.

*mingei.* "Folk art" or "folkcraft." This term was coined by Sōetsu Yanagi and his friends Shōji Hamada and Kanjirō Kawai in the 1920s. They initiated the *mingei* movement in Japan, which brought awareness of the value and beauty of traditional crafts of ordinary people, expressed in objects designed for use in everyday life.

*murasaki.* See *shikon.*

*neri-nuki.* Glossed silk with a distinctive sheen. The warp thread is reeled silk that has not been scoured, and the weft thread (*neri-ito*) is degummed reeled silk.

*nuihaku.* A combination of embroidery and applied gold or silver leaf (see *surihaku*).

obi. Sash worn with kimono. A woman's obi is wide and tied in a large knot or bow. A man's obi is narrow and worn around the hips.

*obiage.* In present-day usage, a decorative silk scarf worn with an obi to cover the thin cord that secures the obi knot. *Obiage* came into fashion during late Meiji (1868–1912), and during the Taishō period (1912–26) shibori became the most popular means of decorating these scarves.

overdyeing. Dyeing one color over another to obtain a desired hue, e.g., yellow overdyed with indigo produces green.

pongee. From the Chinese *benji,* "own loom." A soft, thin silk or a textile made of another fiber (such as rayon) that resembles this silk. Originally the term referred to silk produced in North China from silkworms fed on oak leaves, resulting in soft and nubby, naturally honey-colored cloth.

purple root. See *shikon*

reserve or resist. A substance or technique used to protect an area of yarn or textile from dye.

resist dyeing. Patterning of yarn or fabric by protecting selected areas from dye. Patterns can be created by the application of substances such as wax, paste, and mud, and physically manipulating the cloth. Typical processes are ikat *(kasuri),* batik, paste and stencil dyeing *(katazome),* and shibori.

*rinzu.* Monochrome figured satin-weave silk.

*rōkechi.* Ancient term for wax-resist dyeing. Examples from the seventh and eighth centuries are in the Shōsō-in collection.

*rōketsu.* Wax-resist dyeing (batik). This is not a continuation of the early *rōkechi* but was revived in the early Taishō period (1912–26) by Tsuruichi Tsurumaki, a textile artist and scholar.

*saya.* Light monochrome figured silk with pattern in twill weave.

*seifuku.* During the Heian period, garments of civil employees without rank.

*seikaiha.* Literally "blue ocean wave"; an imbricate scallop or shell pattern considered to be a stylization of waves.

*shaku.* Traditional Japanese unit of length measurement; about (0.994) 1 foot.

*shikon* (or *murasaki*). Gromwell (*Lithospermum erythrorhizon*); literally, "purple root," used in dyeing to achieve shades of purple.

*shinshi.* Flexible split bamboo sticks with needles embedded in each end; used to stretch across warp of fabric for dyeing and drying (see p. 61).

*shippō.* Interlocking circles. Literally "seven treasures"; a design said to symbolize the Seven Treasures of Buddhism: crystal *(hari),* lapis *(ruri),* gold *(kin),* silver *(gin),* mother-of-pearl *(shako),* coral *(sango),* and carnelian *(meno).*

*somewake.* Dyeing in which large areas of ground are dyed in different colors. Typical of *tsujigahana* and Keichō *kosode.*

*suikan.* A large-sleeved upper garment worn over *kosode,* tied at the neck and tucked into the waistband of pants. During the Heian period (794–1185) *suikan* were worn by lower-class men; later the garment became acceptable as casual wear for men of all classes.

*sun*. Traditional Japanese unit of length measurement; 1.193 inches.

*surihaku*. Stenciled application of gold or silver leaf using a special adhesive. *Tsujigahana* textiles and Keichō *kosode* provide examples of *surihaku*.

*tan*. A standard bolt of kimono cloth sufficient to make one kimono. Traditional width of fabric is approximately 36 centimeters (14 in) and length is 10.6 meters (about 12 yards).

*tenugui*. A small, all-purpose towel made of lightweight cotton, often with a stenciled or shibori design and indigo dyed.

*tsujigahana*. Name given to a group of textiles that became fashionable during the latter part of the fifteenth and early sixteenth centuries. Mainly silk garments *(kosode, dōfuku)* are known from the literature and surviving examples. Stitched shibori of both small and large areas is used to achieve the typical effects of *tsujigahana*.

*uchikake*. During the Edo period (1615–1868), an outer robe worn by women of the upper class for formal wear. Now worn only for traditional weddings, thus sometimes translated as "wedding robe."

*uchiki*. A large-sleeved outer robe worn by court ladies of Heian period; it later became part of formal attire, worn over *kosode*.

*ukiyo-e*. Woodblock prints of everyday life during the Edo period (1615–1868), reflecting the culture of the townspeople.

vat dyes. Generally fast dyestuffs that are insoluble in water but in a reduced state form compounds soluble in alkalis. This reduced dyestuff is deposited in or on fabric or yarn immersed in the dye solution (the vat) and is oxidized upon contact with air, becoming the original stable compound in the fiber. This type of dyeing is called mechanical bonding, as opposed to chemical bonding.

viscose rayon. Fiber made from cellulose treated with potassium hydroxide and carbon disulfide; can be dyed in the same manner as plant fiber.

*yogi*. A kimono-shaped quilt.

*yukata*. A single-layered cotton kimono-style garment usually worn after the bath or for casual wear, traditionally embellished by paste-resist, stencil dyeing, or shibori, and indigo dyed. The term is derived from *yu-katabira*, a single-layered bath garment (see *katabira*).

*yūzen*. Complex method of polychrome fabric decoration using paste as the resist medium. The paste is applied with a cone-shaped applicator or through stencils, and dyes are applied with small brushes. Highly popular in the Edo period (1615–1868) and still widely practiced today.

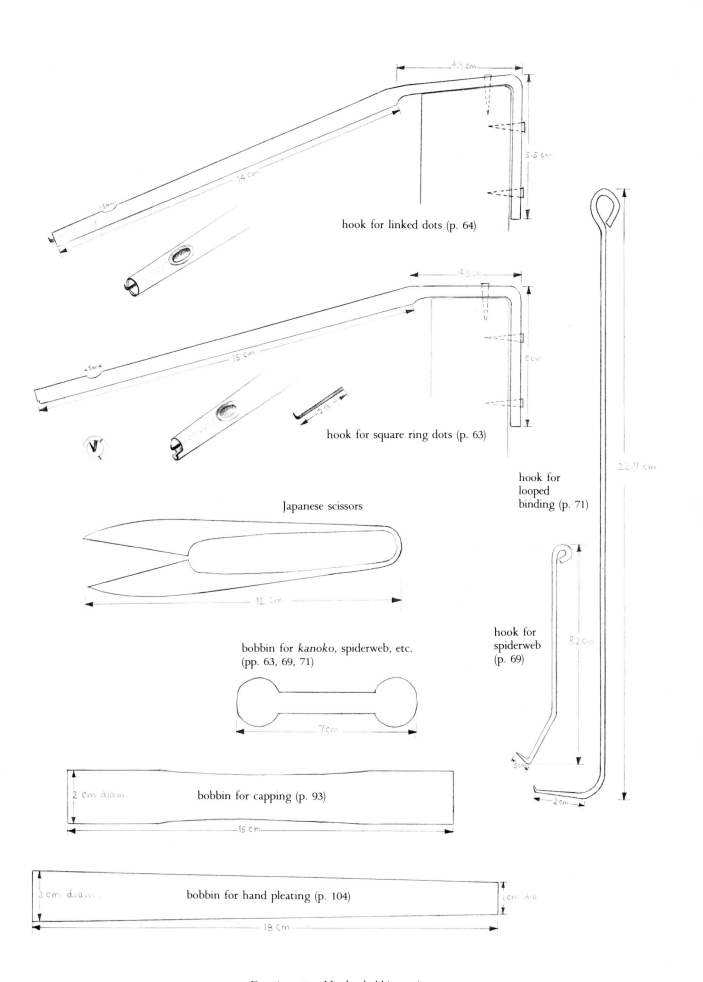

hook for linked dots (p. 64)

hook for square ring dots (p. 63)

hook for looped binding (p. 71)

Japanese scissors

hook for spiderweb (p. 69)

bobbin for *kanoko*, spiderweb, etc. (pp. 63, 69, 71)

bobbin for capping (p. 93)

bobbin for hand pleating (p. 104)

Drawing 43.  Hooks, bobbins, scissors

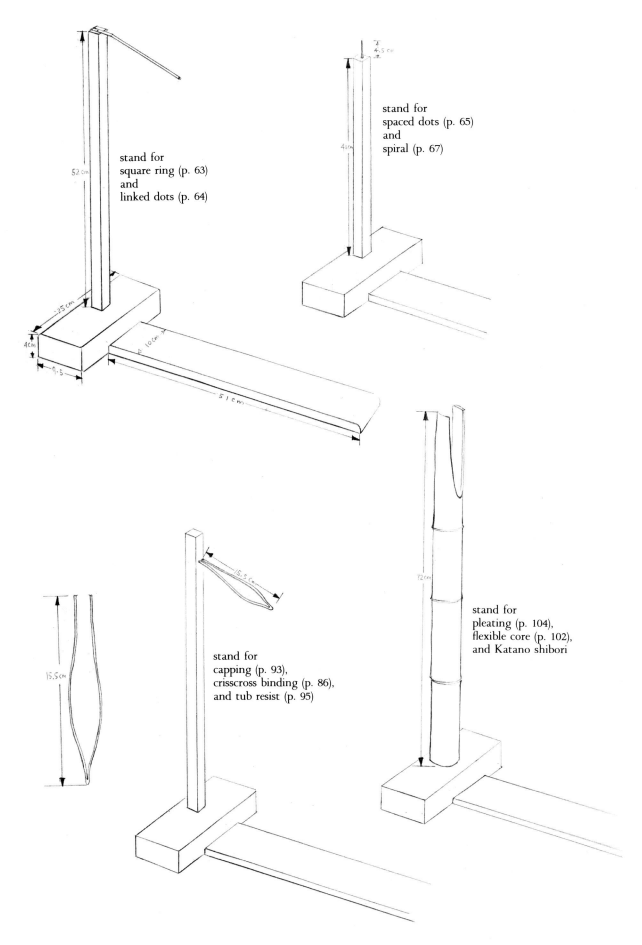

stand for
square ring (p. 63)
and
linked dots (p. 64)

52 cm

25 cm

4 cm

9.5

51 cm

10 cm

stand for
spaced dots (p. 65)
and
spiral (p. 67)

4.5 cm

40 cm

15.5 cm

15.5 cm

stand for
capping (p. 93),
crisscross binding (p. 86),
and tub resist (p. 95)

72 cm

stand for
pleating (p. 104),
flexible core (p. 102),
and Katano shibori

Drawing 44.   Stands

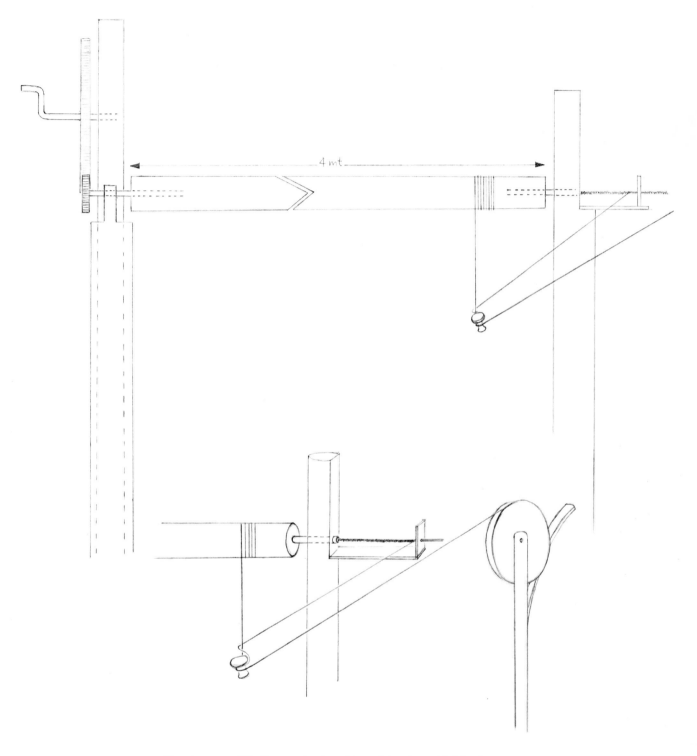

Drawing 45.    Winding mechanism for traditional *arashi* shibori process

# BIBLIOGRAPHY

ENGLISH

Adachi, Barbara Curtis. *The Living Treasures of Japan*. Tokyo: Kodansha International, 1973.

Adrosko, Rita J. *Natural Dyes in the United States*. United States National Museum Bulletin 281. Washington, D. C.: Smithsonian Institution Press, 1968.

Bliss, Ann. *A Handbook of Dyes from Natural Materials*. New York: Scribner's, 1981.

Grae, Idae. *Nature's Colors*. Dyes from Plants. New York: Macmillan Co., 1974.

Hauge, Victor and Takako. *Folk Traditions in Japanese Art*. Catalog organized and circulated by the I.E.F. in cooperation with the Japan Foundation. Tokyo: Kodansha International, 1979.

Hayashi, Ryoichi. *The Silk Road and the Shōsō-in*. Translated by Robert Ricketts. The Heibonsha Survey of Japanese Art, vol. 6. New York and Tokyo: Weatherhill, Heibonsha, 1975.

Horie, Kinnosuke. *Arimatsu Narumi Shibori*. Tōkai Sōsho no. 20. Nagoya: Nagoya Tetsudo Company Limited, 1978.

Hughes, Sukey. *Washi, the World of Japanese Paper*. Tokyo: Kodansha International, 1978.

Hylander, Clarence J. *The World of Plant Life*. New York: Macmillan, 1939.

Hyobu, Nishimura, Jean Mailey, and Joseph S. Hayes. *Tagasode: Whose Sleeves. . . Kimono from the Kanebō Collection*. New York: Japan Society, 1976.

Japan Textile Color Design Center. *Free-Style Designs*. Textile Designs of Japan, vol. 1. Original edition 1959; rev. ed. Tokyo: Kodansha International, 1980.

Larsen, Jack Lenor, Alfred Bühler, and Bronwen and Garrett Solyom. *The Dyer's Art*. New York: Van Nostrand, 1976.

Lubell, Cecil, ed. *Textile Collections of the World: United States and Canada*. New York: Van Nostrand Reinhold, 1976.

Minnich, Helen Benton, in collaboration with Shojiro Nomura. *Japanese Costume and the Makers of Its Elegant Tradition*. Rutland, Vermont and Tokyo, Japan: Tuttle, 1963.

Mizoguchi, Saburō. *Design Motifs*. Translated and adapted by Louise Allison Cort. Arts of Japan, vol. 1. New York and Tokyo: Weatherhill, Shibundō, 1973.

Muraoka, Kageo, and Kichiemon Okamura. *Folk Arts and Crafts of Japan*. Translated by Daphne D. Stegmaier. The Heibonsha Survey of Japanese Art, vol. 26. New York and Tokyo: Weatherhill, Heibonsha, 1973.

Museum of Contemporary Crafts. "Fabric Vibrations" (Tie and Fold-dye, Wall Hangings and Environment), April 14–May 27, 1972.

Museum of the Sinkiang-Uigher Autonomous Region and the Group in Charge of the Exhibition of Cultural Relics, ed. *Silk Road, the Fabrics from the Han to the T'ang Dynasty*. Peking: Wen-wu Ch'u Pan She (Cultural Materials Press), 1972.

Noma, Seiroku. *Japanese Costume and Textile Arts*. Translated by Armins Nikovskis. The Heibonsha Survey of Japanese Art, vol. 16. New York and Tokyo: Weatherhill, Heibonsha, 1974.

Petitt, Florence Harvey. *America's Indigo Blues: Resist Printed and Dyed Textiles of the 18th Century*. New York: Hastings House, 1974.

Robertson, Seonaid. *Dyes from Plants*. New York: Van Nostrand Reinhold, 1973.

Robinson, Stuart. *A History of Dyed Textiles: dyes, fibers, painted bark, starch resist, discharge, tie dye, further sources for research*. Cambridge, Mass.: M.I.T. Press, 1969.

Russ, Stephen. *Fabric Printing by Hand*. London: Studio Vista, 1964.

Schetky, Ethel Jane McD., ed. *Dye Plants and Dyeing—a handbook*, a special printing of plants and gardens, vol. 20, no. 3. Brooklyn: Brooklyn Botanic Garden, 1976.

Simmons, Max. *Dyes and Dyeing*. Melbourne: Van Nostrand Reinhold Australia, 1978.

Sugimura, Tsune. *The Enduring Crafts of Japan*. New York: Walker/Weatherhill, 1968.

Tsunoyama, Yukihiro, ed. *Textiles of the Andes*, catalog of the Amano Collection. Originally published by Dohansha, 1977. Translated by Heian International, Inc., South San Francisco, 1979.

Yanagi, Sōetsu, adapted by Bernard Leach. *The Unknown Craftsman: A Japanese Insight into Beauty*. Tokyo: Kodansha International, 1972.

ENGLISH PERIODICALS

Bühler, Alfred. "Indigo Dyeing Among Primitive Peoples." *Ciba Review*, 1951, no. 85, 3088–3091.

————. "Plangi—Tie and Dye Work." *Ciba Review*, 1954, no. 104, 3722–3748.

Ikle, Charles. "The Plangi Technique." *Bulletin of Needle and Bobbin Club*, 1941, 25 (2), 2–23.

"Japanese Resist Dyeing Techniques." *Ciba Review*, 1967, no. 4, 2–37.

Mailey, Jean. "Four Hundred Winters . . . Four Hundred Springs." *The Metropolitan Museum of Art Bulletin*. 1959, 18 (4), 115–128.

Schuster, Carl. "Stitch Resist Dyed Fabric of Western China." *Bulletin of Needle and Bobbin Club*, 1948, 32 (1–2), 11–29.

Simmons, Pauline. "Artist Designers of the Tokugawa Period." *The Metropolitan Museum of Art Bulletin*, February, 1956, 1–8.

Yamanobe, Tomoyuki. "Dyeing Through the Ages." *Japan Quarterly*, 1966, 13 (2), 207–213.

GERMAN

Bühler, Alfred. *Ikat Batik Plangi: Reservemusterungen auf Garn und Stoff aus Corderasien, Zentralasian, Sudosteuropa und Nordafrika*. 3 vols. Basel: Pharos-Verlag Hansudolf Schwabe, 1972.

JAPANESE

Arimatsu Shibori Henshū Iinkai. *Arimatsu shibori*. Nagoya: Arimatsu Shibori Henshū Iinkai, n.d.

Gotō, Shōichi and Ryōbei Yamakawa. *Senryō shoku-butsu-fu* (Encyclopedia of plant dyes). Osaka: Hakuō-sha, 1972.

The most comprehensive reference of plant dyes used in Japan from antiquity to the present. Lists botanical names and alternative common names in English.

Hinonishi Suketaka. *Fukushoku* (Costume). Nihon no bijutsu (Arts of Japan), no. 26. Tokyo: Shibundō, 1968.

Imanaga, Kiyoshi. *Tsujigahana zome* (*Tsujigahana* dyeing). Nihon no bijutsu (Arts of Japan), no. 113. Tokyo: Shibundō, 1975.

Itō, Shinsui, Mitsukuni Yoshida, and Tomoyuki Yamanobe. *Some* (Dyeing). Nihon no kōgei (Japanese craft series), vol. 1. Kyoto: Tankōsha, 1965.

Itō, Toshiko. *Tsujigahana zome* (*Tsujigahana* dyeing). Tokyo: Kodansha International, 1980.
Best overall reference on *tsujigahana*.

Kamiya, Eiko. *Kosode*. Nihon no bijutsu (Arts of Japan), no. 67. Tokyo: Shibundō, 1971.

Kitamura, Tetsurō. *Shibori*. Tokyo: Unsundō, 1970.

———. *Tsujigahana: Iro to monyō* (*Tsujigahana*: Design and color). Limited edition of 1000. Kyoto: Kōrin Suiko Shoin, 1970.

———. *Yūzen zome* (*Yūzen* dyeing). Nihon no bijutsu (Arts of Japan), no. 106. Tokyo: Shibundō, 1975.

Komura, Osamu. *Arimatsu shibori. Bi to kōgei* (Beauty and craft), vols. 213–16. Special issue. Kyoto: Kyoto Shoin, 1974.

Motoyoshi, Shun. *Shibori zome* (Shibori dyeing). Nihon no senshoku (Japanese dyeing), vol. 12. Tokyo: Tairyūsha, 1961.
Concise information on range of shibori textiles with good technical explanations.

Nakae, Katsumi, *Chijimi to jōfu* (Cotton crepe and fine hemp). Nihon no senshoku (Japanese dyeing), vol. 7. Tokyo: Tairyūsha, 1981.

Nihon Orimono Shimbunsha. *Senshoku jiten* (Textile dictionary). Kyoto: Hakuōsha, 1920.

Okada, Seizo with Kahei Takeda and committee of Arimatsu Shibori Kyōkai. *Arimatsu shibori.* Nagoya: Arimatsu Shibori Gijutsu Hozon Shinkōkai, 1972.

Suzuki, Keizō, Yoshio Takada, and Tomoyuki Yamanobe. *Nihon no fukusō* (Costumes of Japan), vols. I, II, Kyoto: Yoshikawa Kobunkan, 1964.
The most informative book on the construction of Japanese garments and how they were worn.

Takeda, Kahei. *Arimatsu shibori.* Arimatsu: Arimatsu Shibori Gijutsu Hozon Shinkōkai, 1966.

———. *Nihon no shibori zome kireji cho* (Sample book of Japanese shibori). Limited edition of 100. Mingei Orimono Zukan Kankōkai, 1970
Rare book of old swatches of indigo-dyed folk shibori.

Tomiyama, Hiroki, ed. *Nihon no Shibori* (Japanese shibori). Kyoto: Hakuōsha, 1970.

Yamanobe, Tomoyuki. *Nihon no senshoku* (Japanese dyeing). Tokyo: Mainichi Shimbunsha, 1975.
Excellent discussion of folk textiles of Japan and Ryūkyū Islands. Includes 107 swatches.

———. *Some* (Dyeing). Nihon no bijutsu (Arts of Japan), no. 11. Tokyo: Shibundō, 1966.

Yoshida, Mitsukuni. *Kyō kanoko: Bi to dentō* (Kyoto kanoko: Beauty and tradition). Limited edition of 1000. Kyoto: Kyoto Shinbori Kōgyō Kumiai, 1975.
Thorough investigation of shibori tradition in Kyoto.

Yoshioka, Sachio, ed. *Shibori to ai* (Shibori and indigo). Limited edition of 800. Kyoto: Shikosha, 1976.
Presents shibori textiles by Motohiko Katano.

JAPANESE PERIODICALS

"Kimono to yosooi" (Kimono and dress). *Shufu no Tomo,* Fall/Winter, 1979. Special articles on natural dyeing with great photographs.

"Nihon no ai" (Japanese indigo). *Senshoku to Seikatsu,* no. 10.

# SUPPLIERS

Alliance Import Company
1021 R Street
Sacramento, CA 95814
Imported dyestuffs, wholesale and retail. Send stamped, self-addressed envelope for information.

The Arachnid
P. O. Box 1355
Ormand Beach, FL 32074
Imported dyestuffs. Send stamped, self-addressed envelope for information.

Bryant Lab Inc.
1101 Fifth Street
Berkeley, CA 94704
Chemicals for preparing indigo vat and mordants; CMC (carboxy methyl cellulose), a substitute for *funori.* Ask for sodium salt of CMC.

Cerulean Blue Ltd.
P. O. Box 5126
1314 N. E. 43rd Street
Seattle, WA 98105
Wide selection of equipment, natural and chemical dyestuffs, mordants, fabrics. Send for free catalogue.

A. Daigger & Co. of California
10 Harbour Way
Richmond, CA 94802
Parafilm. May be used for capping (*bōshi).*

Dharma Trading Company
P. O. Box 916
1952 University Ave.
Berkeley, CA 94704
Equipment, dyestuffs, mordants, Testfabrics. Catalogue available.

Kasuri Dyeworks
1959 Shattuck Ave.
Berkeley, CA 94704
Japanese natural dyestuffs, indigo, seaweed glue (*funori*), peach bark *shibuki*), dyeing equipment, mordants, fabrics, books on Japanese textiles.

Straw Into Gold
3006 San Pablo Ave.
Berkeley, CA 94704
Natural and chemical dyes, mordants, and equipment. Testfabrics, books on dyes and dyeing.

Testfabrics, Inc.
P. O. Drawer O
200 Blackford Ave.
Middlesex, NJ 08846
Fabrics ready for dyeing. Catalogue available.

VWR Scientific
3745 Bayshore Blvd.
Brisbane, CA 94005
Parafilm. May be used for capping (*bōshi).*

# Acknowledgments

In 1975 Yoshiko Wada first encountered the exceptional book, *Nihon no Shibori-zome*, by Kahei Takeda. This limited edition of one hundred, which contains ninety-five sample swatches of traditional Arimatsu-Narumi shibori, inspired Wada and her colleague Donna Larson to develop a course in shibori for Fiberworks Center for the Textile Arts in Berkeley, California. The following year the class was held, and shibori was introduced for the first time in the United States. It was here that Jane Barton, Mary Kellogg Rice, and Yoshiko Wada met. Subsequent shibori classes have inspired many artists and students and have also led to the organization of the Shibori Society, a group that has continued over the years to share information and to exchange ideas about the art of shibori. The enthusiasm so generated provided impetus for the research and practical collaboration, which, after much learning, hardship, and encouragement, resulted in this volume.

Jane Barton had primary responsibility for the development of the Tradition section. Mary Rice worked with Yoshiko Wada to research further the background of the evolution of shibori in Japan, through sources that are not yet available in English, and with the assistance of Edward Rice completed the writing of this section.

The drawings and text of the Techniques section are the work of Mary Rice, who tested the processes based on information and examples gathered by Yoshiko Wada in Japan. Designs and processes collected and categorized in this book are based on actual samples, some by artisans who have passed away, and with them their techniques. In some cases it was through Rice's experimentation that such lost processes were reconstructed. For the Innovation section, Yoshiko Wada explored the contemporary scene in Japan and the West, gathering representative examples of shibori. These works illustrate applications of the shibori techniques—both conservative and experimental—and form a broad base from which the art of shibori can expand.

This book, the first major project of its kind for the authors, has turned out to be a far more ambitious undertaking than was at first conceived. Its completion could have happened only with the support and input of many people, to whom we offer heartfelt thanks and appreciation.

Mr. Kahei Takeda and Mr. Kōzō Takeda of Takeda Kahei Shōten in Arimatsu have been a major source of information and unlimited, generous assistance, including introductions to craftspeople and local collections. In particular, the rare and extensive Takeda family collection of old Arimatsu-Narumi shibori textiles was invaluable. Mr. Kōzō Takeda was especially helpful in sharing the research completed for his at that time unpublished book *Nihon no te-shibori*. The entire Takeda family provided hospitality and encouragement during many visits.

We would like to thank all the artisans in the Arimatsu-Narumi area for sharing their expertise and knowledge, and particularly for their kindness in taking time from their work. Often anonymous, they are the ones who keep the tradition alive. Mr. Tomokazu Aoki shared his knowledge of *tesuji* shibori and allowed us to use his grandfather's rare *arashi* sample book. Our visits with the Matsuoka family, who work in *tesuji* shibori, were very informative, and Mr. Katsuyuki Matsuoka demonstrated *shirokage* shibori. Mr. and Mrs. Reiichi Suzuki are the only remaining *arashi* artisans. Mr. Yoichi Kanie, liaison *(kageshi)* in the shibori home industry, provided insight into its techniques, designs, craftspeople, merchants, and methods of operation. Ms. Chieko Suzuki and Ms. Kagi Nonoyama work in various stitching and binding techniques such as *nui* shibori and *miura* shibori. We would also like to thank the shibori workshops of Harishō and Sujifuku for professional advice and information about the processes.

In Kyoto, the Fujii Shibori Company and Mr. Masaaki Fujii gave generously their tireless assistance, encouragement, and support, introducing us to the artisans and merchants of Kyoto as well as sharing their samples of Kyoto shibori. They opened their company to us and provided the means to experience firsthand the making and marketing of shibori textiles. Mr. Zensaburō Ueda of the Ueda Zen Shibori Company shared his memories of Kyoto shibori during the Meiji period. Mr. Kokichi Yamagishi and his family, who work in tub-resist shibori and capped shibori, were most helpful in allowing us to observe for many days and in giving valuable samples. Ms. Tazu Takeuchi is an expert in *hitome kanoko*, and Ms. Kisa Naito an artisan in *hitta kanoko*. Ms. Hiromi Tanaka, who is an instructor for the Kyoto Shibori Association, provided directions and samples of shibori. Mr. Kenkō Okitsu, Director of the Kyoto Shibori Association, introduced us to some shibori studios in Kyoto and gave us a greater understanding of the making and marketing of Kyoto shibori.

Mr. and Mrs. Bunichirō Kuriyama of Hanawa have preserved the tradition of purple-root dyeing and still practice the traditional shibori of the Hanawa area.

We would like to express our indebtedness to those who made their collections of shibori textiles available to us. These include Mr. Tsugao Odani and the Osaka Folkcraft Museum, Mr. Hitoshi Fujimoto, who shared his private collection and deep knowledge of folk shibori as well as provided us with several color transparencies, and Mr. Keisuke Serizawa and Mr. Takumi Sugawara, whose collections provided important samples. In addition, Mr. Hiroki Tomiyama and Mr. Sachio Yoshioka, publishers and researchers in textiles, gave us generous assistance in obtaining plates and information regarding contemporary craftspeople. And our thanks to all the artists who cooperated in providing examples and photographs of their work, sharing their creative processes and works of art.

From the earliest stages of our project we have been encouraged and helped by many. Jack Lenor Larsen, whose book *The Dyer's Art* inspired us to undertake this ambitious project, has continually provided the enthusiasm and assistance that enabled us to proceed. During our early planning of the book, Mr. Philip Rosenthal of the University of California Press met with us and gave valuable advice about the field of publishing. Jean Mailey kindly made available to us the Japanese textile collection at the Metropolitan Museum of Art, and Milton Sunday at the Cooper Hewitt Museum gave us the opportunity to study slides of shibori. In addition, we are grateful for the continuing support and advice of Professor Chikara Motoi of the Kyoto Fine Arts University, who provided access to many historical examples. Edward Rice has enriched our understanding through discussions of Chinese written characters, and his experience as writer and historian was essential in the completion of Part I. Our deepest gratitude to Mona Nagai for her professional editorial assistance throughout the project, especially in the writing of Part III, and to Richard Okada for translations of Japanese classic literature. The majority of the photographs appearing here are the work of Kenji Miura and Elaine Farris Keenan, who also contributed great patience and goodwill.

We thank Mr. Saburō Nobuki, Director of Kodansha International, Ltd., for his deep concern for maintaining the quality Kodansha is known for, and his expert staff, particularly our editor Mr. Kim Schuefftan for his boundless patience and enthusiasm and understanding of what we desired to accomplish, and Ms. Takako Suzuki for her editorial expertise and knowledge of Japanese textiles and textile publications. We are also thankful to the Japan Foundation for the professional fellowship that enabled Yoshiko Wada to do extensive research in Japan, which was essential for a deep treatment of the subject.

We acknowledge most gratefully the members of our own families, who endured graciously whatever inconveniences this project has caused, and the numerous friends who have supported us in so many ways.

# Index

定価13,000円
in Japan